The Public Debt
of the United States

The Public Debt
of the United States

An Historical Perspective,
1775–1990

Donald R. Stabile
and
Jeffrey A. Cantor

New York
Westport, Connecticut
London

Library of Congress Cataloging-in-Publication Data

Stabile, Donald.
  The public debt of the United States : an historical perspective,
1775-1990 / Donald R. Stabile and Jeffrey A. Cantor.
      p.   cm.
  Includes bibliographical references.
  ISBN 0-275-93664-3
  1. Debts, Public—United States—History.   I. Cantor, Jeffrey A.
II. Title.
HJ8032.A2S73   1991
336.3´4´0973—dc20   90-37780

British Library Cataloguing in Publication Data is available.

Library of Congress Catalog Card Number: 90-37780
ISBN: 0-275-93664-3

First published in 1991

Praeger Publishers, One Madison Avenue, New York, NY 10010
An imprint of Greenwood Publishing Group, Inc.

Printed in the United States of America

∞™

The paper used in this book complies with the
Permanent Paper Standard issued by the National
Information Standards Organization (Z39.48-1984).

10 9 8 7 6 5 4 3 2 1

Contents

Tables   ix

Preface   xi

Acknowledgments   xv

1. Public Policy and Public Debt   1

        PUBLIC FINANCE   3
        DEBT MANAGEMENT AND ADMINISTRATION   6
        OVERVIEW OF THIS BOOK   8

2. The Beginnings of Debt (1775-1801)   11

        FINANCING THE AMERICAN REVOLUTION   11
        THE CONSTITUTIONAL ERA   15
        THE FEDERALIST ERA   20

3. Keeping the Debt Small (1801-61)   29

        THE JEFFERSONIANS   30
        THE JACKSONIANS   37
        AN INDEPENDENT TREASURY   43

4. The First Growth in Debt (1861-1900)   51

        THE CIVIL WAR   52
        THE POST-CIVIL WAR ERA   59
        EXPANSION OF THE TREASURY   65

5. The Debt Drifts Upward (1900-40)   73

        THE ERA OF REFORM   73
        WORLD WAR I   77

THE RETURN TO NORMALCY   80
THE GREAT DEPRESSION   84

6. Debt Expansion during World War II (1940-45)   91

    FINANCING WORLD WAR II   92
    WARTIME DEBT ADMINISTRATION PROBLEMS   101

7. Postwar Debt Consolidation (1946-60)   109

    THE POSTWAR ECONOMY   110
    FISCAL MANAGEMENT   111
    OPERATIONS AT THE BUREAU OF THE PUBLIC DEBT 113
    FISCAL MANAGEMENT IN THE 1950s   116
    EFFICIENCY IN ADMINISTRATION   122

8. A New View on the Debt (1960-69)   129

    THE ECONOMY AND FISCAL POLICY   130
    DEBT MANAGEMENT POLICIES   133
    DEBT ADMINISTRATION   136
    OPERATIONAL IMPROVEMENT   140

9. Debt Growth in a Stagnant Economy (1970-80)   147

    THE NIXON YEARS   148
    THE FORD YEARS   150
    THE CARTER YEARS   151
    DEBT MANAGEMENT POLICIES   152
    DEBT ADMINISTRATION   156
    THE BOOK-ENTRY SYSTEM   157
    COMPUTER OPERATIONS   158
    ORGANIZATIONAL CHANGES   159
    OPERATIONAL IMPROVEMENT   162
    LOOKING AHEAD   165

10. Economic Experimentation and Debt Expansion   173
    (1981-88)

    THE REAGAN REVOLUTION   173
    THE ECONOMY IN THE 1980s   177
    GENERAL TREASURY ACTIVITIES   180
    THE BUREAU OF THE PUBLIC DEBT KEEPS PACE   185
    TREASURY DIRECT   188
    THE SAVINGS BOND OPERATIONS OFFICE   193
    THE GOVERNMENT SECURITIES ACT   196

11. The Debt in Historical Perspective   207

    DEBT AND GOVERNMENT SIZE   208
    DEBT AND GNP   209

Contents

COMPARATIVE GROWTH RATES   211
INTEREST RATES AND THE DEBT   214
A DEBT REDUCTION PLAN   216

Bibliography   223

Index   235

Tables

2.1   Federal Income to 1780   14

2.2   Hamilton's Estimate of Total Government   20
       Debt (December 1789)

3.1   Government Finance under Jackson   39

6.1   Computed Rate of Interest on the Public   99
       Debt (1941-45)

7.1   Computed Rate of Interest on the Public   114
       Debt (1946-50)

7.2   Employees of the Bureau of the Public Debt   116
       (1945-46, 1948-50)

7.3   Maturity Distribution of Public Debt   120
       (1953, 1956, and 1960)

7.4   Ownership Distribution of the Public Debt   121
       (1953, 1956, and 1960)

7.5   Computed Rate of Interest on the Public   121
       Debt (1952-56, 1959-60)

7.6   Employees of the Bureau of the Public Debt   122
       (1951-53, 1955)

8.1   Computed Interest on Total Debt (1963-70)   134

8.2   Ownership of Federal Securities (1961,   136
       1965, and 1969)

8.3   Employees at the Bureau of the Public Debt   138
       (1960, 1966, and 1970)

9.1   Computed Interest on Total Debt (fiscal   152
       years 1972-80)

9.2   Public Debt Ownership (fiscal years 1970,   156
       1975, and 1980)

9.3   Employees at the Bureau of the Public Debt   157
       (1974, 1976, and 1980)

9.4   Book-Entry Accounts as of December   164
       (1976-80)

10.1   Federal Government Deficits, Fiscal Year   179
       Basis (1980-88)

10.2   Composite Yield on Treasury Bonds of over   180
       Ten Years Maturity (yearly average)

10.3   Savings Bonds Outstanding at Year's End   185
       (1982-88)

10.4   Ownership of Gross Debt, End of Period   186
       (1984, 1986, and 1988)

11.1   Gross Federal Debt Held by the Public   210
       (percent of GNP, selected years)

11.2   Gross Federal Debt Held by the Public   210
       (percent of GNP for the 1980s, 1980-88)

11.3   Growth in Government Debt (change from   211
       previous year)

11.4   Debt at End of Period vs. Debt at Start   212
       (selected periods)

11.5   Comparative Figures on the Public Debt   213

Preface

In recent years there has been a growing concern over
the rapid increase of the national debt, or, to give it
the official title, the Public Debt of the United
States. This concern is not surprising, since the
public debt has tripled over the last decade, and shows
no sign of declining. A belief exists in the country
that action has to be taken to reduce the size of the
debt. As this book goes to press, administration and
congressional negotiators have just approved a plan to
reduce the size of the government's budget deficit in
the coming year, 1991, and for the next five years. The
plan reduces the projected deficits, but does not
eliminate them. The public debt will continue to grow,
and unless further deficit reductions take place, its
present size will double by the end of the century. The
debate over the deficit will continue, and the fear that
the public debt is growing too fast will be of
considerable importance to both sides.

Anxiety over the size of the public debt is nothing
new in the United States. Even before the Constitution
was passed in 1790, our founding fathers worried over
the size of the debt that had developed during the
Revolutionary War, and how they were going to pay it.
Ever since that time, the size of the public debt has
been an issue of concern to government officials, as
well as to the public. This book presents a
comprehensive history of the public debt over the course
of our history as a nation, to the present day. It
describes how the debt was accumulated during wars and
recessions, and what impact macroeconomic policy has had
on its growth. It also details how the debt itself had
an impact on the economy, particularly with respect to
the banking system.

In making this study, our purpose was to describe
as objectively as possible what had caused the debt to

expand and what government officials had done to reduce
it. By placing present-day concerns about the increase
in the public debt in historical context, we hope to
dispel some of the misunderstanding that has been a part
of current debate over the debt. For example, while the
last decade has seen the largest expansion of the public
debt in absolute dollar terms, as a percentage, the
increase is more on par with what took place during the
Mexican War.   Of course, at that time the debt was
smaller, but so was the country. In order to make such
comparisons, we first describe the historical events
leading up to the present debt in chapters 2 through 10,
followed by an overall perspective and summary of what
has happened to the debt in chapter 11.   Two lessons
stand out clearly, however. When the public and the
government wanted to reduce the debt, they were able to
find the means to do so, and when they did not want to,
they were able to live with an expanding debt.

     It has also become clear to us, as a result of this
study, that the way the debt is managed and administered
is as important as the size of the debt itself.   Not
only must the debt be handled fairly and honestly (there
have been no major scandals over this issue in the U.S.)
but it must also be managed in a way that minimizes the
impact of the debt on the economy, and administered in
such a way that accurate records of debt ownership are
maintained,   and   timely   payments   of   interest   and
principal are made.   These are functions performed
within the Treasury Department and the Bureau of the
Public Debt, which have fulfilled their tasks very well.
During the increase of debt during the 1980s, for
example, the Treasury Department and the Bureau of the
Public Debt actually reduced the number of employees
needed to administer it.   The evolution of debt
management and administration policies, from the first
issuance of paper money as a debt instrument to the
electronic transfer of treasury bills, will be another
part of the story of the history of the public debt.

     While this study aims at being descriptive, it also
has a grounding in economic theory. A mere compilation
of facts cannot serve to give a thorough knowledge of a
subject.   Economists   have   a   long   background   in
developing a theoretical approach to the problems of
public finance.   Our history is influenced by this
theory in terms of the issues we have described.
Chapter 1 presents an overview of the economic theory of
public finance for the reader who may be unfamiliar with
what economists have to say.   Throughout the book,
additional reference will be made to developments in
economic thinking, especially as they relate to public
finance and macroeconomic policy.

     It is our belief that history should serve to
illuminate the present. As the nation begins its third

century, it is faced with a number of problems, both
social and economic. Drugs, crime, international unrest
and a growing distrust of government continue to plague
us. At the same time, it appears that we have not yet
eliminated   economic   recession   from   among   our
difficulties. Compared to these, the problem of the
public debt should loom less large, just as it did in
previous eras. The debt can become a problem, as the
following pages will describe, but it is a manageable
problem. All that it will take to solve it is will on
the part of the public and the officials they elect.

Acknowledgments

The authors wish to thank Dr. Cantor's wife, Ruth F. Cantor, for her dedication and assistance to the completion of this project, which involved spending countless hours preparing and editing the original research as well as the final manuscript; and to his children for their support and encouragement. They also wish to thank Professor Andrew Kozak of St. Mary's College, who read parts of the manuscript, offering enthusiastic but critical comments. Two ideal students at St. Mary's College, Lanelle Bembenek and Sara Smith, prepared the index, and to them a grateful thank you.

They also wish to acknowledge the staff of the Bureau of the Public Debt, U.S. Department of the Treasury, for their contributions, cooperation, and assistance during the writing of <u>The History of the Bureau of the Public Debt</u>, the foundation upon which this book is written.

Dr. Cantor would also like to take this opportunity to thank Professor Hollie B. Thomas of Florida State University, for providing the role model which both inspired him, and gave him the skills to pursue a career in research, ultimately leading to this project.

1

Public Policy
and Public Debt

On September 30, 1990, at the close of its fiscal year, the U.S. government was in debt for over $3.22 trillion. This figure, technically referred to as the public debt, remains impressive by any measure. The objective of this book is to document how the public debt has accumulated and provide a history of the methods the government has employed to manage and administer it. The history of the public debt begins with the Revolutionary War in 1775, during which debt was incurred. Since then, the public debt has grown in size, but that growth has been uneven. The figure shows, most of the debt was incurred during periods of war as the government borrowed heavily to finance its defense. Until World War II, efforts were made to reduce the debt during peacetime. For the last four decades, and especially in the 1980s, the growth of the public debt has seemed both inexorable and exponential. Concern over the size of the public debt appears to be growing as fast as the debt itself.

It is beyond the scope of this book to evaluate whether and when the debt has grown too fast, although along the way notice will be given to earlier concerns expressed about the public debt by government authorities, public figures, and economic thinkers. Despite those concerns, public debt is and always has been a fact of life in the United States. The government was in debt even before the passage of the Constitution. It can justly be said that our federal government was founded in debt, and, except for one brief period in the 1830s, has remained so. Figure 1.1 shows the growth of the public debt as a percentage of gross national product (a graph that charted the growth of public debt would be impossible to scale). While there is indication of growth in the debt, given that gross national product has also increased, it is also

Figure 1.1
Government Debt Since the American Revolution

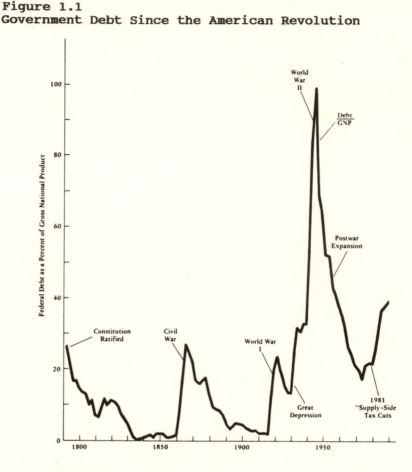

clear that the rate of growth of the debt has varied during different time periods. This book will devote more attention to those periods when the debt showed rapid growth.

Growth in public debt is not absolutely necessary, but the situation of a large debt is not unique to the United States. All governments as a part of their obligations must spend to provide public services, but they have several options for securing the funds they need to spend. Revenues can be raised through taxes, money can be created via the government printing presses, or funds can be obtained through the sale of government securities--the manner through which the government borrows. The choice of which option (or mix of options) to use is a matter of the government's policy of public finance, so a brief survey of the issues involved in public finance is necessary to establish a context for the history that will follow.

PUBLIC FINANCE

Every government has an enormous responsibility
regarding how it manages its finances, as every policy
in this area will have an impact on the economy as a
whole and on individual citizens. A primary source of
finance for the U.S. government comes from its power to
tax as granted by the Constitution. When that power is
used effectively so that the government collects more in
tax revenues than it spends during a given period
(usually the government's fiscal year), its budget will
be in surplus; when the tax revenues equal the amount
spent, the budget is in balance; and when tax revenues
are insufficient to cover government expenditures, there
is a budget deficit. Budget deficits require borrowing,
while surpluses can be used to pay off debt. The
current public debt reflects the total net borrowing
over payoffs of debt by the government for the course of
its history. A high debt reflects a history of deficits
and borrowing.

Federal government budget deficits arise primarily
for three reasons: unforeseen emergencies, economic
recession, and deliberate policy. The classic example
of an unforeseen emergency is a war, although there are
others, such as drought, flood, or the recent efforts to
stop the flow of drugs into the country. War remains
the best example and has been the cause of most periods
of government borrowing in the United States.

When a war is declared, the government needs to
obtain resources to fight it. In a free, democratic
market economy, such as the United States, the national
government cannot commandeer those resources it needs
for the war, but must purchase them. It can raise the
funds it needs for those purchases by increasing the
taxes of its citizens. No matter how willing citizens
may be to pay higher taxes in their patriotic zeal for
the war, there are limits to how quickly they can do so.
Furthermore, taxes will have an impact on the economy.

With taxes, as with any fiscal policy, the
government's actions will help some members of society
and harm others. Those who benefit are the recipients
of the government's spending, either owners of the
needed resources to fight a war or sufferers from a
calamity that the government wishes to redress. Those
who will be burdened must see their disposable income
decreased due to the higher taxes used to cover those
payments.

How the burden of increased taxes will be felt will
depend on the type of tax. Throughout much of its
history, for example, the government of the United

States relied heavily on tariffs--taxes on imports--and excise taxes on certain items (e.g., a tax on liquor) for much of its revenues. Purchasers of those taxed products shared the burden of the tax with the suppliers of the product. When resort was made to an income tax, the burden of the tax was spread wider, but depended on the progressiveness of the tax and the number of exemptions and deductions allowed. There is also a question of how taxes will affect economic decisions to work, save, or invest. High taxes could encourage citizens to work less, for they do not get to keep their earnings, or to work more in order to maintain their standard of living. A concern is that the burden of the short-term high increase in taxes needed to pay for an emergency may be too heavy for taxpayers to bear.

When a deficit is caused by an economic recession, the policy of raising taxes becomes even more problematic. Because of the action of what economists call automatic stabilizers, a recession will push a government's budget toward a deficit (i.e., a larger deficit or smaller surplus). As economic conditions worsen, business sales and profits decline, and unemployed workers lose their wages. The reduction in income and the reduction in purchase of taxed products will cause the government's tax collections to go down. At the same time, the government may be forced to spend more for the relief of the unemployed (in a sense, a recession is also an unforeseen emergency). Using a tax increase to make up for this deficit could worsen economic conditions by further reducing income and consumer spending or business investment. The size and extent of this negative impact will depend on which persons or sectors of the economy the tax burden falls on.

This tendency for the federal government's budget to show a deficit during recessions has existed throughout the history of the United States. In the last four decades, however, fiscal policy in the United States has seen a more deliberate running of a deficit in order to stimulate the economy. Under this policy, as will be described in chapters 6 through 9, taxes may be reduced to stimulate the economy at a time when government spending is being increased. The economic stimulation is expected to come from the encouragement of purchases by consumers, investment by business, and more effort on the part of business or employees as a result of the extra money the tax reduction will give them. In this case deficit is a deliberate policy and there is no direct need to eliminate it.

To avoid borrowing to finance a deficit, the government can resort to the power of the printing press and create money to pay its bills. In the United States, the constitutional authority of the federal

government to print money and declare it legal tender
has been well established and is without limit. As will
be described below, it has used this power in several
wars.   Early in this century, the power to print money
was given to the Federal Reserve Banks, and the process
of using money to finance government activities has
taken on the more complex procedure of monetizing the
debt (also to be described below). But increases in the
amount of money circulating in the economy can have an
impact on economic conditions.

When the economy is in a recession, this impact may
be small and may even stimulate production.   When the
economy is at full employment with all resources being
used, which is usually the case during a war, increases
in the amount of money add to the ability of all persons
holding money to purchase goods and services. Since no
increases in production can be attained, prices will
increase--a condition commonly known as inflation.
Instead of facing a burden of taxes, individuals suffer
from inflation when the government pays its bills by
printing money. Moreover, as with the burden of taxes,
the burden of inflation is unevenly felt, as some
persons gain from its effects while others lose.

Because the burdens of taxation or inflation are
directly if unevenly felt, a portion of government
spending will be financed through borrowing. However,
"even" borrowing imposes a burden on the members of a
society. Whenever a government spends, it must purchase
resources that its citizens also wish to purchase. The
problem facing a government spending program is how to
accomplish this shift of resources to its needs and how
to minimize the costs to its citizens in terms of lost
resources.   The issue of who bears the burden of this
shift when borrowing takes place is the subject of much
debate among the public and among economists.

The popular view is that the burden of government
borrowing (i.e., the public debt) is placed on a future
generation that will have to pay it back.   A more
traditional view among economists is that no matter how
the government finances its purchases--taxes, printing
money, or debt--the real burden is the resources given
up by private citizens for government use.   The real
cost of World War II, according to this view, would be
the cars and refrigerators that were left unproduced in
order to produce airplanes and tanks.[1]   Further,
proponents of this view might contend that the present
generation is the one that presumably would bear the
burden of the debt the government built up during World
War II, but currently no one seems to be worrying about
it.

In opposition to this traditional view, James
Buchanan argues that there is no real burden imposed on
a current generation by deficit finance through

borrowing, because by lending money to the government, private citizens either invested money they were not intending to spend (savings) or volunteered to curtail their spending to make the loan. Since they chose freely to buy government securities, they felt no burden. When a tax is imposed in the future to pay off that debt, those future taxpayers will bear the burden of the debt.[2]

While this argument has merit, it might still be noted that if the government increased the interest rate on its securities to help recruit volunteers, those higher interest rates would impose a cost on the rest of society as they would cause all other interest rates to go up. If the resulting higher interest rates reduce spending on consumption items, then the present generation loses. When investment spending declines due to the higher rates of interest, a future generation will have less capital to work with, giving it a lower level of income than it might otherwise have had.[3]

There is no intention in this book to settle the issues relating to the burden of the debt or of either of the other two methods of public finance. On this issue as on many other issues, the answer to be derived from economists is "It depends." The point here is simply that any policy concerning government spending imposes a burden on the population and has the potential for altering economic conditions.

In choosing which policy or mix of policies to use, government officials throughout the history of the United States have responded as much to political exigencies as to economics; ideology about which type of government was desirable also played a role in government finances. In the history that follows, appropriate mention will be made of the policies chosen at a particular time, and where possible, economic and political reasons for the choice will be provided; the wisdom of those choices will be left for others to determine. The main purpose here, as the title of the book suggests, is to examine closely those cases where the government chose borrowing to pay for its purchases, and to consider the burden the government put on itself in terms of debt management and administration.

DEBT MANAGEMENT AND ADMINISTRATION

When the federal government borrows, it does so by selling its securities--stock, as it was called in the early days, and the bills, notes, and bonds of today. The sale of these securities can also have an impact on the economy, as can their redemption. Debt management is concerned with minimizing the impact of the sale or redemption of government securities on economic conditions and forms a part of public finance. It also includes offering for sale securities that will be attractive to purchasers at minimum cost to the government. Debt administration refers to the detailed work involved with handling the sales of the securities, keeping the records of security ownership, and ensuring that interest payments on the securities are made properly and on time.

Once a decision is made for the federal government to borrow, it becomes a matter of debt management policy to determine the conditions under which the borrowing will take place. To be sure, the government wants to borrow at the lowest cost in terms of the interest rate it must give to lenders, but that interest rate must reflect what prospective purchasers of securities can earn on their money elsewhere. If interest rates on government securities are not competitive with other options, the securities may have to be sold at a discount to attract purchasers. In addition, the life of the security must also be considered. As a rule, short-term securities require a lower interest rate than long-term issues, as purchasers are protected from increases in the interest rate while they are holding the security by being able to get their money back quickly when the security matures. But too much reliance on short-term borrowing can make interest rates rise and also involve frequent sales of securities.

Government securities can also be offered in large or small denominations, depending on whether it is desirable to attract purchasers from among persons of moderate income and wealth. There is also a choice between offering securities that are negotiable and can be resold on the open market, called marketable securities, or those that cannot be sold, which are known as nonmarketable. As will be seen, the debt management policies of the federal government, which are usually determined in the Treasury Department, have evolved as the amount of debt has increased.

Debt management must also be made consistent with the overall policy of public finance. As has been noted above, the sale of government securities can influence the general level of interest rates in the economy, which in turn can affect economic conditions. Higher interest rates can reduce the availability of credit, which means that government borrowing can, as economists put it, crowd out private borrowing.

In addition, even though borrowing negates the need for the printing of money, debt management can create problems for money markets. Government borrowing and spending can shift the supply of money from one section of the country to another. Short-term securities are highly liquid (i.e., readily converted into cash), so they serve as near-money, and it is possible that if too much debt is long-term, budget surpluses will build up in the Treasury until the securities can be redeemed, thus reducing the supply of money.   These are all problems the federal government has faced during its existence, and its ability to solve them has depended in part on the nature of the banking system.   Debt management policy depends on the help of banks in order to minimize its monetary effects.   The history of debt management in the United States is linked to the evolution of the banking industry and central banking, and these topics will form an important part of this book.

Once debt management policies are decided, debt administration can begin.   The more complicated the debt management policy followed, the more difficult debt administration becomes.   Reliance on short-term securities may require frequent sales.   Long-term debt may necessitate elaborate records of ownership and interest payment.   Small denomination securities will heighten the recordkeeping task as more accounts must be opened.   Methods of debt administration have also evolved as the public debt has grown.

OVERVIEW OF THIS BOOK

The primary purpose of this book is to describe the historical events that took place within the U.S. government to bring about the evolution of the functions of managing and administering the public debt.   As described in this introduction, there has been a flow of causation from public finance to debt management to debt administration.   As each chapter title indicates, there have been periods when the attitude toward the size of the debt and the need to pay it off have varied, and efforts to manage and administer it reflected that changing attitude.

For nearly 130 years, the public debt was relatively small, and managing and administering it was concomitantly simple.   The debt was small because prevailing attitudes toward public finance fostered a fiscal system that relied on balanced budgets except for wartime.   A rudimentary level of banking organization supplemented this policy, and at times the Treasury Department acted independently of the banking system. Debt management remained a simple task within the Treasury Department.   Debt administration policies retained the clerical aspect they had from their beginning and did not figure largely in the early years of public debt.   This system will be the focus of chapters 2 through 4.

Over the past 70 years there has been an attitude of less concern over the payment of the public debt, starting with the debt incurred during World War I. There has also been a shift in policy away from balanced budgets and toward functional finance where the government's budget forms part of economic management policy. Starting with the Great Depression and continuing through World War II until the present, federal budget deficits have become the norm. Managing the resulting debt has become a complex job involving cooperation between the Treasury Department and the Federal Reserve. Debt administration became more complex and required greater reliance on modern technology.

Eventually the job of debt administration required the formation of a specialized agency within the Treasury Department, the Bureau of the Public Debt, to undertake responsibility for handling offerings of government securities, accounting for their issuance and redemption, drafting payment checks, and recording sales of U.S. savings bonds. The evolution of the system of debt management and administration that is coordinated by the Treasury Department, the Federal Reserve, and the Bureau of the Public Debt will be an important topic of chapters 5 through 11.

NOTES

1. Campbell R. McConnell, _Economics_ (New York: McGraw-Hill, 1987), p. 296.

2. James M. Buchanan and Marilyn R. Flowers, _The Public Finances_, 6th ed. (Homewood, Ill.: Richard D. Irwin, 1987), pp. 280-281.

3. Richard A. Musgrave and Peggy B. Musgrave, _Public Finance in Theory and Practice_ (New York: McGraw-Hill, 1980), pp. 706-708.

2

The Beginnings
of Debt (1775–1801)

When the American colonists began their struggle for independence from England, they were confronted with the problem of paying for a full-scale war. This problem would plague them throughout the war and the ensuing constitutional era, yet they were very resourceful in solving it. Under the Federalist administration that took office soon after the ratification of the Constitution, government finances would finally be brought into order. Part of that order involved assumption of debt incurred during the Revolutionary War. For this reason it is said that the public debt of the United States originated at the country's very beginning, during the American Revolution.

The task of paying for the war was a pressing one, so when it became organized on May 10, 1775, the Continental Congress immediately went to work setting up the operations of its treasury. Its members selected the first financial Committee of the Congress on June 3, 1775, to estimate the extent of financing needed by Congress. Several successive committees were delegated to deal with finance, until February 17, 1776, when a permanent committee of five was appointed to take charge of the treasury. In those early days of struggle, the work of this committee mainly involved keeping track of the receipts and expenditures related to Congress's financial obligations. There was little public debt.[1]

FINANCING THE AMERICAN REVOLUTION

When it became clear that the war for independence might become lengthy, national finance became a more pressing matter. As with any government, the Continental Congress had the difficult choice of whether to raise taxes, print more money, or borrow. Even among the leaders of the revolution there were differing opinions over which form of finance to use.

In his essay Common Sense, Thomas Paine linked the idea of borrowing to the argument of whether separation from England was an essential outcome of the struggle. Paine felt separation was desirable and that it was worth going into debt to achieve. He noted that while the colonies had no debt, a supposed virtue, they also had no navy. England had the vice of a debt, but also had a navy. By going into debt, the colonists could build a navy to match England's and thereby improve their chances of winning the war. The debt would be worthwhile if it resulted in an established government with its own constitution. As for the virtue of the debt itself, Paine held the view that "No nation ought to be without a debt. A national debt is a national bond."[2] Citizens would be loyal to a government that owed them money.

Although he agreed with Paine over the virtue of debt, Alexander Hamilton understood that the issuance of paper money to finance the war was absolutely necessary, even though this method of finance was to be avoided in peacetime. Ben Franklin, while in agreement with Hamilton on the necessity of printing money, fully recognized that paper dollars as a method of finance were similar to a tax. The people who held them would find that they declined in value due to the inflation their issuance caused.[3] Direct taxes by the national government were not feasible. The individual colonies did not accord the power to tax to the Continental Congress.

Hamilton and Franklin were both right. The American Revolution was financed primarily through the printing of money, and this method led to inflation. On July 23, 1775, three men were appointed by the Continental Congress to oversee the printing of $2 million in currency. In adopting this policy, the Continental Congress was following an established pattern, one that had been used successfully by the separate colonies many times during the previous century. In those days, the colonies had no method of quickly raising taxes. Tax collections were slow and there was always a shortage of specie, (i.e., gold and silver coins), with which to pay taxes. As a short-term stopgap, they printed money to pay their bills directly. It was intended that this money would be redeemed with funds raised through the later payment of taxes, and the legislation authorizing the printing of that money usually stipulated specific taxes that would be paid to redeem the money. In some cases, it was allowable for the taxes to be paid with the new money itself, which would serve to remove it from circulation.[4]

As the war continued, individual colonies and the

Continental Congress employed this method of public
finance in varying degrees. The war lasted longer and
cost more than any of the colonists had anticipated,
resulting in the excessive printing of money.
Consequently, the "Continental" dollars issued by the
Congress suffered a great decline in value during the
course of the war.   They became "not worth a
Continental," in the parlance of the day.   Their value
dropped drastically during the war.   In 1777 it took
$1.25 in Continentals to buy $1 of hard currency
(usually gold coins); by April 1781, $167.50 in
Continentals was needed to purchase the same amount of
hard currency.[5] Still, the Continental dollars were the
most important form of public finance during the war, as
can be seen in Table 2.1, which details all sources of
finance for the war from 1775 to 1781.

When the value of the Continental dollars rapidly
declined, the colonists had to use other methods of
public finance.   It was not possible to raise taxes,
because they had gone to war under the cry of "taxation
without representation is tyranny." The colonists and
the Continental Congress eventually turned to borrowing
on a small scale.   However, the management of the
treasury operations remained cumbersome, and
administration of the public debt was often chaotic.

On July 29, 1775, the Continental Congress jointly
commissioned Treasurers George Clymer and Michael
Hillegas to manage the government's finances.   As
previously mentioned, in February 1776, a committee of
five persons was appointed to control the activities of
the Treasury, with an Office of Audits and an Auditor
General established shortly thereafter.   The committee
operated under several names, including the Board of
Treasury and the Treasury Office of Accounts.   Five
additional members were added during 1776.[6]   Loan
certificates (equivalent to bonds) were first issued in
October 1776, and carried an interest rate of 4 percent.
Loan-office commissioners were appointed in each colony
to oversee the sales of loan certificates, and these
local agents became the fiscal officers of the national
government for their region.   The interest rate on the
loan certificates was soon raised to 6 percent and
remained at this level for the duration of the war.[7]
Additional loans were negotiated with overseas lenders,
mainly from the king of France and from banks in the
Netherlands.   There were even times when loan
certificates were issued as a direct means of payment
for soldiers and suppliers.

The Continental Congress was not given the power to
raise revenues through taxes.   It had to continually
finance a deficit by borrowing, and the resulting debt
continued to grow.   Without the ability to raise
revenues in line with expenditures, the government could

Table 2.1
Federal Income to 1780

Continental Currency	$45,489,000
Government Bonds	5,932,051
State Credit	1,719,315
Total Domestic Income	$53,140,366
Foreign Aid	
France	2,111,528
Spain	69,444
Holland	32,000
Total Foreign Income	2,212,972
Total Federal Income	$55,353,338

Source: Barry W. Poulson, Economic History of the
          United States (New York: Macmillan, 1981),
          p. 107.

---

not accumulate a surplus to pay off prior debt, which made debt management very difficult.   In an effort to achieve some order, the Treasury Office, as it was then called, was reorganized three times between 1777 and 1780.   In February 1779, an Office of the Secretary of the Treasury was formed.   In July of the same year, the office was discontinued, and a Board of the Treasury replaced the Treasury Committee.   These changes, however, did nothing to solve the problem.   A major crisis developed in 1780 when interest payments due in specie had to be suspended.   Some interest payable by bills of credit was continued until 1782.[8],[9]   To address the crisis, the Congress eliminated the Treasury Office and Board of the Treasury and replaced it with a Department of Finance.

Robert Morris, a wealthy merchant and member of Congress nicknamed "the Financier," was chosen as leader of the new department.   His official title was Superintendent of Finance, and his staff was composed of a Comptroller, a Treasurer, a Register, and various clerks.

Morris created some order in Treasury affairs simply by reporting the total debt owed.   This marked the beginning of Annual Treasury Reports to the president.   On January 1, 1783, the public debt totaled $43 million, $7.9 million owed to foreigners and $35.1 million owed at home.   Of the domestic debt, $11.5 million was in the form of loan certificates with two years' interest past due on them.[10]   In 1784, after several years of service, Morris summed up the situation to the president of the Congress by noting that affairs had become so complicated it was hardly possible to say who was at fault.[11] This was a portent of difficult times ahead. Morris then resigned and was replaced by a three-person Board of Treasury. Finances, however, still did not improve.

Throughout this period, the overriding problem for the Treasury was how to raise enough revenue to handle its finances. Even under the Articles of Confederation that had been passed in 1781, the states had not granted the Continental Congress any power to raise money through taxes, jealously guarding that right for themselves. The separate states were each expected to contribute their fair share for expenses. Whenever the Congress did ask the states for money to pay off the debt, it was not forthcoming. Morris and others who later formed the Federalist Party felt that this was a deplorable situation which had to be remedied by a stronger central government with adequate power to raise revenue. A new method had to be implemented to secure a more sound system of public finance. The problem of managing the public debt would become one of the issues in the series of events that led to the passage of the Constitution in 1787.

In 1783, Congress was given the power to raise taxes via an import tariff, and this source of finance was sufficient to meet the normal operating expenses of the national government. Tariffs would come to play a pivotal role in the government's finances for the next 150 years. The states also agreed to pay the interest on the public debt. But in 1785 revenues were still inadequate for debt service, and Congress was forced to suspend payment of interest on debt to France. By 1787 payment of principal was in default as well. This default made it very difficult for the government to borrow money overseas. With the ability of the government to meet its financial obligations called into question, domestic borrowing was also foreclosed. For example, when interest payments were suspended in 1782, the market value of loan certificates dropped to about one-fourth of their stated value, where they remained until 1788. The government's financial structure was so weak that it appeared unlikely that a budget surplus to pay off the debt would ever be generated. In addition to the Federalists, holders of the debt became advocates for a stronger central government that would pay off the public debt at par.

THE CONSTITUTIONAL ERA

Many issues confronted the men who met in Philadelphia in the summer of 1787 to frame a constitution and form a new government. At the heart of these issues lay the overriding question of whether citizens of the states would feel a loyalty to a powerful central government.   Of the public debt, Alexander Hamilton sagely noted that it could form an important bond between holders of the debt and the government.   As he had written in 1781, "A national debt, if it is not excessive, will be to us a national blessing."[12] The key to strengthening that bond was not necessarily payment of the debt, but an assurance that it would be paid.   The framers of the Constitution established measures to provide this assurance.

As one way of improving the finances of the government, the Constitution gave Congress the power "to lay and collect taxes, duties, imposts and excises" and "to borrow money on the credit of the United States."[13] There was a debate in the House of Representatives over whether to continue with a Treasury Commission or to have a department with a single head. Congress finally decided to replace the Board of Treasury, which had been revived in   1784.   They established the Treasury Department, on September 2, 1789, which was to be headed by a Secretary whose responsibilities included preparing "plans for the improvement and management of the revenue, and for the support of public credit."[14] The Secretary would have a staff consisting of an Assistant to the Secretary, a Comptroller, an Auditor, and a Register to assist him in carrying out his duties. Congress named Alexander Hamilton, one of the most active and intellectual Americans of his day, Secretary of the Treasury.

As a young officer during the Revolutionary War, Hamilton had greatly impressed his superiors, especially Washington and Robert Morris, with his abilities and intelligence.   An espouser of very conservative views, he had very strong opinions on the public debt and government fiscal obligations.   Near the end of the war he had even suggested that the army and government creditors unite to compel Congress to take the measures needed to pay what these two groups were owed.   Nor was he shy about what methods should be employed, including the use of taxes. Not only would the public debt be a national blessing in terms of the support it would garner from the wealthy for the national government, the taxes needed to pay and service the debt would also force the masses to work harder to pay those taxes.[15] This was an argument made often at the time, and it fit in with Hamilton's vision of an industrial society fostered by tariffs to protect the elite of businessmen who would run it, while those tariffs would also give the government funds to provide other services for business.

Conservative fiscal management such as Hamilton proposed was exactly what the government needed, so his selection as Secretary of the Treasury was highly appropriate. Hamilton envisioned that his chief responsibility was to establish faith in the new government's ability to meet its obligations. This faith was crucial to a restoration of public credit. The first step in attaining this public credit was to service the debt accrued during the war. As required by law, in 1790 Hamilton presented his first plan to Congress as a "Report Relative to a Provision for the Support of Public Credit," calling for a policy under which the government would assume responsibility for the public debt. This policy would establish faith in public credit.

Hamilton proposed that all of the national debt, both principal and interest, be paid in hard currency. Creditors could exercise an option to take payment in the form of western land, or they could demand hard currency. At the same time, however, Hamilton would lower the interest rate on the debt from 6 percent to 4 percent by exchanging it for a new issue of debt in various combinations with land and lower interest securities. He also proposed that the debt payments be made to current holders of the bonds and that the national government assume the debts incurred by the separate states for fighting the war.[16]

These last two proposals caused an especially heated debate in Congress. One group, headed by James Madison in the House of Representatives, wanted payment to be made to the original holders of the debt, with present holders being accorded only the low market value they had paid for the debt. In this way speculators could be prevented from undue gain based on the full payment of the debt, and those persons who had made the initial sacrifice in fighting the Revolutionary War would be rewarded. They would not suffer because they had been forced to sell their government loan certificates at a loss due to hard times. To give redress to original holders, while not unduly penalizing present holders, Madison proposed to let the present holders "have the highest price that has prevailed in the market; and to let the residue belong to the original sufferers. This will not do perfect justice; but it will do more real justice, and perform more of the public faith, than any other expedient proposed."[17]

Conversely, Hamilton and his followers argued that it would not always be possible to determine the original holders of the debt, as in many cases loan certificates had been issued by agents in each state in direct payment to soldiers and suppliers and the original name on the Treasury register might have belonged to the state agent. Determining the market price paid by the holders of the debt would be equally difficult. In many cases the loan certificates had

changed hands several times.   No one believed that
intermediate holders of the debt should be compensated,
but it would be impossible to determine how the gains or
losses could be allocated among original and present
holders of debt certificates. The simplest plan would
be to pay full value to current holders.[18]

Hamilton's most persuasive argument was related to
restoring confidence in the public credit.   Any
repudiation of payment to present holders of debt, he
argued, would be contrary to the sanctity of contracts
and would call into question the transferability of
federal government debt instruments.   As he put it in
his report,

> The nature of the contract in its origin, is,
> that the public will pay the sum expressed in
> the security, to the first holder, or his
> assignee. The intent in making the security
> assignable, is, that the proprietor may be
> able to make use of his property, by selling
> it for as much as it may be worth in the
> market, and that the buyer may be safe in the
> purchase.[19]

The fact that original holders may have sold from
extreme necessity made for a difficult case.   But if
Congress wanted to aid them it should do so directly and
not at the expense of present holders and of fiscal
prudence.   Hamilton's view prevailed, with Madison's
motion in the House to discriminate between original and
current holders being defeated by a vote of 36 to 13.
This sound policy has remained a part of the U.S.
government ever since.

The issue of assumption of state debts also found
those former allies and collaborators on the Federalist
Papers, Hamilton and Madison, on separate sides.   Here
again, Hamilton thought that fiscal responsibility on
the part of the central government dictated payment by
that government of all debt incurred in the fighting of
the Revolutionary War. The opposition, led by Madison,
believed that such an assumption of state debts
discriminated unfairly between states that had acted
responsibly and those that had not, in terms of funding
their   wartime   activities   and   in   meeting   their
obligations.   Here again Hamilton prevailed, but only
after Madison and Jefferson switched sides and voted for
his proposal.   In return, Hamilton helped the two
Virginia leaders secure a commitment to locate the
capital of the new government on the Potomac River.[20]

The end result of Hamilton's victories was the
Funding Act of 1790, which called for the issuance of
new federal bonds to cover all the old debt.   Each

holder was given two-thirds of his former debt in 6
percent stocks with interest payments to begin
immediately. The remaining third was paid in stocks
with interest deferred for ten years. Interest due from
prior debt was paid in 3 percent stock. Special bonds
with a total value of $21.5 million were issued to be
exchanged for state debt, with four-ninths of the
payment made in 6 percent stock with immediate interest,
two-ninths in 6 percent stock with interest deferred for
ten years, and the remainder in 3 percent stock with
immediate interest payments.[21] Not all the bonds were
exchanged, however, as the amount of state debts
ultimately totaled $18.2 million.[22]

In his report to Congress in 1790, Hamilton had
estimated that there was a total public debt of
$77,124,464 as of December 1789 (see Table 2.2). By
assuming the obligation to pay this debt, the government
firmly reestablished its credit. It also created a
windfall for speculators.

In the years prior to the passage of the
Constitution and the assumption by the federal
government of all debt, government securities sold in
the market at about one-quarter of their face value.
The government, had it acted judiciously and purchased
its securities on the open market, could have retired a
substantial portion of the debt at less than par, saving
the Treasury millions. By assuming the debt at its
stated value, the government instead conferred that
money on holders of the debt. By February 1792, for
example, the 6 percent immediate interest-bearing bonds
were selling in the market at $1.20 on the dollar. A
shrewd speculator who had bought $100 in bonds in 1786
at a market price of about $15 could have sold the
replacement bonds issued by the new government for
$121.50 in 1792, realizing a handsome profit.[23]

It was probably true that a group of speculators,
acting on "inside information" based on what the
Constitutional Convention was proposing in 1787 and what
Hamilton was trying to accomplish in 1790, bought
government securities in anticipation of their
redemption at par. This was plausible especially in
terms of the assumption of state debt, since news of
this proposed policy was slow to reach several states.
It was also presumably true that some members of the
Constitutional Convention, as well as members of the
newly formed government, engaged in speculative
practices. Hamilton himself claimed that he had left
government service poorer than when he had entered it,
but his chief assistant, William Duer, amassed a large
sum of money on speculation in government and state
debt.[24] It is also likely that many of these persons
had purchased their government securities at face value

Table 2.2
Hamilton's Estimate of Total Government Debt
(December 1789)

Foreign Debt	
Principal	$10,070,307
Arrears of interest	1,640,072
TOTAL	$11,710,379
Domestic Debt	
Principal	$27,383,917
Arrears of interest	13,030,168
TOTAL	$40,414,085
State Debt	
Ascertained	$18,201,206
Estimated balance	6,798,794
TOTAL	$25,000,000
TOTAL PUBLIC DEBT	$77,124,464

Source: Louis Hacker, "Secretary of the Treasury,"
          in Thomas C. Cochran and Thomas B. Brewer,
          eds., Views of American Economic Growth: The
          Agricultural Era (New York: McGraw-Hill,
          1966), p. 95.

and were bona fide creditors of the government. In that
case, all they received was full payment of the amount
owed them by the government. In either case, holders of
the debt were still taking a risk. Just because a new
government had assumed the debt, holders of the debt
were not guaranteed payment.

In retrospect, it can be seen that the risk was
worth taking, as the federal government assumed a policy
that assured full creditor security. Although some
individuals may have gained wealth unfairly, the country
as a whole was the biggest gainer. Hamilton's plan for
consolidating and funding the total debt incurred in
fighting the Revolutionary War established once and for
all a systematic method for managing the public debt of
the United States. The general application of that
system is continuing to serve the government today.

THE FEDERALIST ERA

The system of debt management installed by Hamilton
worked well in terms of consolidating the debt and
permitting the government to make payments of interest
as they came due. Hamilton proposed, on May 8, 1792,
and Congress accepted, a sinking fund policy as a means

to meet this obligation. Revenues from post office operations, duties, and public land sales would be vested in a group of Commissioners, comprised of the President of the Senate, the Speaker of the House, the Chief Justice, the Secretary of the Treasury, and the Attorney General. They would use these funds to pay off the debt, either through payment to bondholders at face value of the bonds or through purchase from individual holders on the open market.[25] This fund, which specifically earmarked monies for debt retirement, was little used in actual practice.

With the public credit secured, Hamilton and his colleagues turned to other areas related to government finance. Since a sound system of money was essential for the government as well as for the country and Hamilton's economic plans for it, the Federalists thought it necessary to set up a monetary system based on specie. The Coinage Act of 1792 accepted as legal tender coins from foreign and domestic mints, with gold coins carrying 15 times the value of silver coins of the same weight. It was hoped that this would secure adequate supplies of coin for the country, but the 15:1 ratio gave gold a lower value than production considerations warranted, so many gold coins were withdrawn from circulation.[26] It became crucial to devise a sound system of banking to supplement the money supply and to assist the government's debt management policies.

Banks hold a special place in a market economy. First, they perform the important task of accumulating the savings of a multitude of individuals and making those funds available to a variety of borrowers for investment in productive ventures. Second, and even more important, banks can create money through the issuance of bank notes, as was done in early times, or with checks, as is done today. In principle, under a metallic money system as existed in the United States during this era, banks would gain funds partly from the capital put into the banks by their owners, but mainly from the deposits of gold or silver coin accepted from customers.

Instead of using those coins for making loans, however, banks could issue notes that were backed by the gold and silver reserves they held and payable on demand. When these notes were presented to the banks for payment, gold and silver would be given in return for them. Payment of the loan plus interest might also be made in coin. But as long as the notes were not presented for payment to the banks, they could remain in circulation as another form of money. As long as the banks' reserves of specie remained intact or grew, the banks could issue additional bank notes, until the total of bank notes issued by any bank (and thus all banks) were a multiple of total reserves of specie. As long as runs on the banks were avoided, where every depositor tried to withdraw specie or note holders presented their bank notes for redemption, the process of bank note expansion could continue. The limits to this expansion depended on the prudence of the management of each bank, although a strong central bank could also place limits on the issuance of bank notes by banks, as will be discussed in the next chapter.

In the early years of its life, the U.S. government was the largest financial agent in the country. Its deposits or withdrawals of specie could be very unsettling for the banking system. For example, if the federal government chose to run a budget surplus by increasing taxes, to pay those taxes citizens would withdraw specie from the banks. In addition, since the government's receipts and expenditures did not match up geographically, it faced problems in shifting its funds around the nation.

All of this was fairly well understood by sophisticated experts in finance, such as Hamilton and Robert Morris. But in 1790 there were only three incorporated banks operating in the country,[27] and even though the number of banks would increase to 18 by 1794,[28] the banking system was still inadequate to serve the government's needs.

In response to this inadequacy, Hamilton, in his "Report on a National Bank" given to Congress in 1790, proposed formation of a federally chartered private bank. Using words that echoed Adam Smith's support for the Bank of England in The Wealth of Nations, Hamilton argued "that such a bank is not a matter of private property, but a political machine of greatest importance to the State."[29] Hamilton proposed a bank that was to be owned in part by the government while also holding government deposits. It was expected that such a bank, by issuing its own notes, would be able to establish a national currency.

The bill to charter the Bank of the United States (following convention, it will be referred to as BUS or the Bank) was passed by the Senate on January 20, 1791, and the House on February 8, 1791, both by two-to-one margins. It was signed by President Washington on February 25, 1791.[30]

Despite this seemingly easy passage, the chartering of the BUS actually sparked a heated debate, and the Bank's naysayers would continue to attack it and its successor for the next 45 years. James Madison led the initial attack on the bank by questioning its constitutionality and the country's need for such an institution. The Constitution did not give the government any power to establish a bank, and if it took that power, Madison believed, it would set a precedent that would enable it to establish any other business.

In terms of the BUS itself, Madison had reservations about the impact the bank would have on government finances. He especially worried that having been given the power to borrow under the Constitution, Congress was now creating an instrument to lend to it. If the process of borrowing by the government became as easy as calling on the BUS for loans, there might be no limit as to how much public debt the government could incur.[31]

Thomas Jefferson, although he admitted that the BUS might be a help to the government in organizing its finances, felt the cost of this help would be too high in terms of the power that would be accorded to the government. With his vision of the United States as an agrarian society populated by independent farmers, Jefferson did not care to see concentrations of large amounts of wealth in a few hands, which he feared the Bank would create. He also felt that the Bank would become so powerful that it would eliminate any competition from state-chartered banks, thereby abridging the right of the separate states to charter their own banks.[32]

Proponents of the Bank relied on the doctrine of "implied power." Since the Constitution gave Congress the power to coin money and regulate its value, they argued, this clause implied that Congress had the power to establish the means to accomplish these tasks. The BUS was such a means, they concluded, so its constitutionality was secure. This issue continually resurfaced during the life of the BUS and its successor, but in the original charter debate it was the telling argument.

The BUS was set up to have a total capital of $10 million. Subscriptions were begun on July 4, 1791, and the entire $8 million in stock available to the public was taken. The remaining $2 million was to be held by the federal government, and was purchased only after some tricky financial maneuvering between Hamilton and the BUS involving a loan from the BUS to the government. Hamilton later defended this financing of the government's holding in the BUS very ably.[33]

Headquarters of the BUS were opened in Philadelphia on December 12, 1791. During 1792, it expanded operations with branches in Boston, New York, Baltimore, and Charleston, with additional branches being established in Norfolk (1800), Washington and Savannah (1802), and New Orleans (1805).[34]

In its early years, the BUS did not live up to the fears of its opponents. Despite its existence, the number of state-chartered banks increased to 29 by 1800.[35] And while it did come to hold a portion of the public debt, $6.5 million out of $75.5 million outstanding, the Bank was not an excessive lender to the government.[36]

This last point is important to note, because there was a possibility for abuse of the lending power of the BUS in its early years. During the 12 years of Federalist administration, annual government expenditures exceeded receipts by about a million dollars. As a result, Hamilton's sinking fund plan was not able to operate properly, and the public debt grew by about $7 million, to a total of $83 million by 1801. Some of the increase was offset by cash in the Treasury and by the value of the stock in the Bank of the United States. Interest on the debt was the largest item in the budget, amounting to almost half of all expenditures at the time.

Military expenses associated with fighting Indians, and external conflicts with France, Spain, and Algiers also contributed to the deficit. To meet this deficit, the Treasury borrowed heavily from banks within the United States, as well as in Europe. At one point it became clear that public debt held by the Bank was hampering its ability to make private loans, so contrary to the fears of its opponents, it actually asked the government to reduce the amount of public debt that the Bank was holding. The ability of the Treasury to meet this request was limited. After several disappointing efforts at selling new bonds, in 1796 the Treasury began to issue noncallable, long-term securities. This policy would later cause some difficulties for the Treasury because it would not always be able to match its revenue collection with the periods when debt became payable.[37] This would create special problems in the 1820s, as will be discussed in chapter 3.

By 1795, Hamilton had made too many political enemies to remain effective, and he resigned. By maintaining close personal ties with his successor, Oliver Wolcott, he still remained influential in the government's policy-making, even though his political opponents regarded Wolcott as Hamilton's tool.[38] Hamilton's main contribution was in successfully setting up a debt management system and securing faith in the credit of the government. Conversely, Hamilton was accused by his enemies of not being particularly interested in the detailed aspects of Treasury operations, and it was not possible to get a clear statement of the public debt from the accounts he presented to Congress. The mundane details involved in the day-to-day operations of the Treasury Department were sadly neglected during the Federalist era.

To some extent this lack of clarity resulted from the budgeting procedure used by the government. Appropriations were lumped into a small number of categories, and until 1809, the Executive could transfer

unspent funds to different categories at will. Since
Hamilton never sent regular reports to Congress on the
government's finances, it was easy to assign him fault.
Still, it should be noted that when Wolcott resigned in
1800, at his request a committee of the House examined
Wolcott's conduct and found no discernable problem. The
Act of May 10, 1800, required the Secretary of the
Treasury to prepare an annual report to Congress.[39]
These annual reports became a concise summary of
activities at the Treasury and provided Congress with
sufficient information to judge how the government's
finances were being handled.

   Under Hamilton's overall guidance, the Treasury
Department established itself as the preeminent
administrative agency of the government. By controlling
the purse, the Treasury exercised a degree of fiscal
authority over other agencies and departments. This
growing authority was matched by a growth in the number
of employees in the central office of the Treasury
Department. In 1790 there were 70 employees. By 1792
that figure rose to 90. By 1801, when the seat of
government moved from Philadelphia to Washington, the
Treasury employed 78 persons in the Capital and 1,615 in
the field, mostly in the Customs Service. At the time,
this was considered an exceptionally large department to
administer.[40] The organizational system by which this
entire fiscal system was managed, basically the product
of Hamilton's genius, remains an outstanding achievement
of the Federalist period.[41]

   Because Hamilton resigned under political pressure,
it is important to note that in 1794 his operations as
Secretary were investigated by the House of
Representatives. He was absolved of any wrongdoing and
was declared innocent of any misuse of power.[42] Perhaps
the greatest testament to Hamilton's administrative
achievements came from his successors and former
enemies. Thomas Jefferson once lamented about
Hamilton's policies, "We can never get rid of his
financial system."[43] Albert Gallatin, Jefferson's
Secretary of the Treasury, was more complimentary,
asserting in 1801 that under the previous administration
less abuse in government had been practiced because "it
has been most closely watched."[44] These men would
establish equally high standards within their own
administrations.

NOTES

   1. Albert S. Bolles, The Financial History of the
United States, From 1774 to 1784 (New York: D. Appleton,
1892), pp. 9-11.

2. Thomas S. Paine, <u>Common Sense and Other Political Writings</u> (Indianapolis, Ind.: Bobbs-Merrill, 1953), p. 35.

3. Bray Hammond, <u>Banks and Politics in America</u> (Princeton, N.J.: Princeton University Press, 1957), p. 29.

4. James E. Ferguson, <u>The Power of the Purse</u> (Chapel Hill, N.C.: University of North Carolina Press, 1961), pp. 78-79.

5. Ferguson, <u>Purse,</u> p. 32.

6. Bolles, <u>Financial History,</u> p. 13.

7. Ferguson, <u>Purse,</u> p. 35.

8. Ferguson, <u>Purse,</u> p. 115.

9. Gene Gurney and Claire Gurney, <u>The United States Treasury: A Pictorial History</u> (New York: Crown, 1978), pp. 2-3.

10. Bolles, <u>Financial History,</u> p. 317.

11. Ferguson, <u>Purse,</u> p. 179.

12. Arthur M. Schlesinger, Jr., <u>The Age of Jackson</u> (Boston: Little, Brown, 1950), p. 11.

13. Margaret G. Myers, <u>A Financial History of the United States</u> (New York: Columbia University Press, 1970), p. 55.

14. Davis R. Dewey, <u>Financial History of the United States</u> (New York: Longmans, Green, 1934), p. 85.

15. Joseph Dorfman, <u>The Economic Mind in American Civilization, 1606-1865</u> (New York: Viking Press, 1946), p. 408.

16. Ferguson, <u>Purse,</u> pp. 293-295.

17. George R. Taylor, ed., <u>Hamilton and the National Debt</u> (Boston: D.C. Heath, 1950), p. 32.

18. Taylor, <u>Hamilton,</u> pp. 1-3.

19. Taylor, <u>Hamilton,</u> p. 12

20. Ferguson, <u>Purse,</u> pp. 306-323.

21. Taylor, <u>Hamilton,</u> pp. 3-4.

22. Ferguson, <u>Purse,</u> p. 330.

23. Ferguson, <u>Purse,</u> p. 330.

24. Taylor, <u>Hamilton,</u> pp. 93-96.

25. David F. Swanson, The Origins of Hamilton's Fiscal Policies (Gainesville, Fla.:   University of Florida Monographs, Winter 1963), pp. 50-51.

26. Susan Previant Lee and Peter Passell, A New View of American History (New York: W. W. Norton, 1979), pp. 110-111.

27. Lester V. Chandler, The Economics of Money and Banking, 4th ed. (New York: Harper & Row, 1964), p. 133.

28. Chandler, Money and Banking, p. 6.

29. Richard H. Timberlake, Jr., The Origins of Central Banking in the United States (Cambridge, Mass.: Harvard University Press, 1978), p. 5.

30. Hammond, Banks and Politics, pp. 209-210.

31. Timberlake, Origins of Central Banking, p. 7.

32. Hammond, Banks and Politics, p. 120.

33. Hammond, Banks and Politics, pp. 123-124.

34. Hammond, Banks and Politics, pp. 125-127.

35. Hammond, Banks and Politics, p. 144.

36. Timberlake, Origins of Central Banking, p. 5.

37. Paul Studenski and Herman E. Kroos, Financial History of the United States, 2nd ed. (New York: McGraw-Hill, 1963), pp. 54-56.

38. Dewey, Financial History, p. 117.

39. Dewey, Financial History, pp. 115-117.

40. Leonard D. White, The Federalists (New York: Free Press, 1965), pp. 122-123.

41. White, The Federalists, p. 126.

42. White, The Federalists, pp. 352-354.

43. Leonard D. White, The Jeffersonians (New York: Free Press, 1965), pp. 146-147.

44. White, Jeffersonians, pp. 146-147.

3

Keeping the
Debt Small (1801–61)

With the change of administration that took place in 1801, there transpired one of those dramatic shifts in political philosophy that are both epoch making and rarely seen in the United States. The Federalist program, which is often labeled Hamiltonian in honor of its chief advocate, had deemed it proper to use the powers of the central government to foster industrial growth in the private sector. If the government and its debt grew large in the process, that was of little concern. The Jeffersonians and their successors the Jacksonians, as agrarians, were disinterested and even distrustful of the accumulation of wealth the growth of industry might bring, especially when it ended up in banks.

In addition, they were fiscally conservative where the federal government was concerned. As James D. Savage points out, an underlying theme of the Jeffersonians was that government debt was corrupt and had the potential to subvert democracy. In support of this interpretation, Savage cites Jefferson's opinion on balanced budgets, expressed in a letter written to John Taylor in 1798: "I wish it were possible to obtain a single amendment to our constitution. I would be willing to depend on that alone for the reduction of our government to the genuine principles of it's [sic] constitution: I mean an additional article, taking from the federal government the power of borrowing."[1] By calling for a balanced budget amendment, Jefferson anticipated by 200 years the fiscal views of Ronald Reagan and his followers. But unlike them, he and his followers, even without constitutional backing, were able to keep the federal government small and to reduce the public debt. The next 60 years would be a period of low government expenditures and debt reduction.

THE JEFFERSONIANS

When Thomas Jefferson took office as President, he placed the Treasury Department in very capable hands. His Secretary of the Treasury, Albert Gallatin, had served on finance committees in the House of Representatives, where he had been the chief critic of Hamilton's methods of debt management. In 1796, Gallatin had authored "A Sketch of the Finances of the United States" to present his own opinion of how the public debt should be managed. In general, he opposed the idea of the public debt and especially its increase, on the grounds that it would make government insolvent. Recognizing that a rapid payment of the debt would impose a heavy tax burden on the population, Gallatin favored its gradual reduction through taxes and from proceeds due to the sale of public lands.[2] He also favored reductions in government spending.

Once in office, Gallatin was able to place some of his ideas in operation. He operated in a manner similar to Hamilton, using his position to guide the fiscal policies of the entire administration.[3] But the thrust of that policy changed, for Gallatin assumed as his chief responsibility the reduction of the public debt. He recognized that a sinking fund built from surplus revenues could not be consistently relied on to pay off the debt. He devised a plan whereby $7.2 million would be appropriated annually to pay off the debt. The money would be derived from reductions in expenditures. He was able to carry out this plan for the first six years of his term of office, and by 1811 the total debt had been reduced to $45.2 million. During that year, debt interest payments amounted to less than one-third of government expenditures, down from one-half under the Federalists in 1801. The foreign debt that had been contracted during the Revolutionary War was completely paid by 1810.[4]

The Jefferson administration was not totally concerned with fiscal prudence, however. In 1803, Jefferson and Gallatin both supported the expenditure of $15 million for the Louisiana Purchase, emphasizing their agrarian preferences. The new land would provide for further expansion of agriculture. The purchase price was paid with $2 million in cash from current revenue, $1.75 million in temporary debt, and $11.25 million of 15-year 6 percent stock.[5] This expenditure, however unwise it appeared at the time, proved to be a bargain.

The Louisiana Purchase also added the busy port of New Orleans to the nation. During the Jeffersonian period, customs collections continued to be the primary source of government revenue. As the nation grew and developed more overseas trade, tax collections increased. As part of his fiscal management, Gallatin was not only able to reduce the debt, he was also able to cut taxes. But he soon found this policy difficult to reverse.

Starting in 1807, as a result of a trade embargo aimed at isolating the United States from the Napoleonic Wars of Europe, customs revenues declined. Jefferson's imposition of the embargo was unpopular in many areas of the country, especially those reliant on trade for their livelihoods. When Gallatin proposed to increase customs rates, Congress refused to act, and total revenues fell. In 1809 the government had a $2 million deficit, the only one of Jefferson's administration.

The Jeffersonians were also made victims of their own fiscal conservatism on the issue of banking. The charter of the BUS came up for renewal in 1811, and the Jeffersonians discovered that the Bank had not performed badly. During the time Gallatin was pursuing his debt reduction program, the BUS also decreased its holding of public debt from $6.2 million to $2.23 million.[6] The Bank was not a dominant force in the market for government securities.

In addition, by acting like a central bank the BUS was found to be an ally of the Treasury in keeping the state banks in check. As noted in the last chapter, banks had the power to issue their own bank notes based on their reserves of specie. While prudence should hold the issuance of bank notes to a reasonable multiple of reserves, the longer the time and wider the area in which the notes circulated, the more tempting banks found it to issue more of them. A central bank could impose prudence on banks, however. By collecting notes issued by individual banks and presenting them for collection, a central bank could reduce the reserves of specie of individual banks and thereby limit their ability to issue notes. Banks would then have to curtail their lending to protect their reserve position.

A central bank can also assist individual banks during tight periods by helping to increase their reserves. Under a specie system, for example, a central bank can refrain from presenting bank notes for collection, in a sense making loans to individual banks, or find ways to deposit specie into the individual banks. In 1811, only two agencies existed with the concentrated fiscal operations required of a central bank: the BUS and the U.S. Treasury Department.

While its powers in this area were limited, the BUS had at times restrained other banks by presenting their notes for collection. At other times it helped expand credit by issuing its own notes and holding on to notes of other banks. Much of its accumulation of individual bank notes came from its role as the government's bank, for it received all monies collected by the Treasury in the form of individual bank notes.[7]

As fiscal agent for the government, the BUS paid interest on the public debt, took subscriptions for new issues of the debt, made salary payments to government officials, including the President, and helped the Treasury manage its foreign exchange operations. In evaluating the Bank's performance, Gallatin listed three advantages it secured for the government:

> 1st. A safe place of deposit for the public moneys.
> 2nd. The instantaneous transmission of such moneys from any one part of the continent to another, the Bank giving us immediately credit at New York, if we want it, for any sum we have at Savannah, or any other of their offices, and vice versa.
> 3rd. The great facility which an increased circulation and discounts give to the collection of the revenue.[8]

Despite Gallatin's support and growing praise for the Bank from around the country, the attempt to recharter it failed. On January 24, 1811, the House voted by 65 to 64 to put off indefinitely debate on the recharter bill, which effectively killed it. On February 20, 1811, the bill was defeated in the Senate by 18 to 17. Many Jeffersonians supported the recharter; Jefferson himself had given the bank de facto recognition by using it, while Madison, who had opposed the original charter of the BUS as a member of the House, as President came to support it. Still, there were enough Jeffersonian diehards, who, in combination with business and banking interests that feared the conservative policies on credit expansion of the BUS, were able to defeat its rechartering.[9]

With the cessation of the Bank's operation, the Treasury began placing its deposits with state banks. It also lost a valuable ally in its efforts to control the nation's finances. This lack would become readily apparent in the government's efforts to finance its next war.

When he became fearful that the country faced the prospect of another war, in 1807 Gallatin formulated a policy for coping with the financial strains of a possible war. The policy was simple. During a war the government should use its revenue to pay normal peacetime expenses, interest on existing debt, and interest on new wartime debt. It should borrow the remaining amounts it needed and thereby manage its finances. Gallatin's effort to anticipate the financing of war was never realized because customs revenues were not raised prior to the War of 1812, even though the eventuality of war seemed apparent. With its revenues reduced, and without the Bank to supplement its financial activities, the government was ill-equipped to handle the financial burden placed on it by the War of 1812.

The War of 1812 was financed mainly through the use of borrowed funds. Without the help of the BUS, the government found that its loan offerings were taken up very slowly by the public and the state banks. As a stopgap, the government did issue a large amount of small denomination Treasury notes, which were only slightly different from the "Continentals" of the Revolutionary War. They were declared legal tender for government transactions and were convertible into long-term securities in denominations of $100 or more. Even though they paid interest of 5.4 percent, many of them circulated as money, adding to inflation. The total of these notes outstanding at any time never exceeded $17 million.

During the war, Congress did enact new taxes. Tariffs were increased and internal taxes were placed on sugar, "spirits liquors," retailers of alcoholic beverages, bank notes and other financial instruments in excess of $50, and "all carriages for the conveyance of persons." As the war continued, the list of taxable items was expanded to include duties such as, "On every gold watch kept for use, $2. On every silver watch kept for use, $1."[10] As extensive and encompassing as they may sound, these taxes were insufficient in raising the large amount of funds needed to finance the war.

Five loans were also authorized in addition to the new taxes. A total face value of $55 million was sold, but because several issues were sold at a discount, they brought in only $48 million, or about $28 million in gold. The total public debt increased from $45.2 million on January 1, 1812, to $119.2 million as of September 30, 1815. Interest on the new debt ranged from 5.4 percent to 7 percent.[11] Following the practice of the time, the securities were of a high denomination issued to wealthy individuals and banks.[12]

The number of state-chartered banks grew greatly during this period, from 117 in 1811 to 338 in 1818.[13] Their earlier policy of indiscriminate issuance of notes increased as well. In addition to issuing bank notes based on specie reserves, many banks began to issue notes backed by their holding of Treasury notes. Since these were expanding during the war, the supply of money in circulation went up dramatically. During the inflation that followed, hard money began to be hoarded, and the banks had to stop redeeming notes in gold. In the absence of central bank control, there appeared to be no other alternative. The Treasury might have performed that function, but its effectiveness was limited because its own financial needs dictated a policy of issuing notes.[14]

The Treasury also had a difficult time collecting its taxes and other revenues in hard money, therefore having to accept state bank notes instead. In addition, the Treasury had no central fiscal agent or depository, functions that the Bank had previously performed, so its deposits were scattered in many different state banks, making access difficult. It often became impossible to get money to the geographic areas where it was needed. An attempt to revive the BUS was made during the war, but it failed.

The lack of a central bank and national currency created special problems of debt finance during the war. With the suspension of payment in specie, the only form of currency available was local bank notes. These local notes, however, circulated at different values in different areas. As a result, "differences in the rate of exchange arose between the several states, and even between several districts of the same state."[15] The Treasury was not always able to pay its obligations in a particular region for want of that region's currency. To gain local currencies, the Treasury offered bonds at below par in return for the currency it needed, "but where local funds had so accumulated as to approach the probable amount of the local demands, the price of the stock was raised at the Treasury."[16] In Boston and New York, for example, local funds were insufficient to pay Treasury notes that were due, so holders of those notes had the option of exchanging their notes, both principal and interest, for new notes (at a price of $95 old for $100 new) or accepting drafts on Philadelphia or Baltimore banks. In the absence of a central bank, all debt transactions took place at state loan offices.[17]

Having seen the problems the Treasury faced without the help of a fiscal agent, officials started a movement to charter a second Bank of the United States (hereafter referred to as 2BUS, or the Bank). By this time, the constitutionality of the Bank did not trouble its former opponents. President Madison set aside any objections to the Bank on constitutional grounds, even those he had raised 25 years earlier, because of "repeated recognitions, under varied circumstances, of the validity of such an institution, in acts of the legislative, executive and judicial branches of the government, accompanied by indications in different modes of the concurrence of the general will of the nation."[18] In short, if everyone wanted a national bank, it was constitutional. Current holders of the philosophy that the Constitution should be interpreted on the basis of the "original intent" of its framers should be wary of any imputation of "original intent" that might be derived from Madison's views on national banks.

The bill to charter the 2BUS passed the House in a series of votes including a final vote on April 5, 1816, which confirmed the Senate's approval of the charter on April 3 by a 22 to 12 vote. Madison signed the bill on April 10, 1816. The head office of the Bank opened in Philadelphia on January 7, 1817, with a total capital of $35 million; by 1830 it would operate 25 branches throughout the country.

In addition to having powers similar to that of the First Bank, the Second Bank took on direct responsibilities for the Treasury. In 1790, Congress had passed a law authorizing a loan commissioner located in each of the original states to issue or liquidate government certificates or notes to the public, pay interest and pensions, and maintain records. The loan commissioners entered transfers in their books, supervised subscriptions for and issued new certificates, calculated and transcribed the dividends payable to owners of outstanding stock, and in some cases paid the dividends.[19] These various duties were transferred to the Bank of the United States by an Act of March 3, 1817. Government funds were required to be deposited with the Bank, and the Bank made transfers of government funds without charge.

This latter service was especially important, since by this time New York City had become the most important port in the nation and a high proportion of customs revenues were collected there. These funds had to be made available to other areas on a timely basis. The Office of the Register, however, continued to act as recordkeeper for the Treasury.

The Bank got off to a slow start, which may be seen as a fault of its first president, William Jones.[20] But there was also a necessary adjustment to be made to the new system, and Jones's chief disability seems to have been his failure to prevent the Treasury from overpowering the Bank. In 1817, for example, Secretary of the Treasury William Crawford began urging state banks to cancel outstanding Treasury notes and send them to the Treasury. The Treasury had a surplus balance because its revenue in 1816 was $48 million, three times what it had been the prior year, and expenditures were reduced. Much of this surplus was in the form of bank notes. In 1817, the Treasury used $17 million to reduce its own outstanding notes and to cut down on its deposits with state banks as part of the transfer to the 2BUS.

This policy would have the effect of contracting the supply of money and credit, so the Treasury allowed the state banks to make transfers as best they could. In this way, as Esther Taus concluded, "The leadership in the money market was held, not by the National bank

or central bank, but by the United States Treasury."[21]
  Professor Richard H. Timberlake's assessment is more
blunt: "The Treasury was indeed the central bank."[22]
The 2BUS could ease the credit problems the Treasury was
creating, but could not offset them. It had to push the
state banks for a resumption of specie payment. The
overall effect of the policy was to create a period of
deflation and panic leading to a recession in 1819-20.
As a result, the Treasury saw deficits for the next
three years.
     Meanwhile, in 1819 the constitutionality of the
Bank was established by the Supreme Court in the famous
case of McCulloch v. Maryland. Maryland had tried to
limit the effectiveness of the Bank by placing a tax on
it. In the unanimous decision of the court, written by
Justice John Marshall, the federal government's ability
to set up the Bank or any other institution needed to
meet its constitutional obligations was affirmed.
     At the same time, Jones resigned as president of
the 2BUS. Under the able leadership of his successors
Langdon Cheves, who served four years, and Nicholas
Biddle, whose presidency spanned the remainder of its
life, the Bank kept the fluctuations of receipts and
payments of the U.S. government from seriously affecting
cash resources of banks and tightening the credit
markets of the country. Through the innovative device
of "branch drafts," checks drawn by an officer of a
branch of the Bank circulated like bank notes, and thus
the Bank enabled businessmen to send money inexpensively
from one part of the country to another.
     The Bank also helped the government control its
finances, which for the next several years after the
recession again had a surplus of $5 million to $8
million a year, starting in 1822. Some of that surplus
was spent on pensions to Revolutionary War veterans and
on internal improvement projects. The National Road and
several canals are examples of projects that were
started during this time with the surplus money. Effort
was also made to reduce the debt.
     After 1822, some debt reduction took place, but an
unusual problem arose because the debt did not become
due in an even pattern. From 1822 to 1825 the Treasury
had surplus cash because the debt was not redeemable on
call, while in 1824 and 1826 the debt would be $18
million more than the Treasury would have. From 1829 to
1831, surplus cash would again accumulate as there was
no debt due in those years.
     William H. Crawford, the Secretary of the Treasury
in 1822, anticipated this problem and asked Congress to
let him purchase public debt at the market price to even
out its payment.   Crawford recognized that the
accumulation of a surplus in the Treasury was harming
credit conditions in the economy.[23]   When Congress

declined, Crawford tried a plan whereby holders of debt could exchange their holdings due in 1825 and 1826 for 5 percent stock payable at a later time. Congress agreed, but few exchanges were made. Richard Rush, Secretary of the Treasury in 1825, paid off as much of the debt as the surplus allowed, exchanged a portion for new debt, and continued to pay interest on the remaining debt. By 1828, the total public debt had been reduced to $58.5 million. Despite the accumulation of debt during the War of 1812, the Jeffersonians' debt management program had left the country with less debt than the Federalists had 28 years earlier. Additionally, during this same period, the number of Treasury employees increased to 181 in Washington in 1826, with an increase of 894 persons employed in the Customs Service.[24]

THE JACKSONIANS

When Andrew Jackson entered office, his views on government debt and banking were so severe that even Jefferson might have found them overdone. Writing in 1824, Jackson had labeled the public debt "a national curse" and promised that if elected President his policy would be "to pay off the national debt."[25] He also made known his opposition to the 2BUS as fiscal agent for the Treasury, once--just before taking office--going so far as to tell Alexander Hamilton's son the odd notion, "Your father was not in favor of the Bank of the United States."[26] More importantly, Jackson, the war hero and man of action, was willing to fight for any cause in which he believed, and in this case, economic and political conditions were on his side.

The financial state of the government was in excellent condition when Andrew Jackson took over as President in 1828. The "Tariff of Abominations" of 1828 had raised the average tax rate on dutiable items to 41 percent. A new tariff act in 1832 reduced the rates on imports, but not enough to placate radicals in the South. A crisis was set off when South Carolina issued its Ordinance of Nullification whereby it attempted to declare the Constitution null and void and raised the menace of secession. Jackson countered the ordinance by taking a forceful stand on enforcing the Constitution as the unbreakable law of the land. It also helped when Congress passed a compromise tariff in 1833, reducing rates further.

To a large extent, the Jackson administration represented a culmination of the agrarian policies started by the Jeffersonians. Under Hamilton, the Federalists wanted a policy wherein the federal government would foster economic growth through tariffs,

internal improvements, and central banking. The
Jeffersonians were opposed to this system on the grounds
that it would lead to a concentration of wealth in a few
hands. However, they had learned to accommodate
themselves to various components of the policy. Albert
Gallatin had written a report on the need for a system
of canals and roads and had supported renewal of the
charter of the first Bank of the United States. By the
1820s, the Hamiltonian policy had been revived as Henry
Clay's "American System." Andrew Jackson remained loyal
to the agrarian system, however, and did not support
federal government funding of internal improvements.

As part of that agrarian system, the sale of public
land was encouraged. In the 1830s, there was a boom in
the sale of public land. The proceeds from those sales,
along with revenue from the high tariffs, would soon
enable Jackson to fulfill his promise to pay off the
public debt. As Table 3.1 indicates, the Treasury was
experiencing large surpluses by the middle of the 1830s,
mainly due to funds from land sales. By 1835, when the
surplus was larger than the total government budget, it
was possible to extinguish the public debt. But first
the issue of the recharter of the 2BUS had to be
resolved.

The battle over the rechartering of the 2BUS is one
of those historical events that still is clouded in the
mystery of what it was all about. It is doubtful, for
example, that Jackson's motives in fighting the Bank
will ever be established. The debate itself took place
at several levels. At a legal level there was still
some question in many minds about the constitutionality
of the Bank. In terms of economics, the Bank under
Biddle had taken on more and more of the role of a
central bank. Politically the 2BUS had made enemies,
especially among the rising business classes interested
in easy credit to finance their investment plans. Even
personally, there appears to have been a great distrust
and dislike between Jackson and Biddle.

It is clear that by 1828 the 2BUS had evolved into
a central bank, even though nothing in its charter
specified it as such. It alone through its branches had
a national network of contacts with state banks, and due
to its large reserves, on its own account and as agent
for the government, it had the wherewithal to keep a
check on state banks. Secretary of the Treasury Richard
Rush noted in his Annual Report for 1828 that the 2BUS
was a great aid in helping the Treasury "to apply the
public funds at the proper moment in every part of a
country of such wide extent" as the United States. He
went on to acknowledge the Bank's expansion and
contraction of its notes in response to the needs of the
economy, making it "the instrument alone by which

Table 3.1
Government Finance under Jackson

Year	Customs	Public Land Sales	Total Receipts*	Expenditures
1828	$23,200	$ 1,000	$24,800	$16,400
1829	22,700	1,500	24,800	15,200
1830	21,900	2,300	24,800	15,100
1831	24,200	3,200	28,500	15,200
1832	28,500	2,600	31,900	17,300
1833	29,000	4,000	33,900	23,000
1834	16,200	4,900	21,800	18,600
1835	19,400	14,800	35,400	17,600
1836	23,400	24,900	50,800	30,900
1837	11,200	6,800	25,000	37,200

*The total includes other, minor revenue.

Source: Bray Hammond, Banks and Politics in America
         (Princeton, N.J.: Princeton University Press,
         1957), p. 451.

Congress can effectively regulate the currency of the nation."[27]

Biddle was more blunt in his own appraisal of the Bank's power. When asked in 1832 by a Senate committee whether he pushed state banks too hard, he replied, "Never." But he continued, "There are very few banks which might not have been destroyed by an exertion of the power of the bank."[28] Biddle played right into the hands of his foes, for he admitted to a potential power that they feared. The key issue over the Bank was whether a private bank in competition with other banks should also have the power to regulate their activities.

To some extent this control was discretionary, as the 2BUS had a choice of presenting state bank notes in its own accounts for collection or holding on to them. As fiscal agent for the government, the Bank had less flexibility. Bank notes paid to the government had to be presented to the state banks to be redeemed in specie. It was especially important that specie be accumulated in the government's accounts when the government wanted to redeem its debt. Too much redemption of debt in a short period, especially since some of it was foreign-held, could lead to a withdrawal of specie from the banks and a curtailment of credit.

The assistance of the 2BUS in avoiding an undue

influence of Treasury actions on the money markets was well known. In his message to Congress in 1829, Jackson himself observed that in the last payment of the public debt,

> It was apprehended that the sudden withdrawal of so large a fund from the banks in which it was deposited, might cause much injury to the interests dependent on bank accommodations. But this evil was wholly averted by an early anticipation of it at the Treasury, aided by the judicious arrangements of the officers of the bank of the United States.[29]

Here can be seen the sort of cooperation later to be arranged between the Treasury and the Federal Reserve.

At the same time, however, Jackson was warning Biddle: "Ever since I read the history of the South Sea Bubble, I have been afraid of banks. I have read the opinion of John Marshall. . . and could not agree with him."[30]   Jackson's distrust of banks could have come from financial difficulties he had experienced in his youth.

It is possible, as Professor Robert Remini argues, that Jackson might have been willing to compromise and permit the rechartering of the 2BUS under modified terms.[31]   But Biddle apparently rejected any plan for compromise by pushing for a vote on the recharter in 1832, hoping to make it an issue in the presidential election. Jackson took up the challenge and determined to destroy the "Monster." Public support for the Bank was presented to Congress in the form of petitions, although some of these may have been at Biddle's instigation. The recharter application was approved by both houses of Congress (by 28 to 20 in the Senate and by 107 to 85 in the House). On July 10, 1832, however, Jackson vetoed this approval, and the Bank could not secure sufficient votes to override the veto.[32]

Supporters of the Bank hoped to be able to launch a new charter in the four years that the old charter still had to run. But Biddle undertook several actions that angered Jackson. In the 1832 elections Biddle spent about $100,000 in opposition to Jackson; Jackson's stand on the Bank may have cost him popular support, as his vote total declined, making him the only President to lose votes in an election campaign.[33]   In August 1833, the Bank sharply reduced its loans, arguing that it did so in anticipation of losing its charter. The Bank also mishandled a payment of the public debt in 1833, forcing it to resort to some unseemly financial scrambling to cover itself.[34],[35]

In response, Jackson announced on September 18, 1833, a policy of withdrawing government funds from the

Bank as a means of retaliation. Two successive
Secretaries of the Treasury refused to go along with
this policy, so Attorney General Roger Taney was
appointed Secretary of the Treasury. Starting in
October 1833, he began depositing fresh government
revenues in state banks, the so-called "pet banks,"
while paying expenditures from funds in the Bank.

Biddle retaliated with a further curtailment of
credit, putting more pressure on the state banks.
Initially there were seven "pet banks," but the number
expanded to 22 by the end of 1833 and over 100 within
three years. Even though the impact of the Bank's
actions were spread out, it was necessary for the
Treasury to help the "pet banks" by sending them
additional deposits. Treasury Secretary Woodbury
reported in 1835, "The public money continues to be
collected and deposited, under the present system of
selected banks, with great ease and economy in all
cases."[36]

It appeared that the government could function
without the 2BUS, but appearances soon proved to be
wrong. Meanwhile, in 1837 the second Bank of the United
States was liquidated. The federal government's
original investment was returned along with a profit.[37]

The government did not really need the extra
revenue at this time, as it was experiencing an influx
in revenues which resulted in large surpluses. As noted
in Table 3.1, annual federal revenue doubled during the
Jackson administration, from $25 million to $50 million.
As an opponent of Hamilton's view on government debt,
Jackson had once proclaimed, "I am one of those who do
not believe a national debt is a national blessing."[38]
In 1835 the $17.9 million budget surplus was greater
than total government expenses for the year; the next
year the surplus reached $20.4 million. By January
1835, for the first and only time, all of the
government's interest bearing debt was paid off.
Secretary of the Treasury Levi Woodbury enthusiastically
announced, "An unprecedented spectacle is thus presented
to the world, of a Government . . . virtually without
any debt."[39]

A reduction of the budget surplus was not possible
without a reduction in taxes, but the compromise that
had been reached over the tariff in 1833 would not allow
for any tax reduction. Expenditures for internal
improvements could have been increased, but Jackson was
opposed to these. Ever since his decision in 1830 to
veto government funding of the Maysville Road, internal
projects had become local matters. Secretary of the
Treasury Levi Woodbury thought the surplus should be
maintained as a fund to meet future deficits.

Instead, Congress decided to distribute the surplus
to the states, many of which were heavily in debt at the

time.   In 1836, Congress passed the Act to Regulate the Deposit of Public Money. The last three sections of the act ordered the transfer of Treasury deposits to accounts of the separate states. As a result, in the early months of 1837, a total of $28 million of the surplus was loaned to the states, although no one expected the loans to be repaid.

The Deposit Act of 1836 also set up requirements for banks to meet if they were to hold Treasury deposits.   Under provisions of the act, on July 11, 1836, Jackson issued the executive order known as the Specie Circular, which stated that only specie would be used for buying plots of public land in excess of 320 acres.

By itself, the Specie Circular might not have caused a problem for banks. But taken in combination with the closing of the 2BUS and the flow of funds to and from state banks as part of the distribution of the surplus to the states, there were just too many shocks for the banking system to cope with. The depository banks had only $15.5 million in specie reserves as against $45 million in government deposits.[40] International outflows of specie were also a problem at this time. Many banks had to suspend payment in specie, and the resulting panic brought about a recession in 1837.   Equally damaging, Secretary Woodbury had to report that the Treasury under the Deposit Act had "to give notice to such of the selected banks as had suspended specie payment that they could no longer be considered depositories of the public money."[41] But by that time Jackson had retired to Hermitage.

The Jackson administration ended with the government out of debt and with the country rid of the 2BUS. But his success in these accomplishments must be weighed against the costs. In his message vetoing the Bank's rechartering, Jackson challenged the Bank because of its power and questionable constitutionality.   Both arguments were overdone, especially the constitutional issue. He also argued that since the public debt was being paid off, there was no longer a need for a national bank to help manage and administer it.   Here Jackson was on solid logical ground. There was only one problem: What would happen if the government had to go back into debt?

Despite Jackson's optimism about the government's being able to stay out of debt, within a year of his departure it had to begin borrowing again. But now it faced a perplexing question, aptly posed in retrospect by Esther Taus: "How could the Nation provide itself with central banking service without the establishment of an institution called a central bank?"[42]

AN INDEPENDENT TREASURY

Martin Van Buren, as next president and party designee, expected to continue Jackson's policies. The Van Buren administration (1837-41) began with a financial crisis for the federal government. The decline in government revenue caused by the depression of 1837 turned the recent budget surpluses back into a deficit; the last distribution of the surplus to the states had to be cancelled, and the Treasury issued almost $20 million in securities during 1837-39. Because state banks that had suspended specie payment were prohibited from acting as government depositories, federal revenue agents were forced to store funds in the mint or temporarily in strongboxes and vaults.

Van Buren called a special session of Congress in September 1837 to deal with the crisis. He dismissed any possibility of forming a new central bank and considered it impossible to use state banks. Secretary Woodbury proposed that either the existing offices of the government, from mints and custom houses to land offices and post offices, be expanded to keep and disburse government funds, or that a new commission be established to oversee these activities.[43] To provide a vehicle for disbursing and collecting government funds, Congress passed the Independent Treasury Act of 1840, which provided that government funds would be kept in its own subtreasuries.[44] This new measure would not be implemented for several years.

In the next election, Van Buren was replaced by William Henry Harrison and, after his death a month after inauguration, by John Tyler (1841-45). With a new party in power, change was anticipated. The Independent Treasury Act was repealed before it ever became operable.

By 1844, government funds were being deposited in 39 different state banks. The Congress, now controlled by the Whig Party, passed a bill to create a new national bank along the lines of the second Bank of the United States, to be called the Fiscal Bank of the United States. The bill was vetoed by Tyler, much to the surprise of his party. The bill was reintroduced with a name change to Fiscal Corporation of the United States, as a way of sidestepping Tyler's mistrust of banks, but he again vetoed it. During the Van Buren and Tyler years, deficits totalling $25 million accumulated, financed by long term and short-term notes carrying interest of 5 percent to 6 percent.

The Democratic Party returned to office with the election of James K. Polk in 1844. Among its first acts was passage of a second Independent Treasury Bill in 1846, creating a system that remained in place until 1921. Under its provisions, money due the government had to be paid in specie or Treasury notes, and government funds were to be kept in subtreasuries around the country. Revenue agents were forbidden to deposit any funds in private banks. In this way, the groups most distrustful of banks had their way, and government fiscal operations were separated, at least in theory, from the banking system. When Congress neglected to authorize funds to pay for the construction of facilities for holding government revenues, Treasury agents reverted to using banks as depositories. This was especially true in New York, where two-thirds of government revenue was collected at the Customs House. The hard money had to be transported to the rest of the country for disbursement. A decade later facilities for holding Treasury deposits were still lacking, and often, as in one case in Indiana, were nothing more than a wooden enclosure located next to a tavern.[45]

The country went to war with Mexico in May 1846 over the issue of the annexation of Texas and California. The total cost of the war was estimated at $64 million, of which $49 million was borrowed and $15 million paid out of current revenue. The war, lasting only two years, did not allow for any substantial increases in taxes to catch up with the rapid escalation of military expenses. In settling the war, the United States paid the Mexican government $15 million and received land comprising California, Nevada, Utah, New Mexico, Arizona, and portions of Wyoming, Colorado, and Texas. In addition, the United States agreed to take over about $3.5 million in debts owed to U.S. citizens by Mexico, as had been established by a treaty in 1839.[46]

Congress decided to authorize additional debt in order to meet all these obligations. For the first time, the Treasury acted on its own in selling bonds. This put the Independent Treasury to a severe test, as Treasury Secretary Robert J. Walker pointed out: "During the last 11 months the Government has received, transferred, and disbursed more specie than during the whole aggregate period of fifty-seven years preceding-- since the adoption of the Constitution."[47] Walker therefore initiated an innovative policy to help in placing this loan. As he put it,

> It had been usual heretofore with my predecessors, in advertising for loans, to emit no sum to any individual under $25,000; but with a view to insure the largest possible subscription, and at the best rates, and so diffuse the loan as far as practical throughout all classes of the community, bids were authorized to be received by the advertisement as low as the lowest

denomination of Treasury notes permitted by
law--namely, fifty dollars.[48]

Here in embryonic form is the concept that would later
underlie the Savings Bond Program. As a result of this
campaign, the Treasury was able to sell its entire loan
for hard money at a price above par.

Moreover, by keeping its funds in its own vaults,
the Treasury prevented an issuance of bank notes by
state banks that might have led to inflation. After the
war a new set of problems arose.   Congress had
determined that none of the war debt could be
repurchased by the Treasury at a market price above par.
But in 1847, Secretary Walker was being pressured by New
York banking interests to purchase government securities
with government funds to ease a credit difficulty they
were having.   Since the securities were selling above
par, Walker purchased $800,000 of them and agreed to
resell them to their previous owners at the same price,
in essence making them a loan with the securities acting
as collateral.[49]

Despite this increase in Treasury responsibilities,
the scale of operations in the government remained very
small by today's standards.   President Polk, for
example, retained an interest in government functions
sufficient to cause him to write to Treasury Secretary
Walker, reminding Walker, "There is no duty which
appears to me more imperative, than to take care that
officers who receive the public money shall promptly and
fully perform the duties for which the law appropriates
their particular salaries."[50]

The President was also concerned that

the distribution of labor among the Clerks
shall bear a fair proportion to their
compensation, and it is unjust that the
meritorious and faithful should have to
perform the duties of such as may be found to
be negligent, idle or incompetent.   To
prevent this injustice, it is essential that
each Clerk shall attend regularly in his
office, and discharge his own appropriate
duties.[51]

Polk suggested that bureau heads keep records of
absenteeism among clerks and ensure that the clerks paid
all their debts to avoid embarrassment in the
performance of their public duties.[52] It is intriguing
to think of a government on so small a scale that the
President would be concerned with the daily activities
of lower-level employees.   It would be nearly half a
century before civil service procedures were set up to
provide a more effective system of managing government

employees and eliminate some of the problems referred to by Polk.

With the election of a new administration under Presidents Zachary Taylor and Millard Fillmore, Walker and his innovative spirit were removed from the Treasury. The ruling Whig Party cared little for the Independent Treasury. While they did not destroy it, neither did they improve its operations. By the end of 1849, the public debt totaled $63.1 million, with interest payments amounting to little more than 6 percent of the total government budget.

For the eight years starting in 1850, the federal budget was again in surplus, with revenues exceeding expenditures. Tariff rates remained high and were well above the financial needs of the government. These surplus funds could have been used to pay off debt accumulated during the budget deficits of the previous decade. But none of the debt was due for payment, and as the Treasury was still forbidden to buy at prices above par, purchase in the open market was not possible. Instead, under the Independent Treasury system the surplus accumulated in the Treasury, thus reducing the amount of hard money available for circulation in the country. To put some of these funds back into circulation, Secretary of the Treasury James Guthrie asked Congress for permission to buy government bonds on the open market, even if he had to pay a price above par. He was granted this permission in 1853 when Congress repealed the provisions of the Loan Act of 1847 that had forbidden purchase above par. He used this permission to immediately start purchasing bonds, paying as much as a 21 percent premium, to help avert a banking panic.[53]

Guthrie had argued that the Treasury had the potential to "exercise a fatal control over the currency . . . whenever the revenue shall greatly exceed the expenditure."[54] By pulling in money the Treasury could cause economic problems as the policy caused a tightening of credit markets. Despite the purchase of government bonds by the Treasury, what today would be called "open market operations," since customs collections remained high in 1854 and 1855, large amounts of specie continued to pile up in the Treasury.

By the late 1850s banks were again in a tight spot, while additional surpluses were building up in the Treasury. Late in 1856, several New York banks had to suspend specie payments. Treasury Secretary Howell Cobb continued buying bonds to help these banks out, believing that the government should use all of its surplus, if need be, to retain liquidity in the banking system.[55] By 1857, the debt had been reduced to $28.7 million.

It is possible that the Treasury's actions

emboldened the banks to make further loans and get themselves back in trouble. In any event, by 1857 the country was hit by a financial panic and recession. In the beginning months of that year, the balance of hard money held by the Treasury reached a high of $15.7 million. This policy of holding on to reserves reduced the nation's money supply, which may have been a contributing factor in the panic. Cobb continued to purchase bonds, but as government revenue fell and the surplus turned to a deficit, he lost faith in the effectiveness of his actions and ceased. Very shortly, the Treasury began borrowing again, with the result that by the end of 1860, on the eve of its greatest challenge, the federal government was in debt by $64.8 million.

NOTES

1. James D. Savage, <u>Balanced Budgets and American Politics</u> (Ithaca, N.Y.: Cornell University Press, 1988), p. 106.

2. Joseph Dorfman, <u>The Economic Mind in American Civilization 1606-1865</u> (New York: Viking Press, 1946), p. 30.

3. Leonard D. White, <u>The Jeffersonians</u> (New York: Free Press, 1965), p. 135.

4. Secretary of the Treasury, <u>Annual Report</u> (Washington, D.C.: 1815), p. 20.

5. Margaret G. Myers, <u>A Financial History of the United States</u> (New York: Columbia University Press, 1970), pp. 63-64.

6. Richard H. Timberlake, Jr., <u>The Origins of Central Banking in the United States</u> (Cambridge, Mass.: Harvard University Press, 1976), p. 9.

7. Timberlake, <u>Origins of Central Banking,</u> p. 10.

8. Bray Hammond, <u>Banks and Politics in America</u> (Princeton, N.J.: Princeton University Press, 1957), p. 20.

9. Hammond, <u>Banks and Politics,</u> pp. 210-211.

10. Secretary of the Treasury, <u>Annual Report</u> (1815), pp. 8-13.

11. Paul Studenski and Herman E. Kroos, _Financial History of the United States,_ 2nd ed. (New York: McGraw-Hill, 1963), pp. 78-79.

12. Secretary of the Treasury, _Annual Report_ (1815), pp. 25, 54-61.

13. Timberlake, _Origins of Central Banking,_ p. 15.

14. Esther R. Taus, _Central Banking Functions of the United States Treasury, 1789-1941_ (New York: Columbia University Press, 1943), p. 27.

15. Secretary of the Treasury, _Annual Report_ (1815), pp. 24-27.

16. Secretary of the Treasury, _Annual Report_ (1815), p. 53.

17. Secretary of the Treasury, _Annual Report_ (1815), pp. 24-27, 53, 58-59.

18. Hammond, _Banks and Politics,_ pp. 233-234.

19. Leonard D. White, _The Federalists_ (New York: Free Press, 1965), p. 350.

20. Robert Remini, _Andrew Jackson and the Bank War_ (New York: W. W. Norton, 1967), p. 27.

21. Taus, _Central Banking Functions,_ p. 27.

22. Timberlake, _Origins of Central Banking,_ p. 23.

23. Taus, _Central Banking Functions,_ p. 31.

24. White, _Jeffersonians,_ p. 139.

25. Savage, _Balanced Budgets,_ p. 104.

26. Remini, _Jackson and the Bank War,_ p. 46.

27. Timberlake, _Origins of Central Banking,_ pp. 30-31.

28. Hammond, _Banks and Politics,_ p. 297.

29. Hammond, _Banks and Politics,_ p. 375.

30. Hammond, _Banks and Politics,_ p. 373.

31. Remini, _Jackson and the Bank War,_ p. 70.

32. Arthur M. Schlesinger Jr., The Age of Jackson (Boston: Little, Brown, 1950), pp. 88-90.

33. Remini, Jackson and the Bank War, pp. 99, 106.

34. Hammond, Banks and Politics, p. 411.

35. Remini, Jackson and the Bank War, pp. 120-121.

36. Secretary of the Treasury, Annual Report (Washington, D.C.: 1835), p. 646.

37. Schlesinger, Jackson, pp. 103-114.

38. Schlesinger, Jackson, p. 36.

39. Secretary of the Treasury, Annual Report (1835), p. 643.

40. Timberlake, Origins of Central Banking, pp. 50-58.

41. Secretary of the Treasury, Annual Report (Washington, D.C.: 1837), p. 10.

42. Taus, Central Banking Functions, p. 41.

43. Secretary of the Treasury, Annual Report (1837), pp. 11-13.

44. Studenski and Kroos, Financial History, U.S., pp. 110-112.

45. Myers, A Financial History, p. 132.

46. Alexander DeConde, A History of American Foreign Policy (New York: Scribner, 1963), pp. 196-205.

47. Secretary of the Treasury, Annual Report (Washington, D.C.: 1847), pp. 129, 135.

48. Secretary of the Treasury, Annual Report (1847), pp. 129, 135.

49. Timberlake, Origins of Central Banking, p. 78.

50. James K. Polk, handwritten letter to Robert J. Walker (Washington, D.C.: located in files at the Bureau of the Public Debt, April 11, 1845).

51. Polk, Letter to Walker.

52. Polk, Letter to Walker.

53. Taus, <u>Central Banking Functions,</u> p. 53.

54. Taus, <u>Central Banking Functions,</u> pp. 52-55.

55. Taus, <u>Central Banking Functions,</u> pp. 52-55.

4

The First Growth
in Debt (1861–1900)

The period marked by the American Civil War, 1861-65, has long been thought of as a watershed in the country's life. The political and social changes brought about by the war, such as the abolition of slavery and the reduction in influence of the agrarianism of the southern states, certainly give credence to that thought. In economics, it is clear that this period saw the beginning of a great economic expansion; at the outbreak of the war the United States was what today would be called a less-developed country, still reliant on imports of manufactured goods and of investment funds. That would soon change. Estimates of national production show a fivefold increase between 1870 and 1910, for an annual growth rate of 4 percent, fueled in part by a sevenfold jump in the amount of capital used by the country as a whole. In this case, however, economists disagree as to whether the war served as a stimulus to this takeoff in growth, for it is very likely that the same growth path might have taken place without the war.[1]

In terms of government growth, there is much less dispute. The public debt in 1860, totaling $64.8 million, was about equal to the federal government's annual budget of $63.1 million. This quantity of money would appear insignificant compared to the amount the national government would owe at the end of the War between the States. Moreover, budget levels would never be reduced to their prewar levels. One indicator of the change in government finance was the loans given to the railroad companies building the transcontinental line, a total of nearly $65 million,[2] or as much as the government's entire prewar budget just cited. This support of a transportation project also was evidence of a shift in attitude about the government's role in economic development. For the next half century, under primarily Republican administrations, there would be a variety of public works projects undertaken to assist the development of industry, such as harbor development and waterway improvement.   In this respect the government moved away from the Jeffersonian principles of the previous half century and became more of what Hamilton would have wanted.   But first there was a war to be fought and financed.

THE CIVIL WAR

At the outset, it was believed by many in the government that the war would be of very short duration. The greater resources of the northern states were expected to overpower the southern states in rebellion. As the war continued, however, the federal government was forced to completely overhaul its financial organization.   It was even likely that the rudimentary nature of the government's fiscal management itself proved to be a disadvantage in the early stages of the war and may have prolonged it.

The nation began the march toward war with the election of Abraham Lincoln as President in 1861.   As a politician, Lincoln had no doubts about the role government should play in economic affairs.   In his early years he had been in favor of federal spending for internal improvements, supported the 2BUS, and took a protectionist attitude toward tariffs.[3]   He also took a benign attitude toward the public debt, arguing, "The great advantage of citizens being creditors as well as debtors, with relation to the public debt, is obvious. Men can readily perceive that they cannot much be oppressed by a debt which they owe to themselves."[4] Lincoln may have been overly sanguine about his fellow citizens' perception of the debt, but he was right about its being owed to themselves.   At the outset of the war it became quite clear that the government would not be able to secure funds from abroad.[5]

Even worse, the new administration was starting office with the treasury virtually empty.   Among Lincoln's first appointments was that of Salmon P. Chase as Secretary of the Treasury.   Chase was a "hard money" advocate and an adherent of the principle of the Independent Treasury.   In the initial phases of the war, he was able to sell a small amount of securities authorized during the previous administration.   As conditions worsened, Congress met in a special session in July 1861 to consider ways of financing the war, which Chase estimated would amount to $318,519,581.87 during the coming year. He proposed that $80 million be raised by taxes, mainly through an increase in tariffs, and the rest be borrowed.   In formulating this plan,

Chase was reverting to Gallatin's old view that the government should use current revenue to pay for its normal operations and interest, and borrow whatever was needed to pay for the war.[6]

On July 16, 1861, Congress authorized $250 million in loans in a variety of forms, carrying interest in the 7 percent range. It also allowed the issuance of noninterest-bearing Treasury notes, to be used to pay government salaries and to be deemed acceptable in payment of money owed the government. A Division of Loans was created in the office of the Secretary to perform certain administrative debt management functions. Chase then negotiated loans of $150 million with a group of major banks in the latter half of 1861.

At the time of the loan, the banks had only $63 million in hard currency available and were afraid that a transfer of a large portion of that supply to the government would shake public confidence in their ability to redeem their own notes. They wanted the government to keep its proceeds from the loan in the banks until the banks could resell their holdings of government bonds to the public for additional amounts of hard money. Then, as the government spent the money, the recipients of that money would deposit it back into the banks, where it could be used to finance additional issues of government debt.

Several problems intervened to lay waste to this plan. The Trent Affair, wherein it appeared that England might go to war against the North, and early battlefield losses by the North caused a crisis of confidence toward the federal government, resulting in a hoarding of gold. Banks had problems in reselling their bond holdings, and government spending of specie was not returned to the banks. In addition, Chase, under the Independent Treasury Act, felt it necessary to insist upon full payment in hard currency to be kept by the Treasury.

As the banks could not accommodate this demand, a compromise was reached. Chase permitted the banks to have the extra time needed until sales of government securities could replenish their gold supplies. This they could not do, which brought about the suspension of specie payment in December 1861.[7]

Meanwhile, Chase had to revise his estimate of expenditures for the first year of the war upward to $532 million. At the same time, his assessment of anticipated revenues was amended downward to $55 million. To make up for this huge deficit, Chase proposed that Congress increase taxes and approve additional loans. Partly as a provision to establish a national currency and partly as a financing device, Chase very reluctantly recommended that Congress create a class of interest-free notes that would serve as legal tender for all transactions.

In summing up his case for these notes, Chase admitted their benefit as being "practically a loan from the people to their government without interest."[8] He also admitted that the notes were being resorted to because of difficulty in selling interest-bearing bonds at par, estimating that current loans "could not be had, in coin, at better rates than a dollar in bonds for eighty cents in money." In the place of loans, he concluded that no better way of funding the immediate needs of the war seemed "likely to effect the object with so little public inconvenience and so considerable public advantage as the issue of United States notes adapted to circulate as money, and available, therefore, immediately in government payments."[9]

Chase entered into this approach as a "hard money" man and noted the potential for abuse. He acknowledged the possibility of inflation, but felt that prices were and would remain steady. He also fretted about the long-term implications of government-issued notes, for this would mean that the money supply of the nation would depend on the government's fiscal management to a great degree, which "would convert the Treasury into a government bank, with all its hazards and mischiefs."[10] For this reason, he supported the use of notes as a necessary evil, although as Wesley Mitchell long ago observed, they were only necessary to avoid paying a higher interest on bonds.[11]

Congress, with Chase's support, passed the Legal Tender Act on February 25, 1862. This act authorized the Treasury to issue $150 million in U.S. notes and authorized the sale of up to $500 million in 6 percent bonds. The Treasury notes, which eventually were referred to as greenbacks, were declared legal tender for the payment of all public and private debts, even though they were not backed by gold. This was the first paper money issued by the federal government. The next year, Congress authorized the issuance of an additional $300 million in greenbacks, a necessary measure since the government was spending $1 million a day.

As might be expected, the value of the greenbacks declined over the course of the war. Gold prices nearly doubled in terms of paper money by the end of the war, and the cost of living rose by 50 percent. Although the issuance of paper money added to the inflation, the rapid increase of government demand for goods and services was also a contributing factor. Mitchell concluded that because real wages (i.e., payments to workers adjusted for inflation), declined, there was a significant inflation tax imposed on the population by the issuance of greenbacks.[12] More recent scholarship has found evidence of a wage gap, but determines that it was not as important as Mitchell had thought, primarily because wage earners did not make up a high proportion of the population given the structure of the economy at the time. Still, an estimate that a wage gap accounted for "(at most) 25 percent of total federal expenditures during the war"[13] cannot be considered insignificant.

As the government's finances were stretched, Congress turned to increased taxes to help pay for the war. Congress passed a comprehensive tax act on July 1, 1862, designed to raise $150 million. The act included internal taxes such as an excise tax on spirits and tobacco, specific taxes on manufactured goods, stamp taxes, and income and inheritance taxes. By 1865, these taxes were contributing over $200 million to the northern cause. The office of Tax Commissioner, which had been established in 1861, was superseded by a Commissioner of Internal Revenue.[14]

Since even these taxes were inadequate to raise the necessary funds to fight the war, a continued reliance on borrowing was inescapable. In a manner similar to the policy advocated by Secretary Walker during the Mexican War, Chase's view on public finance was also a portent of the Savings Bond Program; he called for "the general distribution of the debt into the hands of the greatest possible number of holders."[15] Chase justified this view on the grounds of loyalty and fairness. As he summed up the case, "every holder of a note or bond, from a five cent fractional note to a five thousand dollar bond, has a direct interest in the security of national institutions and in the stability of national administration."[16] Chase further held that it was another advantage of a wide distribution of the debt that its burdens on the economy would be diminished if the receivers of interest were also those who paid the taxes that supported interest payments.

Chase began executing this approach to borrowing by employing "a large number of agents in many places, and directing their action from the Department."[17] The plan was initially very effective, but soon became inadequate to raise the amount of money the government needed.[18]

As a result of this inability of the Treasury to market its own securities to the general public, Chase negotiated a deal in October 1862 with the banking house of Jay Cooke. Cooke was to be paid .5 percent on the first $10 million and .375 percent on the balance for his efforts in selling the bonds. Calling himself "General Subscription Agent of the Government Loan," Cooke began a sales campaign that employed 2,500 salesmen operating in every community and selling bonds in denominations of as little as $50. By January 1864, this approach had produced sales of $362 million. Despite Cooke's claim that after expenses he had only made $220,000 on the deal, public opinion had it that he had profited too greatly, so Chase was forced to end the arrangement.   Later on, William P. Fessenden, Chase's successor as Secretary of the Treasury, was forced to use Cooke's services again to arrange the sale of $700 million in notes, this time at an even higher rate of commission of .75 percent on the first $50 million and .625 percent on the remainder.

The war eventually forced the government into making some reforms in its financial operations.   It was finally realized that a national banking system was needed to handle the many transactions of the Treasury. Therefore,   in   February   1863,   Congress   passed   the National Bank Act, permitting the charter of national banks and establishing the Office of the Comptroller of the Currency to supervise national banks.   Many state banks refused to become nationally chartered, however, until Congress passed a series of amendments, including several increasingly harsh impositions of a tax on notes issued by state-chartered banks.   By October 1866, 1,644 banks had received a national charter.[19]

One purpose of the creation of the national banks was to provide a ready market for government bonds. National banks were given the exclusive right to issue bank   notes,   which   were   printed   for   them   by   the government;   these notes, in turn, had to be backed by government bonds held by the banks.   The total of national bank notes that could be issued, however, was limited to $300 million.[20]   It was felt that national bank notes and greenbacks would give the country an adequate money supply, but it also meant that national banks would have to buy and hold government securities in order to issue any of their own notes.

The   increased   activity   in   Treasury   operations caused a need for more employees.   Consequently, all Secretaries of the Treasury during the war continually lobbied Congress for appropriations to hire more clerks and to raise the pay of all employees.   One incident reported by Secretary Fessenden highlights the problems that   were   caused   by   this   burden   of   work   and   also indicates   the   environment   within   which   the   work   of handling securities took place.

On June 5, 1864, C. P. Bailey, chief clerk and superintendent of the loan branch, wrote to Fessenden to report   that   100   bonds   of $1,000   denomination   were missing   from   his   office.   An   inquiry   was   held   that brought out the facts, as summarized by Fessenden.

On the 29th of September previous, Mr. Bailey
sent the bonds in an open basket, with a
weight placed on them, by two messengers, one
of whom was an old clerk of established
character, to the Register's office, and
there offered them to the clerk who usually
received the coupon bonds in the Register's
room, who objected to taking charge of them
on the ground that there was no place in the
office where they could be safely kept, and
requested that they might be taken back to
the loan branch, where there were good safes.
Mr. Bailey was sent for, and after some
consultation as to the proper place of
deposit, consented that they be taken back,
and deposited in the safe in his office, and
they were accordingly carried back by the
same messengers, taken out of the basket,
laid on the table, and in the course of the
day placed in the safe, where they remained,
as supposed, until called for by the
Register. They were called for and delivered
from time to time, from March 7 to June 5,
1864, when the loss was discovered.[21]

The bonds had not been signed or sealed by the Register,
so they were not negotiable. The coupons had been
completed, but no evidence existed that they had been
paid.[22]

No claim of wrongdoing was laid to any employees;
the event was more readily construed as an inadvertent
lapse on the part of overworked and underpaid workers.
As Treasury Secretary Hugh McCulloch later stated, "The
custody of vast amounts of government securities printed
and issued from the Treasury Department is imposed upon
the Chief of the First Division of the Currency Bureau,
who receives an annual compensation of only three
thousand dollars."[23] As the sums involved in the public
debt transactions were indeed vast for the time, the
possibility of future theft could not be ignored.

A Senate committee was formed because of the many
opportunities that existed for irregular operations,
fraud, or theft. They investigated the operations of
the Treasury Department during the war. While the
report concluded that no extensive losses had taken
place, it did give some glimpses into the caliber of the
operations in the Treasury at that time. The committee
was especially concerned with careless accounting
procedures such as the one previously cited. During the
transfer of securities from one bureau to another,
vouchers would be taken for the interchange of
securities, recorded on slips of paper, and released
when settlements were made, leaving no recorded evidence

of the transaction.

The potential difficulties caused by this poor recordkeeping were described in great detail:

> This want of proper accounts led in some of the bureaus and particularly in the Register's office, to other evils. A leading one will be mentioned. It was the course of practice in printing and transmitting securities to that office . . . to transmit with each thousand impressions a quantity, usually ten, of extra impressions not numbered, and intended to be used to supply those of the regular class which from time to time might be erroneously filled up or accidentally defaced. These extra impressions were called the "stock package," and whenever there was occasion in the course of business to use one of them, the bond or note injured, or said to be injured, would be thrown in the fire or otherwise destroyeda s is stated by all clerks and one taken to supply its place from the "stock package" without any account or record being kept of the performance, and without any proof or method of proof of the one so actually or ostensibly disposed of. [24]

As a result, it was impossible to determine which bonds were actually issued, except by a careful review of later interest payment records.

There was also some concern over duplicated numbers on some issues of securities. It was agreed that these oversights were probably due to errors on the part of the clerks who operated the numbering machines. They might have issued the same number twice, and would then omit a number to compensate for the error. The investigators were concerned because these mistakes should have been remedied when the securities were listed in the numerical registers. As a result, the investigators concluded, "the numerical registers of issue are rather theoretical than actual records of transactions."[25] This was due to clerks assuming that all bonds were numbered consecutively and making the register by taking the first and last numbers in a batch of securities and then basing the intervening numbers, on them, instead of matching the bonds with the numbers they recorded.[26] Despite these problems, few losses were experienced and no difficulty was encountered in managing the massive war debt.

It is estimated that the Civil War cost the nation $5.2 billion in direct expenditures ($3.2 billion for the North and $2 billion for the South). In the North, the war was financed primarily by loans and paper money. Taxes contributed 22 percent of the cost of the war (a little over half a billion dollars), and $450 million in greenbacks was issued. The balance was financed through debt, with a peak of about $2.8 billion borrowed. At the end of 1865 interest-bearing debt stood at $2.2 billion, and the interest payments of $77.4 million in that year were higher than the total expenditures of the entire government in 1861. An enormous leap in the methods and amount of public financing had taken place, and the Union had been preserved.[27]

THE POST-CIVIL WAR ERA

With the war successfully over, attention at the federal level turned to the problem of debt management. In his report for 1865, Secretary of the Treasury McCulloch took a conservative approach to ordering the government's finances. In order to correct policies that had been undertaken under the exigencies of war, he recommended a program of redeeming the legal-tender issues as quickly as possible, pointing out the inflation they had caused.[28] He also pushed for a rapid reduction of debt of short maturity and "to provide for raising, in a manner the least odious and oppressive to taxpayers, the revenues necessary to pay the interest on the debt, and a certain definite amount annually for the reduction of the principal." He estimated that if $200 million per year were set aside for interest payments and debt reduction, the public debt could be paid off in about thirty years. He even provided calculations for national wealth and production to establish that "the total estimated charges of the national government for payment of the debt in 30 years, and all other ordinary expenses, begin at less than 5 percent of the resources of the country, and end in seven-eighths of one percent."[29]

In modern terms, McCulloch was suggesting that the government let economic growth pay for the debt. As the economy grew, more tax receipts would be collected, and if government expenditures remained constant, the public debt could be eliminated. In terms of economic growth, he was proven correct.

The United States underwent an economic transformation following the Civil War. During the remaining 35 years of the nineteenth century, new agricultural areas opened up as the west was settled. Railroad construction created employment and spawned steel-making and machine-tool building industries. The railroads made cross-continent traveling considerably easier. Advances in communications such as the dispersion of the telegraph and the invention of the telephone linked the country. The country underwent an industrial revolution, turning the great organizers of business into heroes and giving urban workers and rural homesteaders access to work as factory employees.

The national government played a part in this economic transformation. It provided land grants and subsidies to the railroads and inexpensive land to farmers through the Homestead Act. It also embarked on a program of internal improvements. As a result, government expenditures never fell to their prewar level of $65 million. Immediately after the war, in 1866, annual federal expenditures fell from $1.3 billion in 1865 to $520 million; they gradually declined over the next decade to about $250 million a year. Interest on the debt alone accounted for nearly 40 percent of total expenditures, and it did not fall below $100 million a year until 1880. Government spending averaged $325 million per year for the period 1865-1900; from 1869 to 1890, for example, nearly $160 million was spent on river and harbor improvements. Pensions for the veterans of the war and a patronage system of expanding the post office also took large amounts of money.[30]

As a result of this increase in government spending, new taxes were in order. McCulloch was sensitive to the need for taxes to be fair, but he relied very heavily on the one tax that had been traditionally used in the past, the tariff. As he put it, "Free trade, although in accord with the principles of government and the instincts of the people, cannot be adopted as a policy as long as the public debt exists in anything like its present magnitude."[31]

In many ways, a tariff on imported goods is a useful way of raising revenues. It is hidden in the sense that it is not collected directly from consumers, so they are less aware of its existence and magnitude. To some extent it can be seen as a levy on foreigners, who do bear some of its burden. And it is even a tax that has popular support in that some members of society, those who are protected by it, derive benefits from its introduction and increase. In the case of the Republican era of 1860 to 1932, the chief beneficiaries of the tariff, manufacturing capital and organized labor in those protected industries, were also the chief constituents of the party. Whatever the reason, for the period 1870 to 1900, customs receipts were substantial and averaged over 50 percent of total government revenues; in absolute terms, the tariff brought in a sum that was always greater than the government budget surpluses that were the dominant fiscal policy of this period.

The Treasury's fiscal management plan was also helped by foreign credit. During the war, foreign loans were not available to the federal government, and

Treasury Secretaries expressed satisfaction on their ability to do without foreign loans as evidence of the country's self-sufficiency. It was a fact that the debt was owed internally. After the war, with the future of the Union secure, government securities became desirable to foreign investors. In 1866, the Secretary of the Treasury estimated that foreigners held about $350 million in bonds (13 percent of the federal debt). The amount of government bonds held by foreigners in 1869 increased to about $1 billion (45 percent of the total).[32] Just as today, when foreign holdings of the public average around 11 percent, this influx of borrowing from abroad was regretted, especially as it was viewed as being used to finance purchases that could have been made at home. As McCulloch put it, "Our importations of goods have been increased by nearly the amount of the bonds that have been exported."[33] The same concerns would be expressed 120 years later, when the trade deficit would be on the same order of magnitude as the federal budget deficit.

The Funding Act of April 12, 1866, gave the Secretary of the Treasury the authority to convert short-term notes into long-term bonds and to begin retiring greenbacks. Soon after, the Public Credit Act of March 1869 was passed; its main purpose was to restore faith in government credit by paying all interest-bearing obligations in hard money.

But reduction of the debt and restoration of hard money were not readily accomplished. During the war, the Treasury had continued to receive gold as customs payments, keeping it in the Independent Treasury. At the end of the war it had a large stock of gold reserves on hand, which McCulloch began to sell. In this way he hoped to add to bank reserves of gold and hasten the return to hard money. But the gold was still needed for customs payments by importers, so it soon returned to the Treasury.[34] At the same time, the policy of debt reduction and greenback redemption was diminishing the supply of money. Banks, it will be recalled, could issue notes based on their reserves of government securities; in modern terms, then, these securities served as high-powered money, meaning they could support an expanding amount of notes. When they were called in, they could cause a contraction of bank notes. Since they were not being replaced by gold reserves, which kept returning to the Treasury, and since greenbacks, the other form of currency, were also being reduced, tight money and credit became a problem. Prices declined rapidly, and the Treasury's actions were blamed for the poor economic times that began to appear by the late 1860s. Plans for a quick reduction in debt were curtailed and few greenbacks were redeemed. Due to widespread complaints, the Funding Act of 1866 was repealed in 1868. Greenbacks remained a debt obligation of the government, about 15 percent of the total public debt.

In addition, the Treasury needed to keep revenues high in order to attain debt relief and to reduce the interest payments. However, there was much opposition to the system of internal taxes that had been used during the war. Shortly after the war ended, in July 1866, Congress either repealed or reduced excise taxes on a variety of items. The income tax was also reduced and totally eliminated by 1872. The primary source of revenue remained the tariff on imported goods. The Treasury managed to accumulate a total surplus of $1.3 billion from 1866 to 1885. This made possible elimination of a large portion of the public debt, but the pace of that reduction was not as rapid as McCulloch had planned.

In 1870 and 1871, Congress authorized a refund of the debt using lower interest securities, ranging from 4 to 5 percent. The 4 percent bonds were due in 30 years and were not callable. This policy was based on the mistaken assumption that interest rates would not get much lower. At the same time, Treasury activities were still influencing the money markets. In the early 1870s, Treasury Secretary George Boutwell began letting banks act as depositaries for funds the government received for the sale of gold. In addition, he felt obligated to adjust the supply of money to seasonal needs, so the Treasury would accumulate gold reserves during the summer and then use them to buy bonds during the autumn, when more money was needed to handle large crop sales.[35]

The constitutional problems surrounding the issuance of greenbacks were only slowly resolved. In 1869, in the case of <u>Hepburn v. Griswold,</u> the Supreme Court in a 4 to 3 decision declared that greenbacks were not legal tender and were thus unconstitutional, on the grounds that their designation as legal tender voided contracts that had called for payment in specie. Ironically, Salmon Chase, as Chief Justice, voted to declare unconstitutional the same policies he proposed and implemented as Secretary of the Treasury. This decision was reversed shortly afterwards when the composition of the Court changed through the resignation of one justice and the addition of two more. In 1870 the Court decided by 5 to 4 (<u>Parker v. Davis</u>) that Congress could declare paper money legal tender during war. The Court held in 1884 (<u>Julliard v. Greenman</u>) that Congress had the authority to declare fiat money legal tender in peace or war.

The Resumption Act, which became effective in January 1875, required that greenbacks be redeemable in gold after January 1, 1879. The Refunding Act of July

14, 1870, had given the Treasury the authority to accumulate budget surpluses and to sell bonds in anticipation of redemption and the return to specie. In August 1876, the sale of $40 million in bonds at 4.5 percent for this purpose was negotiated with a team of underwriters led by August Belmont & Co.; members of the group were given a commission of .5 percent for handling the sale.[36]

Very few greenbacks were turned in when the date for resumption of specie payment arrived. The idea that the greenbacks were redeemable in gold on demand was sufficient to keep individuals satisfied with holding them. They became as good as gold and as readily acceptable. It should be noted that at this time currency (i.e., greenbacks), was carried on the Treasury books as noninterest-bearing debt.

Monetary reform also marked this era. The Bland-Allison Act of February 1878 required the Treasury to make monthly purchases of $2 to $4 million in silver, to be minted into coin and used by the Treasury for spending when its other revenues were lacking. On May 31, 1878, Congress fixed the total amount of greenbacks at $346 million.[37]

By 1880, the public debt and interest charges on it had been reduced substantially through the refunding program. Thereafter, when market rates of interest fell to 3 percent, the noncallable government bonds of higher interest rates sold at a premium and could only be retired through open market purchase at that premium. As had happened previously in the 1830s and 1850s, the Treasury was in command of a surplus that could not be used to retire its debt.[38] In 1882, Treasury Secretary Charles J. Folger remarked, "What now perplexes the Secretary is not where from he may get revenue and enough for the pressing needs of the government, but whereby he shall turn back into the flow of business the more than enough for those needs, that has been drawn from the people."[39]

As the surplus built up in the Treasury, a tightening of credit and money took place. As had been done by his predecessors in the 1850s, Secretary of the Treasury Charles Fairchild began buying bonds on the open market, paying premiums as high as 29 percent. But to some extent these purchases were counterproductive because the bonds were still used by national banks as a reserve against their issuance of bank notes, which had to be contracted. When the surplus grew so large that even bond purchases were insufficient to disburse it, Fairchild began depositing gold directly in national banks.[40]

With debt reduction being limited because of the due dates of bonds, there were only two other options for reducing the size of the government's surplus:

spending increases or tax decreases. President Grover Cleveland (1885-89) followed a policy of keeping expenditures down, so no help was to be had from fiscal policy. By 1887 all of the callable debt had been paid, leaving only the prospect of open market purchases at a premium. All Secretaries of the Treasury disliked this practice, as it wasted tax money. Unfortunately, a sinking-fund law required annual retirements of debt, so in fiscal years 1888 and 1889 the Treasury purchased about $170 million in its securities, paying a premium of about $26 million. There were also proposals to distribute the surplus to the states, to use it for internal improvements and to pay out veterans' pensions, but Cleveland refused. He sought to eliminate the surplus through reduction of tariff rates, but that suggestion met with little success.

In 1889, the Harrison administration (1889-93) took office, with the contradictory aims of increasing protection and reducing the surplus. The McKinley Tariff of 1890 raised the customs rates on a variety of goods. The duty on raw sugar, however, which had brought in $50 million a year, was eliminated. Not surprisingly, in 1894 the Treasury began showing a deficit. To make up for the loss of tariff revenue, Congress tried to levy an income tax. The Supreme Court, in 1895, determined in a 5-4 decision that the income tax, which had been used fairly effectively to raise revenue during the war, was unconstitutional. This decision necessitated the eventual passage of the Sixteenth Amendment to the Constitution in 1913.[41]

Secretary of the Treasury John Carlisle placed blame on the Supreme Court for the government's fiscal problem, arguing, "If the income-tax provision contained in the Act of August 29, 1894, had been sustained by the courts, it is believed that the deficiency for the year would not have exceeded the amount estimated in my last annual report." Rather, there would have been "a surplus of nearly $29,000,000."[42] Instead, the government was forced to issue new securities, but under favorable conditions. Of the $50 million offered during the previous year, 486 bids totaling $179 million were made at rates of 3 percent or less. A single bid for the offering at an effective yield of 2.878 percent was accepted, netting nearly $60 million in proceeds.[43]

The deficits continued for the rest of the century. Poor economic conditions caused by a recession starting in 1893 added to the government's low revenues, and the Spanish-American War in 1898 was financed by additional debt issue, offered through an underwriting syndicate headed up by National City Bank and J. P. Morgan.

As a result of these conditions, during the 1890s the Treasury found its gold reserves declining. To help ease the strain on the Treasury's finances, which were worsened by a banking panic that accompanied the recession of 1893, Congress on November 1, 1893, released the Treasury of its obligations to buy and mint silver. But problems remained. The Treasury was still obligated to redeem outstanding greenbacks for gold, but since the amount of greenbacks in circulation had been fixed at $346 million, it had to put redeemed greenbacks back into circulation. They could then be handed in for gold again. This process could have taken up the Treasury's entire reserve of gold, and its holdings did get low enough to require it to have to ask banks for gold. Sales of bonds finally brought in enough gold to offset the drain, and when public confidence was restored, the gold reserves were returned to safe levels.[44]

At the close of fiscal year 1899, gross debt, which included Treasury notes, stood at $1.9 billion, with the interest-bearing portion at just over $1 billion. Due to low interest rates, interest paid out during the year was $39.9 million, less than 10 percent of total expenditures.[45] The government ended the century with its finances in very good order.

EXPANSION OF THE TREASURY

Within the Treasury the operating bureaus responsible for the public debt had been expanded during the war by adding the Division of Loans in the office of the Secretary of the Treasury, the Currency Division, and the Bureau of Engraving and Printing. In 1870, the Register reported that his office had 229 employees (including 28 in the Loan Division). This number continued to rise and then gradually reduced, until by 1875 the total was 208. The Register, John Allison, cited this as a significant reduction of staff over the previous six years. Further reductions brought the total employees in the Register's office to only 137 by 1878.[46]

The number of persons working in the area of handling the debt was even smaller. The type of work being done and the salaries and duties of persons employed in this area can be seen in the following account, given in 1872 by James Gilfellen, chief of the Division of Loans:

Adams, R.D., $1400--keeps journals and ledgers of bond purchases and record of five-twenties of 1862, redeemed; makes charge tickets for cashier, daily; assists in drawing quarterly checks.

Anderson, John. S., $1,600--draws all checks on New York, Philadelphia and Boston;

also quarterly checks for interest on funded loan; makes credit ticket for cashier.

Rowling, E. M., $1,600--represents the Treasurer on counting committee.

Brown, J. E., $1,600--represents the Treasurer on burning committee.

Kingdom, John, $1,400--schedules five-twenties received for redemption and views all checks issued, and all letters, inclosing checks, and keeps record of funded loan of 1881.

Stieilin, Carl, $1,600--keeps the record of 7 3/10 notes redeemed and converted, of which there are now few; receipts of five-twenties for redemption, and keeps numerical registers of purchased five-twenties of 1862, and consols of 1865.

Weiler, Fred, $1,800--makes up the slips for redemption of five-twenties; makes computations for back of debt statement; keeps register of quarterly interest checks, and has immediate oversight of redemption and conversion of five-twenties.

Wilson, W. W., $1,800--keeps registers of coin coupons paid; record of five-twenties redeemed; record of bond purchases.

Cross, C. E., $900--has charge of the coupon room, in which there are eleven lady counters, and keeps the record of five-twenties received.

Pierce, Mrs. R. A.--examines purchased bonds, and keeps the numerical registers of the five-twenties on 1865, June 1864 and consols of 1867 and 1868.

Steel, Mary C., $900--makes schedules of five-twenties sent for redemption and computations of interest, and writes all letters enclosing checks on that account.[47]

The report also listed 11 people as employed in the coupon room, and earning a salary of approximately $900.

Management procedures were also being streamlined. To consolidate the handling of the large amount of wartime debt, the Division of Loans in the office of the Secretary of the Treasury was formed in 1861. It and the Currency Division, formed in 1862, were combined into the Division of Loans and Currency by an act of Congress on August 15, 1876. The new Division had responsibility for taking care of the public debt and the issuance of currency.[48] The Dockery Act of July 31, 1894, specified the duties of the Register of the

Treasury to make them conform with the many activities that were already being performed, including issuing and transferring bonds, keeping ledger accounts with each bondholder, and keeping a general account for each loan.[49]

In addition to organizational changes, operations at the Treasury were also affected by the civil service reforms that took place during this era. The post-Civil War era might be called a "golden age" of political patronage. Because there were no specific qualifications for government employment, jobs at all levels in the federal government were handed out by victorious candidates as rewards for their political supporters. The Treasury was especially vulnerable as a source of jobs in return for political favors. Between 1873 and 1896, the number of persons employed by the Treasury increased from 4,000 to 24,000; many of these were employed by the Customs Service to collect the high tariff duties of this period. These jobs entailed the handling of large quantities of money, so charges of corruption against customs collectors were frequent occurrences. In addition, many subordinate officers at the Treasury, even the comptroller and auditors, were subject to confirmation by the Senate. When an administration changed political parties, new appointments were made; it was difficult to maintain continuity of service in these offices.[50]

The Civil Service Act of 1883 marked the beginning of a new government policy, granting job appointments based on examinations and establishing a Civil Service Commission to manage the new personnel policy. It also provided for promotional examinations, efficiency records for employees, and a standard salary scale. In 1889, Treasury Secretary William Windom noted in his annual report that compared to the former system, "The present condition of affairs [is] preferable in all respects. Under the old plan appointments were usually made to please some one under political or other obligations to the appointee, and the question of fitness was not always the controlling one."[51] Moreover, he continued, there was always pressure to remove someone to secure a patronage spot, which "did much to distract and disturb the even current of routine work"[52]

Approval of all features of the civil service system was not unanimous among Treasury Department officials. In 1892, W. S. Rosencrans, Register of the Treasury, maintained that competitive examinations for promotion "have given very unsatisfactory results."[53] This dissatisfaction reflected Rosencrans's opinion on the nature of clerical work. As he put it,

> The public service does not, as prime qualities, demand that employees be quick-witted, of all-around intelligence, able to give pedagogic instruction on Department and general matters; it requires efficient clerical service. Therefore the monthly record of efficiency is greatly superior to the haphazard results of the competitive examination . . . But this record of efficiency counts for only 20 percent, while the competitive result counts for 80 percent.[54]

Rosencrans recommended that the relative weights of efficiency reports and examinations be reversed. He also complained about the problem of promoting clerks when no openings appeared at the upper levels and asked for higher pay for all the employees in his operation.[55]

Rosencrans's comments reflect the small size of his operation, for the total employees in the Register's office was 108 in 1892. He had intimate knowledge of those employees, which was demonstrated in a letter written to the Secretary of the Treasury, elaborating on a report by the captain of the watch discussing a safe used for currency being prepared for destruction that was found open. Investigation showed that because the room where the safe was located had been overfilled with currency from the Treasurer's office, another place for storing the money had to be found. The clerk in charge had not locked the door of the safe, and he returned to do so later. The currency was recounted, with no losses recorded, and Rosencrans exonerated the man in charge of the safe by stating, "he was and is esteemed as a man of strict integrity."[56]

Rosencrans was able to comment about the clerical staff in general, "to testify to the zeal and fidelity with which, generally, they have performed their duty, clerks sometimes cheerfully doing work as messengers and even laborers in handling and moving files, when our already inadequate force of messengers and laborers was weakened by casualties."[57] Such were the pleasures of working at a time when the scale of government operations was quite small.

NOTES

1. Susan Previant Lee and Peter Passell, A New View of American History (New York: W. W. Norton, 1979), pp. 266-270.

2. Edward Chase Kirkland, Industry Comes of Age (Chicago: Quadrangle Books, 1967), p. 61.

3. James D. Savage, _Balanced Budgets and American Politics_ (Ithaca, N.Y.: Cornell University Press, 1988), p. 123.

4. Savage, _Balanced Budgets,_ p. 128.

5. Wesley Clair Mitchell, _A History of the Greenbacks_ (Chicago: University of Chicago Press, 1903), p. 20.

6. Paul Studenski and Herman E. Kroos, _Financial History of the United States_, 2nd ed. (New York: McGraw-Hill, 1963), pp. 137-156.

7. Mitchell, _Greenbacks,_ pp. 23-41.

8. Secretary of the Treasury, _Annual Report_ (Washington, D.C.: 1862), p. 2.

9. Secretary of the Treasury, _Annual Report_ (1862), pp. 7-8.

10. Secretary of the Treasury, _Annual Report_ (1862), pp. 16-17.

11. Mitchell, _Greenbacks,_ pp. 73-74.

12. Mitchell, _Greenbacks,_ pp. 347-351.

13. Lee and Passell, _American History,_ p. 233.

14. Studenski and Kroos, _Financial History, U.S.,_ pp. 137-156.

15. Secretary of the Treasury, _Annual Report_ (Washington, D.C.: 1863), pp. 13-16.

16. Secretary of the Treasury, _Annual Report_ (1863), pp. 13-16.

17. Secretary of the Treasury, _Annual Report_ (1863), pp. 13-16.

18. Secretary of the Treasury, _Annual Report_ (1863), pp. 13-16.

19. Studenski and Kroos, _Financial History, U.S.,_ pp. 137-156.

20. Richard H. Timberlake, Jr., _The Origins of Central Banking in the United States_ (Cambridge, Mass.: Harvard University Press, 1976), pp. 86-88.

21.   Secretary   of   the   Treasury,   <u>Annual   Report</u>
(Washington, D.C.: 1864), pp. 27-28.

22. Secretary of the Treasury, <u>Annual Report</u> (1864),
pp. 27-28.

23.   Secretary   of   the   Treasury,   <u>Annual   Report</u>
(Washington, D.C.: 1865), pp. 41.

24.   U.S.   Congress   (40th),   Select   Committee   on
Retrenchment of the Senate, <u>Report</u> (Washington D.C.:
March 3, 1869), pp. 95-98.

25. Select Committee, <u>Report,</u> 1869, pp. 95-98.

26. Select Committee, <u>Report,</u> 1869, pp. 95-98.

27. Studenski and Kroos, <u>Financial History U.S.,</u> pp.
137-156.

28. Secretary of the Treasury, <u>Annual Report</u> (1865),
pp. 4-9.

29. Secretary of the Treasury, <u>Annual Report</u> (1865),
pp. 17, 23, 25.

30. Savage, <u>Balanced Budgets,</u> pp. 131-132.

31.   Secretary   of   the   Treasury,   <u>Annual   Report</u>
(Washington, D.C.: 1866), p. 19.

32. Margaret G. Myers, <u>A Financial History of the
United States</u> (New York: Columbia University Press,
1970), p. 175.

33. Secretary of the Treasury, <u>Annual Report</u> (1866),
p. 23.

34. Esther R. Taus, <u>Central Banking Functions of the
United States Treasury, 1789-1941</u> (New York: Columbia
University Press, 1943), pp. 65-66.

35. Timberlake, <u>Origins of Central Banking,</u> pp. 100-
101.

36.   Secretary   of   the   Treasury,   <u>Annual   Report</u>
(Washington, D.C.: 1876), p. x.

37. Timberlake, <u>Origins of Central Banking,</u> p. 117.

38. Studenski and Kroos, <u>Financial History, U.S.,</u> pp.
161-175.

39. Davis R. Dewey, _Financial History of the United States_ (New York: Longmans, Green, 1934), p. 415.

40. Taus, _Central Banking Functions,_ pp. 80-81.

41. Studenski and Kroos, _Financial History, U.S.,_ pp. 161-175.

42. Secretary of the Treasury, _Annual Report_ (Washington, D.C.: 1895), p. lxvi.

43. Secretary of the Treasury, _Annual Report_ (Washington, D.C.: 1894), p. lxx.

44. Taus, _Central Banking Functions,_ pp. 93-94.

45. Studenski and Kroos, _Financial History, U.S.,_ pp. 212-235.

46. Secretary of the Treasury, _Annual Report_ (Washington, D.C.: 1870, 1875, 1878).

47. U.S. Congress (42nd), _Report on the Condition of the Office of the Treasurer of the United States_ (Washington, D.C.: May 2, 1872), p. 33.

48. Linda Baziluik, ed., "Division of Securities Operations: Look Where We've been," _Public Debt Newsletter,_ 1973-1975, chap. 3.

49. Baziluik, _Public Debt Newsletter,_ chap. 4.

50. Leonard D. White, _The Republican Era_ (New York: Macmillan, 1958), pp. 110-114.

51. White, _Republican,_ p. 131.

52. White, _Republican,_ p. 131.

53. U.S. Government, _Report of the Register of the Treasury_ (Washington, D.C.: 1892), pp. 15-16.

54. U.S. Govt., _Register of the Treasury,_ 1892, pp. 15-16.

55. U.S. Govt., _Register of the Treasury,_ 1892, pp. 15-16.

56. W. S. Rosencrans, letter to the Secretary of the Treasury (Washington, D.C.: copy in the files of the Bureau of the Public Debt, October 15, 1888).

57. U.S. Government, <u>Report of the Register of the Treasury</u> (Washington, D.C.: 1889), p. 16.

5

The Debt Drifts
Upward (1900–40)

Despite the string of deficits that took place during the late 1890s, the post-Civil War era is considered to be a sound financial period. Under predominantly Republican administrations, the federal government did increase its spending. However, public authorities were willing to pay for those increases with higher taxes, albeit these taxes were mainly the result of tariffs and a protectionist policy. Over the next four decades the government would not be as successful in ordering its finances. To be sure, there would be periods of budget surplus--20 to be precise, but deficits would also become more acceptable. As part of a continuous trend, the federal government would be called on to perform more services for its citizens, and its ordinary expenditures would rise. As the government's budget increased, it became less possible to finance it effectively from tariff revenues. New sources of internal revenue had to be explored, and these had never proved popular. Overall this would be a period of great change in government institutions and in popular perception of what government should be doing to protect its citizens.

THE ERA OF REFORM

At the turn of the century, many citizens began to perceive that the industrial system that had developed over the previous three decades created a variety of social problems. A group of civic-minded reformers, called progressives, began worrying over the ills created by urbanization, industrialization, and concentration of economic power. Inspired by the activism of President Theodore Roosevelt, these progressives were willing to use the government as a

tool of action. New laws and regulations were passed to
handle the problems facing society. The Pure Food and
Drug Act, which required the national government to
employ more civil servants, was one of these measures.
Other actions included stricter enforcement of the
Sherman Act to break up business trusts and greater
regulation of railroads.

In addition, the government began taking on more
international responsibilities. The Spanish-American
War resulted in acquisition of several remote
territories. Cuba required political administration for
a time, and the Philippines saw a period of military
intervention. The Panama Canal, one of the largest
public works projects ever undertaken by the government,
was built during this period. This was also the time
when Roosevelt sent the American fleet on a cruise
around the world.

As a result of these increased activities, by 1914
federal expenditures were double what they had been in
the 1890s. The rise was gradual, with the budget at
$520 million in 1900 and $735 million in 1914. Customs
receipts, which had made up over half of the budget for
most of the past century, slipped below that figure.
The government was able to show budget surpluses except
during periods of economic disorder, but by 1914 gross
debt totaled nearly $3 billion, with the interest-
bearing portion at just under $1 billion. Interest,
however, was very low, at only $23 million, about 3
percent of the total budget.

Even without that increase in debt, debt management
problems were becoming exceedingly complex. The
Independent Treasury law was still in effect in 1902,
although it had been modified to permit under certain
conditions the deposit of government funds in national
banks. Still, in principle, the Treasury was supposed
to remain distinct from the banking system. However,
the size of Treasury operations made this principle
impossible to achieve. Anytime the Treasury collected
or expended revenues, there was a noticeable impact on
the money supply.

Under banking law at the time, national banks were
still required to deposit government securities with the
Comptroller of the Currency as a reserve against any
bank notes they might issue. Payment of the debt had
two adverse effects on money and banking. First, while
the Treasury began accumulating money to pay off debt,
that money was withdrawn from the banking system.
Second, when the debt was redeemed, it reduced the
amount of bank notes that national banks could issue.

National banks, too, had flexibility in their use
of government securities to back their notes. Their
issuance of notes was based on the lesser of the market
value or par value of bonds. When bonds sold below par,

banks found it profitable to buy them and issue additional notes. Otherwise they did not find it profitable. Treasury operations that influenced the market value of bonds affected the banks' willingness to issue notes. Outstanding bank notes fluctuated as a result, going from $352 million in 1882 to $162 million in 1891 to $714 million in 1914.[1] This was not a good way to control the money supply.

Secretary of the Treasury Leslie M. Shaw was well aware of these conditions and strove to do something about them. He stated in his annual report in 1906 that the Treasury should conduct its operations with an eye toward having a positive influence on the economy. For financial panics to be minimized, methods had to be devised to place more reserves into the banking system. As Esther R. Taus puts it, "Mr. Shaw considered himself the permanent guardian of the money market and looked upon the Treasury as a central bank."[2] Some of the methods used were deposit of government funds in banks, prepayment of interest and principal on government securities that the banks could hold as reserves until final payment was made, and the buying and selling of bonds.[3]

These actions reached a peak, under Treasury Secretary George Cortelyou, when the Treasury increased its deposits in banks by about $80 million during the panic of 1907, in an effort to help banks remain liquid. On October 21, 1907, the Knickerbocker Trust Company, with $50 million in deposits, had suffered a run and had been forced to close, causing runs on other banks. The Treasury also sold $150 million in securities on November 1, 1907. Not only did this enable banks to expand their issuance of bank notes, but the Treasury also allowed the banks to keep a large portion of the money they had collected for the sale of the securities.[4]

The aftermath of the panic of 1907 caused many financial experts to begin rethinking the need for a central bank in the United States with powers and responsibilities similar to those that had been held by the first and second Banks of the United States. Many worried that too much power in the money market was being accorded to the Treasury, especially when it came under the leadership of an individual as activist as Shaw. Some wondered how far this intervention could go, querying whether the Treasury might buy "stocks in support of the stock market." From the academic sphere came concern over the difficulties of the Independent Treasury system itself, especially in a period of budget surpluses when receipts would lay idly in the government's vaults. As Professor Eugene Patton of the University of Chicago put it, "This is an argument for revision of the sub-treasury law, not for granting autocratic power to the secretary of the treasury."[5]

The solution to the problem of managing the government's effect on the money market as well as finding a substitute for intervention in those markets as Shaw had done was the subject of several years of debate and the formation of numerous committees. Finally, in December 1913, legislation passed both houses of Congress that enabled the formation of the Federal Reserve System, a quasi-government central bank, created in 1914. The responsibilities of the Federal Reserve Banks were to maintain flexibility in the money supply, to provide a way to rediscount bank loans, and to oversee the functioning of the banking system.

What Congress seemed to want was a neutral policy-making agency that could monitor the banks and the money supply, but not be politically partisan as the Secretary of Treasury, a presidential appointee, might be. At the same time, there was a feeling of distrust for private bankers, who often monitored themselves through their regional clearinghouses. The Federal Reserve compromised between these two aims. It was headed up in Washington, D.C., by a Federal Reserve Board to make overall policy. (This agency was changed to the present Board of Governors during the 1930s.) To keep the banking system from becoming centralized, the country was divided into 12 Reserve Districts, each with its own Federal Reserve Bank, although the New York Reserve Bank was accorded a dominant role in line with its location at the country's financial center.

The Federal Reserve Banks were made the fiscal agents for the Treasury in November 1915. The Treasury kept its working balances in Federal Reserve Banks after January 1916. Treasury deposits in the Federal Reserve System eventually replaced the need for regional subtreasuries, and the Independent Treasury was eliminated as a legal requirement in May 1920. Academic experts in the area of banking have made the Treasury's activities in the money markets a key variable in the formation of the Federal Reserve System. According to Professor Richard H. Timberlake, "Creation of the Federal Reserve system was a clear reaction to the treasury policies, mild as they were, that Shaw had developed."[6] Taus's explanation is more elaborate, but equally concise:

> The Federal Reserve System had been created to relieve the Treasury of all respon-sibilities in money market crises, to keep politics from entering into the distribution of Government deposits, to cut the connection between Government debt and the currency, to eliminate the manipulation of the public debt in order to increase or decrease funds in the

money market, and to prevent the receipt and disbursement of Government revenue from influencing bank reserves.[7]

With the advent of the Federal Reserve, the national currency became more reliant of its issues of notes. Thus national bank notes, which were tied to the size of the public debt, became less important. At the same time, many of the details involved with managing the public debt, such as sales, redemptions, and interest payments, could be delegated to the Federal Reserve as part of its fiscal agency obligations. The Treasury could let the Federal Reserve worry about debt management and its impact on the banks.

At the time when the formation of the Federal Reserve System was being debated, the debt administration operations at the Treasury underwent reorganization. The work of the Office of the Register and the Division of Currency and Loans was redistributed according to an order of the Secretary on March 11, 1911. The duties of the Register dealing with individual holders and transfers were given to the Division of Loans and Currency, making it the transfer agent for the Treasury. The Office of the Register kept those duties related to bond accounting. It continued to sign the bonds and ensure that their total did not exceed the sum authorized by Congress.[8]

WORLD WAR I

Much of the initial work of the Federal Reserve System and of the rearranged Treasury Department was done under pressure, for by the time they began operating, the country was starting to feel the effects of World War I. The dramatic beginning of the war, with the assassination of Archduke Ferdinand, set off an international financial panic that eventually caused a small recession in the United States. Soon orders for supplies from the belligerent nations reversed that situation and our exports boomed. This rapid increase in business had to be financed by the American banking system, and by the end of the war the United States had been transformed from a nation that owed money to the rest of the world to one that was owed. Foreigners held $5.4 billion in American securities in 1914. After the war that figure had declined to $1.6 billion. By the end of 1920, the rest of the Allies owed the United States about $9 billion.

Starting in 1916, the government prepared for possible entrance into the war by raising taxes and authorizing the Treasury to borrow up to $300 million. When war was declared on April 6, 1917, the problem

faced by the Treasury was how to make large-scale
purchases of the necessary materiel. William Gibbs
McAdoo, Secretary of the Treasury, estimated that the
war would cost $8.5 billion in the first year. McAdoo
hoped to finance almost 50 percent of these costs from
taxes, to keep the demand for goods and services from
private sources from interfering with the government's
purchasing plans. Whenever a country goes to war, it
pays out income to its members. If those members try to
spend their income at a time when government purchases
are high, inflation can result. High taxes could reduce
the income available for personal spending, but McAdoo
was persuaded that a too-high tax rate would hinder the
levels of personal effort needed in war work. He soon
revised his goal of tax finance downward and resorted to
heavier borrowing.

The problem of how to raise taxes was exacerbated
by several conditions. Reliance on tariffs as a way to
raise revenue was out of the question. Tariffs had been
reduced by the Underwood Tariff of 1913, and with the
disruption of the war the amount of products being
imported was declining. Resort was made to internal
taxes, but even here a shift was made.

Ever since the Civil War, the primary source of
internal revenue had been taxes on liquor and distilled
spirits, which in 1912 had contributed 68 percent of
internal collections. But there were limits to how much
could be collected from this source. More revenue was
derived from the income tax, which had been approved
under the Sixteenth Amendment to the Constitution and
initiated in 1913. In 1917, the government collected
$800 million in income tax from 780,000 income-tax
returns, while in 1918 the figure turned out to be $3.7
billion from six million returns.[9,10]

As a result of the income tax, even though
collections of the tax on liquor and spirits rose, they
amounted to less than 12 percent of tax receipts.[11]
Despite this large increase in tax collections from all
sources, it was estimated that only 32 percent of the
war spending was met with tax receipts.[12] Recourse was
made to borrowing.

On April 24, 1917, to start off the wartime
borrowing program, Congress authorized the First Liberty
Loan of $5 billion and permitted the Treasury to sell $2
billion in short-term certificates to generate operating
revenues until bond sales and taxes brought in higher
revenue.

The First Liberty Loan was offered for public
subscription on May 14, 1917. The Treasury itself
handled the sales, marshalling a campaign that rivaled
Jay Cooke's during the Civil War. By relying on the
patriotism that the war had fostered, the Treasury was
able to secure $3 billion in subscriptions for $2

billion in bonds, more than had been sold during the entire Civil War. Bonds were sold in denominations as low as $50, and purchase on an installment plan was permitted. Interest and principal payments on the bonds were exempted from the federal income tax.

The Second Liberty Loan Act of September 24, 1917, gave the Treasury authority to borrow, with approval of the President, on the basis of Treasury loans. Previously, Congressional approval was needed for every loan. Congress retained authority over the total amount of debt.

Under the direction of the Secretary of the Treasury, a War Loan Organization was set up to conduct the five Liberty Loan campaigns. The organization consisted of three branches: sales, speaking, and publicity. Subcommittees of the War Loan Organization were formed using the facilities of the 12 Federal Reserve districts. These subcommittees extended into individual communities. This entire sales network relied on volunteers who worked in coordination with local banks collecting subscriptions for bonds. Subscriptions were combined by the local banks and sent to Federal Reserve Banks, which in turn combined them further, and sent them to the Treasury. Bonds were then delivered to the communities by reversing this system.

The Treasury began offering War Savings Certificates, War Savings Stamps, and Thrift Stamps in the fall of 1917. The Thrift Stamps cost as little as 25 cents each. The purpose of these small denomination issues was to allow persons of little means to help finance the war and to promote savings. A special campaign to sell these issues was organized, with a corps of volunteers forming a network throughout the country. In the case of the stamps, a folder was provided for holding each stamp as it was purchased. Sixteen 25-cent Thrift Stamps would fill a folder, which could then be turned in for a War Savings Stamp worth $5 at maturity, if desired. War Savings Stamps were also sold at a discount in denominations of $5 at maturity, and 20 of them could be exchanged for a War Savings Certificate.

Both types of stamps were sold in every post office and were even available through rural mail carriers. Additional volunteer sales agents for the stamps included stores, banks, and manufacturing firms. By October 31, 1918, a total of 233,287 agents had been appointed by the Treasury. The sales of the War Savings Certificates and Stamps operated independently of the War Loan Organization until late in the war, when both were joined under the Federal Reserve System. Both efforts were very successful. The War Savings Plan raised $1.6 billion at a cost of about $10 million, and provided a way to draw loans from persons with low

income.   Consumer purchasing power was also reduced.
The five Liberty Loans raised over $21 billion at a cost
of $46 million.[13]

Bond sales during the war were greatly aided by the
activities of the Federal Reserve, which helped banks
maintain   sufficient   liquidity   to   buy   bonds   for
themselves   or   to   finance   the   purchase   of   bonds   by
individuals.   During the war, large amounts of short-
term certificates were sold to banks through the Federal
Reserve System, to be refunded later by the government.
Since   banks   paid   for   them   from   their   own   excess
reserves,   more   money   was   added   to   circulation.   In
addition,   the   Federal   Reserve   gave   banks   preferential
rates   on   loans   that   were   secured   by   government
securities.

While there was no direct recourse to finance the
war by the issuance of money, as in the Revolutionary
and Civil wars, Federal Reserve support of government
borrowing   did   bring   forth   an   increase   in   the   money
supply.   It has been estimated that between early 1915
to   the   end   of   1918,   the   supply   of   money   more   than
doubled;   there was a corresponding increase of the same
magnitude in prices.[14]

It has been estimated that it cost over $30 billion
to   fight   the   war.   At the end of 1919, total debt
exceeded $25 billion.   Interest payments alone totaled
$616 million for that year, not much less than the total
prewar   budget.[15]   A   great   burden   of   debt   had   been
accepted and managed in a short time period and without
greatly disrupting the economy.

THE RETURN TO NORMALCY

The   end   of   the   war   found   the   American   people
yearning for a return to the days of little government
interference in their lives.   The war itself had marked
the   period   of   greatest   government   control   over   the
economy up to that time.   Government agencies had been
set   up   to   allocate   basic   resources   such   as   food   and
fuel,   and   the   railroad   system   had   been   temporarily
nationalized.   In the area of finance, a Capital Issues
Committee   was   formed   to   examine   every   request   for
capital to make sure that only funds needed in the war
effort   would   be   borrowed   by   the   private   sector.[16]   No
one   would   be   allowed   to   compete   with   the   Treasury's
borrowing program unless it was absolutely essential.

After the signing of the Armistice on November 11,
1918, the control over the economy was quickly returned
to the private sector. At the same time, the transition
to   peacetime   enabled   the   government   to   bring   its
finances   into   order. From   the   end   of   the   war   until
fiscal year 1920, the federal budget declined to $6.1

billion, because the Wilson administration was interested in further cuts in order to generate a surplus to pay off the debt.

The immediate postwar period also saw effort being made to reorganize the government's debt administration agencies. During the course of the war, the Treasury sold five Liberty Loans and one Victory Loan for a total of $21.5 billion. The Treasury organizations handling public debt at the beginning of the war included the Division of Loans and Currency in the Secretary's Office and the Office of the Register in the Treasury. These two small offices had sufficed for servicing of normal debt transactions when the debt was fairly constant. They were not adequate for the large issues of the war. In April 1917, the two offices had just over 100 employees. They were both greatly expanded during the war and new procedures were devised to take care of the large number of subscriptions for Liberty Loans and war saving issues.[17] To give an idea of the workload faced in administering the new debt, the third Liberty Loan was subscribed to by 18.3 million persons and the fourth by over 21 million.[18]

The total issue of Liberty Loans amounted to almost 100 million certificates and required the processing of more than 66 million subscriptions. Because of this volume of transactions, the Division of Loans and Currency had expanded its activities during the war. However, further reorganization of its duties was required. By the end of the war, the number of Public Debt Service employees totaled 3,061, approximately two-thirds of whom were employed in the Division of Loans and Currency (1,939) and one-third in the Office of the Register (945).[19]

To smooth out the administration of this large and widely held debt, Secretary of the Treasury Carter Glass approved a plan set forth on November 11, 1919, designating a Commissioner of the Public Debt to take general charge of public debt transactions conducted by the Division of Loans and Currency, the Office of the Register, and a new division to be created and designated as the Division of Sinking Fund and Investment.[20] Included in the plan was the nomination of William S. Broughton, head of the Division of Loans and Currency, to be appointed as the first Commissioner of the Public Debt at a salary of $6,000. The purpose of this plan was to reorganize the public debt activities which had expanded in a disorderly fashion during the war, when the number of employees was increased from under 100 to nearly 3,000, and operations were housed in nine separate buildings.

Secretary Glass further elaborated on the plan on January 6, 1920, by adding a Division of Accounts, and detailed the duties and procedures to be followed by each division, as well as the relationships that would exist among the separate divisions, the Treasury, and the Federal Reserve System.[21]   Before this final reorganization could be put into place, however, a change in administration was made.

A total return to normalcy was not felt until the election of Warren G. Harding as President late in 1920. The emphasis in government finance changed with the inauguration of Harding's new administration in March 1921.   The new administration faced economic difficulties, however, for the economy had entered a recession in January 1920 and was still far from recovery. Nevertheless, the federal government was able to run a budget surplus as a result of high taxes as part of the program for paying off the war debt. President Harding stated his own views on this fiscal policy as a sound practice. He told a conference on unemployment, "There has been vast unemployment before and there will be again. There will be depression and inflation just as surely as the tides ebb and flow. I would have little enthusiasm for any proposed remedy which seeks either palliation or tonic from the Public Treasury."[22]

Harding's opinion of government finance was shared by his Secretary of the Treasury, Andrew Mellon, who was even more fiscally conservative. Mellon continued with the plan to cut government expenditures, but he gave tax reduction a higher priority than debt reduction. He was able to cut the budget to $3.6 billion by 1922, and it remained at that level for the rest of the 1920s.

Throughout the 1920s, Mellon presented several tax reduction plans to Congress. Mellon's overall policy was to reduce the tax burden in the upper brackets as well as for corporations, arguing that this policy would stimulate business and create many middle-class jobs on which taxes could be levied. This policy, which might be called old-time Republicanism, was an earlier version of the trickle-down tax policies offered by Ronald Reagan in the 1980s. Only Mellon was conservative enough to want to avoid the revenue losses this policy would entail. To offset some of those revenue losses, in 1922 the Fordney-McCumber Tariff was passed, raising tariff rates from an average of 15 percent to over 35 percent. By 1928, most of Mellon's tax recommendations had been followed.

Mellon's fiscal management policy was helped by good economic conditions during most of the 1920s. The recession of 1921 ended in July and except for two minor downturns the economy expanded vigorously for the rest of the decade. During this period, the federal budget produced surpluses ranging from $184 to $689 million. As had happened in the post-Civil War period, however, tariff collections were equal to the size of the surplus, ranging from $300 to $600 million. As a result, the public debt was gradually reduced from $24 billion to about $17 billion during the 1920s.

Additional changes in the government's budgeting and debt planning agencies were made in the 1920s. Congress passed the Budget and Accounting Act in 1921, which established an executive budget and formed a Bureau of the Budget in the Treasury Department.[23]

In accord with a memo from Commissioner Broughton dated August 20, 1921, Secretary Mellon agreed that the Public Debt Service be designated by that name and that its operations include the following divisions: the Office of the Commissioner, the Division of Loans and Currency, the Division of Paper Custody, the Office of the Register of the Treasury, the Division of Public Debt Accounts and Audits, the Distribution Unit, the Savings Unit, and the Destruction Committee. As these divisions indicate, the Public Debt Service retained a diverse set of operations, ranging from the registration of securities to the procurement of distinctive paper for the printing of currency and securities.

The consolidation of these functions enabled the Public Debt Service to eliminate many duplications of work that had existed when the divisions operated independently. The main functions of the Service were more readily separated under the new system, with the Division of Loans and Currency issuing new securities, the Register handling retired securities, and the Division of Audits and Accounts controlling the accounts of the other two divisions. The Division of Audits and Accounts was also given the responsibility of overseeing the public debt transactions performed by the Federal Reserve System, acting as fiscal agent for the Treasury. It is also of interest to note that both operating divisions maintained a system of efficiency ratings for employees.[24]

The activities of the Public Debt Service were housed in five buildings by April 1921. The Commissioner's office and portions of the Division of Loans and Currency and the Division of Public Accounts and Audit operated from the main Treasury Building. Additional units of the Division of Loans and Currency were located in the Liberty Loan Annex (14th and D St. S.W.), and the Auditor's Building (14th and B St. S.W.), while the Tracing Unit of the Division of Public Accounts and Audit worked in the Bond Building (14th and New York Ave. N.W.). The entire staff of the Register of the Treasury was situated in the Register's Annex (119 D St. N.E.), and the Custodian of Paper was attached to the Bureau of Printing and Engraving. A Treasury official noted at the time, "It is hardly necessary to describe in detail the many disadvantages and inconveniences which arise as a consequence of this

wide separation of forces."[25] It was further hoped that
some day the operations would be assembled in one
building.   The total work force for the Service was
3,061 persons at this time, and during the fiscal year
ending June 30, 1920, $46.3 billion in securities had
been handled and nearly 6 million interest checks had
been issued.[26]

The payment methods involving these securities as
part of the debt reduction program also needed to be
rethought.   As had happened in the past, the
government's collections of taxes did not always
coincide with its payment of debt.   To solve this
problem, a plan was set in place to refund the debt with
issues whose redemption dates took place at the same
time as quarterly tax payments. To help in this effort,
on June 15, 1921, the Treasury introduced the three-year
Treasury note, which was then issued in exchange for
Liberty and Victory bonds.[27]

For the rest of the decade, refunding of the debt
took place without any problems. Some issues of Thrift
Denomination Savings Certificates were offered to
attract small savers, but when complaints were received
that these competed too heavily with private borrowing,
the issues were withdrawn.   Congress later authorized
the Treasury in 1929 to issue Treasury bills to be sold
at a discount for 61-90 days.   Congress gave the
Treasury control over the forms, maturities,
distribution, and interest rate on its issues, finally
admitting that the job had become too complicated for
Congress alone to handle.   Congress retained control
over the total amount of debt.

THE GREAT DEPRESSION

The prosperous years of the 1920s ended in a
spectacular fashion, as the stock market suffered its
great crash and the economy entered into the worst
depression ever known or experienced. The causes of the
depression remain obscure.   Some economists have held
that the 1920s had seen a large investment boom brought
about by the expansion of the automobile and electric
power industries, and when these were completed there
was a decline in business spending. Other economists
believe that declines in consumer spending, brought
about by the uneven prosperity of the 1920s, wherein
blue-collar workers suffered, is the leading culprit.
Government policy can be held at fault to some extent,
for despite efforts by the Federal Reserve to tighten
the money supply in the late 1920s, the Treasury cut
taxes too quickly. By placing extra funds in the hands
of investors, this policy may have encouraged excessive
and speculative stock market activities.   As economic

historians Susan Lee and Peter Passell summarize their own findings: "Regrettably, no clean and quick explanation for the Depression survives close examination."[28]

Business activity had started to decline in the summer of 1929, and the stock market crash followed in October. At first it was thought the decline would be minor, but by mid-1930 it was apparent that a major economic crisis was in progress. Thereafter it was all downturn: Real gross national product fell by 30 percent, prices fell by about 25 percent and unemployment went to 25 percent until the economy hit bottom in 1933.

Although the administration of Herbert Hoover (1929-33) believed in balancing the budget, its first efforts during the downturn were to cut taxes at the end of 1929, as there was still a budget surplus. The times forced a deficit, however, and the tax cut was rescinded in 1930. Thereafter, the Hoover administration sought tax increases, including the notorious Smoot-Hawley Tariff of 1930, and heavy increases in excise and income taxes in 1932. Since the sale of alcoholic beverages had been prohibited by the Nineteenth Amendment, this usual source of tax revenue was not available. At the same time, an estimated $2 billion in public works projects were funded from 1930-33 and a billion-dollar veteran's bonus was voted by Congress in 1931. By 1933, there was a budget deficit of nearly $3 billion, including funds for mandatory debt retirement, and the debt had risen to more than $22 billion.

Despite these deficits, economists today cite the failure of the federal government to do more as contributing to the severity of the depression. Using the concept of a full-employment budget, (i.e., looking at what the government's budget would have been if full employment had been accomplished), Hoover's fiscal policy has been deemed conservative.[29] In addition, blame has been laid on the Federal Reserve for mishandling the money supply, especially during 1931 when interest rates were pushed upward to help keep the dollar backed by gold.[30]

To be sure, these criticisms have the benefit of hindsight. In the area of fiscal policy, for example, a new set of ideas, drawn from the writings of the English economist John Maynard Keynes, was developing. This view held that a general depression was as great a national emergency as a war, so the federal government should be willing to use deficits to stimulate the economy, just as it would borrow money to fight a war.

The election of Franklin D. Roosevelt as President in 1932 was a factor in the older view remaining in effect, at least in principle, for Roosevelt strongly believed in a balanced budget. If he forgot the

principle of balanced budgeting, his director of the
budget reminded him: "I hope, and hope most fervently
that you will evidence a real determination to bring the
budget into actual balance, for upon this, I think,
hangs not only your place in history, but conceivably
the immediate fate of western civilization."[31]
Reminders such as this were redundant where Roosevelt
was concerned. The full-employment budget method shows
that his fiscal policy was even more conservative than
Hoover's.[32] During his first days in office, Roosevelt
was too involved with the banking crisis and the first
flurry of New Deal legislation to concern himself with
budgetary matters. Besides, the ability to balance the
budget was basically out of the control of the
government, since the depression had caused a sharp
decline in tax receipts.

Roosevelt persisted in trying to balance the budget
for several years, but the need for spending on welfare
and public works, as well as the reduced tax revenues,
prevented this from happening. Economic conditions
improved, with a slow sluggish recovery from 1933 to
1937. At that point efforts were made to reduce the
deficit, and it did fall to $1.8 billion; at the same
time, the Social Security Act was being put into
operation, and collection of taxes under the act further
reduced the effective deficit of the federal government.
A downturn in economic conditions began in March 1937.
For the rest of the 1930s, the Roosevelt administration
abandoned its efforts at budget balancing,[33] and its
attitude toward the budget became more pragmatic. In
discussing changes in tax policy in 1939, Secretary of
the Treasury Henry Morgenthau felt it necessary to be
sure "that the change promotes and does not retard
business recovery, and that the change makes easier and
not more difficult progress toward the establishment of
a balanced relationship between revenues and
expenditures."[34] In short, the need for a balanced
budget should not take priority over economic recovery,
and a balanced relationship in fiscal affairs was not
the same as a balanced budget.

Regardless of his fiscal philosophy, Roosevelt
never achieved a budgetary surplus. Deficits ranged
from $2.3 to $3.5 billion from 1933 to 1940. During
this same period, $26.3 billion in total deficits was
incurred and the debt rose to $43 billion.

In order to manage that debt, changes had to be
made in the government's security offerings. The growth
in debt was greater than that financed during World War
I, and the war was a time of prosperity. Finding
sources for borrowing required greater resourcefulness
during a depression.

The sale of U.S. savings bonds was of great help in
managing this increased debt. A Division of Savings

Bonds was set up in the Public Debt Service to promote
the sale of savings bonds, the first "Series A bond"
being issued on March 1, 1935.   Bonds were issued in
denominations of $25 to $1,000, carrying interest at 2.9
percent.   The idea was to reactivate the World War I
strategy of tapping the resources of small savers, which
this time would help to fund programs to reduce
unemployment. In addition, Morgenthau, following in the
footsteps of his predecessors Robert J. Walker and
Salmon P. Chase, expected that the Savings Bond Program
would give citizens an interest in their government's
affairs.[35]   Obtaining citizen support for government
action was important during the dark days of the
depression,   when   other   ideologies   were   being
contemplated as offering better hope and economic
security, and would become vital when the nation entered
World War II.
     Cumulative sales of Series A, B, C, and D bonds
were about $4 billion through April 1941.[36]   The
recording of all transactions was handled by the Public
Debt Service, which in fiscal year ending June 30, 1936,
had 2,458 employees with salaries and wages totaling
$3,702,548, including $7,470 for the Commissioner.[37]
     Congress   began   considering   legislation   to
reorganize   the   executive   branch   of   the   federal
government in the late 1930s, at the request of
President Franklin Roosevelt.   As one senator put it,
"Reorganization of the Federal Government for economy,
simplification and efficiency is one of the most
urgently   needed   responsibilities   confronting   the
Congress, the Executive, and the Nation as a whole."[38]
The legislation was duly enacted on April 3, 1939, as
the Reorganization Act of 1939.
     The President created the Fiscal Service of the
Treasury to be headed by the Fiscal Assistant Secretary
under the Reorganization Plan III of the act, as
transmitted to Congress on April 2, 1940.   As part of
this plan, the Public Debt Service was redesignated the
Bureau of the Public Debt and was made part of the
Fiscal Service.   Effective June 30, 1940, under the
direction of the Commissioner of the Public Debt, the
reorganization began affecting the previous operations
of the Public Debt Service, the Division of Loans and
Currency, the Office of the Register of the Treasury,
the Division of Public Debt Accounts and Audits, and the
Division of Paper Custody, with the addition of the
Division of Savings Bonds.[39]   The total public debt was
$50.7 billion at that time, but with the advent of World
War II, that figure and the operations of the Bureau
would be greatly altered again.

NOTES

1. Lester V. Chandler, <u>The Economics of Money and Banking,</u> 4th ed. (New York: Harper & Row, 1964), pp. 147-148.

2. Esther R. Taus, <u>Central Banking Functions of the United States Treasury, 1789-1941</u> (New York: Columbia University Press, 1943), p. 120.

3. Taus, <u>Central Banking Functions,</u> p. 131.

4. Taus, <u>Central Banking Functions,</u> p. 124.

5. Richard H. Timberlake Jr., <u>Origins of Central Banking in the United States</u> (Cambridge, Mass.:   Harvard University Press, 1976), p. 179.

6. Timberlake, <u>Origins of Central Banking,</u> p. 221.

7. Taus, <u>Central Banking Functions,</u> p. 142.

8. Linda Baziluik, "Division of Securities Operations: Look Where We've Been," <u>Public Debt Newsletter,</u> 1973-1975.

9. Secretary of the Treasury, <u>Annual Report</u> (Washington, D.C.:   1917), p. 43.

10. Secretary of the Treasury, <u>Annual Report</u> (Washington, D.C.:   1918), p. 44.

11. Secretary of the Treasury, <u>Annual Report</u> (1918), p. 44

12. Secretary of the Treasury, <u>Annual Report</u> (Washington, D.C.:   1919), p. 25.

13. U.S. Department of the Treasury, The Commissioner of the Public Debt, <u>Report to the Secretary of the Treasury,</u> (Washington, D.C.:   December 20, 1940), p. 4.

14. Milton Friedman and Anna Schwartz, <u>A Monetary History of the United States</u> (Princeton, N.J.:   Princeton University Press, 1963), p. 206.

15. Paul Studenski and Herman E. Kroos, <u>Financial History of the United States,</u> 2nd ed. (New York: McGraw-Hill, 1963), pp. 280-301.

16. Taus, <u>Central Banking Functions,</u> p. 164.

17. U.S. Dept. of Treasury, Commissioner of the Public Debt, Report, December 20, 1940, p. 4.

18. Secretary of the Treasury, Annual Report (1918), p. 1.

19. Baziluik, Public Debt Newsletter, 1973-1975.

20. R.C. Leffingwell, Memorandum to Carter Glass (Washington, D.C.: Public Debt Files, Important Data File D-120.94, November 11, 1919), vol 1.

21. Secretary Carter Glass, Memorandum (Washington, D.C.: Bureau of the Public Debt), January 6, 1920.

22. Robert A. Gordon, Economic Instability and Growth: The American Record (New York: Harper & Row, 1974), pp. 21-22.

23. James D. Savage, Balanced Budgets and American Politics (Ithaca N.Y.: Cornell University Press, 1988), p. 145.

24. U.S. Government Pamphlet, The Public Debt Service (Washington, D.C.: April 1921).

25. U.S. Govt., Public Debt Service, pp. 43-44.

26. U.S. Govt., Public Debt Service, pp. 43-44.

27. Taus, Central Banking Functions, p. 180.

28. Susan Previant Lee and Peter Pasell, A New View of American History (New York: W. W. Norton, 1979), p. 382.

29. Lee and Pasell, American History, pp. 385-387.

30. Freidman and Schwartz, Monetary History, chap. 7.

31. Alonzo Hamby, ed., The New Deal: Analysis and Interpretation (New York: Weybright and Talley, 1969), p. 17.

32. Lee and Pasell, American History, p. 386.

33. Gordon, Economic Instability and Growth, pp. 66-67.

34. Esther R. Taus, The Role of the U.S. Treasury in Stabilizing the Economy (Washington, D.C.: University Press of America, 1981), p. 93.

35. Taus, <u>Role of the U.S. Treasury,</u> p. 72.

36. U.S. Department of the Treasury, <u>A History of the United States Savings Bond Program</u> (Washington, D.C.: September 1984), p. 5.

37. U.S. Department of the Treasury, <u>File D100.4, Subject: Treasury Department</u> (Washington, D.C.: 1936).

38. U.S. Congress (76th), Senate Report No. 142, <u>Reorganization Act of 1939</u> (Washington, D.C.: 1939). See also House Report No. 120, 76th Cong., 1939, on the same topic.

39. Franklin D. Roosevelt, <u>Third Plan on Government Reorganization</u> (Washington, D.C.: House Document No. 681, 76th Congress, April 2, 1940) p. 2.

6

Debt Expansion during World War II (1940–45)

If the Great Depression of the 1930s began altering the nation's attitude toward government budget deficits, World War II would serve the same function in terms of the public debt. At the beginning of the war the level of public debt, while at an all-time high, still was in a range that, at least in principle, made payment of it a feasible political option. By the end of the war, the public debt reached a level that made its eventual repayment virtually impossible; it became a debt that would never be paid. To be sure, total repayment of the debt had been a distant goal ever since the Civil War, and the country had not suffered as a result. A growing economy and expanding financial markets had made refunding of the debt an easy task. The mountain of debt piled up during World War II would also be handled easily, although there was little appreciation of this possibility as the war began.

Nothing in our nation's history could have prepared the people and the government for those activities entailed in the massive effort to achieve victory in World War II. It has been estimated that total government expenditures during the war were $323 billion, about 40 percent of the gross national product (GNP) during that period. In comparison, it was estimated that World War I expenditures were only one-quarter of the GNP during that timespan.[1] The effort to fight the war required a total mobilization of our financial resources. It is doubtful that any citizen of the country was untouched by the handling of the financing for the war effort, which also put great pressure on the fiscal agencies of the government.

The government and industry were not totally unprepared for the war. Many industries had already been selling war materiel to England and France, and the U.S. government began increasing its own defense expenditures during 1939-40, particularly after the fall of France. Fortunately, Selective Service (the "draft" for the armed forces) was in effect before our entrance into the war, and plans also were made for purchasing strategic materiel. Fifteen percent of the nation's industrial production was geared toward the military. This was only a small amount of what would be needed.

The economy performed remarkably well during the war. Total output (GNP) more than doubled between 1940 and 1945, and the unemployment rate fell to a record low of 1 percent. The government's share of total output during the war reached half of GNP by 1944. This meant that by 1945 defense expenditures were 15 times what they had been in fiscal year 1941. Despite this massive increase in government spending, personal consumption did not decline during the war. At the outset of the war there was still enough unused capacity left over from the depression that a guns-versus-butter choice was not immediately required. As the war continued, measures such as price controls were needed to keep consumption expenditures from expanding, however.[2]

FINANCING WORLD WAR II

Despite the solid performance by the economy, a large growth in the public debt took place during the war, as approximately $190 billion of the estimated $323 billion spent in fighting the war was borrowed. As had happened in previous wars, efforts were made to pay for a portion of this war through increased taxes. The first in a series of tax increases went into effect on June 25, 1940. Individual personal exemptions were lowered and the tax rates were raised. This trend continued through 1944, and by the end of the war, revenue from the personal income tax had increased twentyfold. Personal withholding deductions were introduced during the war under the Current Tax Payment Act of 1943. Corporate taxes were increased and an excess profits tax was added; estate and gift taxes were also increased. Overall, government tax collections in 1944 were eight times what they had been in 1940.[3] All of these tax increases were significant, as taxes paid for 46 percent of World War II, as compared with 35 percent in World War I. The rest had to be borrowed.

An overall plan for managing this borrowing, with an eye toward minimizing its impact on the economy, was established at the Treasury. Treasury officials had always been sensitive about the effect that their financial policies had on money markets. This massive spending program meant that they had to be concerned about avoiding inflation, maintaining reasonable rates of interest, and attaining a widespread ownership of the public debt. Each of these complex technical problems will be considered in turn.

It is doubtful that a war has ever been fought without inducing some inflation. Through its expenditures the government creates income for individual consumers and businesses, money that they would like to spend. However, the government's purchases reduce the available supply of goods and services. Therefore, when consumers and businesses attempt to use their rising incomes for purchases, demand becomes greater than supply, resulting in upward pressure on prices. Economists call this condition an inflationary gap. One goal of debt management during the war was to eliminate this gap.

Total income in the economy was $833 billion during the war. The federal government spent $323 billion of that income, with all but $16 billion going to fighting the war. This figure, $323 billion, represented the inflationary gap that needed to be eliminated. If the government could have taxed away the entire amount of the inflationary gap, there would have been no reason to fear inflation. This aspect of the problem was recognized by Secretary Morgenthau, who, in arguing for higher taxes, observed, "If, in an attempt to protect the incomes of our people we hold down taxes and as a result the cost of living rises, we shall have taxed them just as fully as if we had levied on them directly."[4]

Morgenthau's appreciation of the problem notwithstanding, taxes accounted for only $133 billion of the gap, leaving an inflationary gap of $190 billion. It seems to be an axiom that wars cannot be fought on a "pay-as-you-go" plan. The Treasury officials recognized this problem and planned accordingly. The Secretary of the Treasury summed up the wartime experience by stating, "One of the major goals of the Treasury financing was to try to channel back into the Treasury as much as possible of this $190 billion that people were accumulating as a result of this Federal deficit."[5]

The manner in which these funds were channeled to the Treasury was very important, and requires a brief review of the relations between the Treasury and the banking system. Under the principles of banking and the regulations of the Federal Reserve System, banks are required to keep only a small portion of their customers' deposits on reserve to meet withdrawal requests. The rest of those deposits, as loaned, add to the total money supply. Each loan that is made generates an additional deposit that can then be loaned out again and again, until the amount held in reserves is exhausted. When banks are holding excess reserves, this money-creating capability is only a potential problem. Anything that translates these inactive reserves into active reserves can create money, lead to an increase in purchasing power, and an increase in the inflationary gap.

It would have been very efficient for the Treasury simply to sell the bulk of its debt to commercial banks to finance the war. To do so, however, would have been inflationary. Idle funds that were already being saved would then be spent. What was needed was to reduce current demand by inducing individuals to save their extra income.

The Treasury employed a strategy of tailoring its securities to meet the needs of purchasers to encourage current saving through the purchase of government securities by individuals. A broad mix of securities was offered, ranging from short-term to long-term. A class of debt that was restricted as to its purchase by banks was sold to keep too much debt from going to banks. Special Tax savings bonds, enabling individuals and corporations to set aside funds for future tax liabilities, were sold until 1943, when withholding taxes were imposed. The Third War Loan, for example, contained a mix of seven securities dated September 1, 1943: 7/8 percent certificates due September 1, 1944; 2 percent Treasury bonds due September 15, 1953; 2 1/2 percent Treasury bonds due December 15, 1969; Series E, F, and G savings bonds; and Series C savings notes.[6]

The inclusion of savings bonds in a loan drive was a marked departure from previous financing methods. As noted previously, Alexander Hamilton had stressed the need to have holders of public debt feel secure in the transferability of their securities, and his advice had since been followed. But efforts to encourage purchase of government securities by small savers created a new situation. While a government security is marketable (i.e., able to be sold in a securities market), it does not follow that it can be sold at its par value. As with any other security, the price of a government issue can fluctuate, and a purchaser who wants to sell a bond prior to maturity may lose money if bond prices fall.

Many small savers, for example, had been brought into the government securities market during World War I through the sale of small-denomination Liberty bonds, which were completely negotiable. Immediately after the war, the price of Liberty bonds fell; the 4 1/4 percent bonds of the Fourth Liberty Loan, for example, fell to a low of $82.75 for a $100 par bond on May 20, 1920. Many of the purchasers of these bonds were unsophisticated investors who, when they sold their bonds at a loss, felt cheated and blamed the government for their losses. They also had a difficult time understanding why the government could not readily replace negotiable bonds that were lost or stolen.[7]

Even though the Treasury's goal was to keep interest rates constant during the war, which would have protected small investors from changes in rates, it was still felt that small denominations of marketable securities would provide tricky problems in cases of sudden large liquidations in the securities markets. The Treasury, in an effort to appeal to small savers during World War II, placed greater reliance on nonmarketable securities in the savings bond series, especially Series E.   They were available in small denominations, redeemable in cash two months after issue, and carried interest in fixed amounts depending on when they were redeemed.   As they were nonnegotiable their value would not change, and because they were redeemable before maturity at the option of the holder, they could easily be turned into cash.[8]   They were sold in registered form, which meant that they could be replaced if lost, stolen, or destroyed.   They were designed this way to make the small saver feel very secure in purchasing them.   This effort was so successful that savings bonds constituted 17.6 percent of total public debt outstanding by the end of the war.[9] Comparatively, savings bonds comprised about 10 percent of the debt just before the war began.[10]

With a goal of wartime fiscal policy being the reduction of consumer spending, and with the level of taxes being used to their fullest in meeting this goal, a main focus of the effort to reduce the purchasing power of consumers was the Savings Bond Program. The sale of nearly $50 billion in savings bonds during the war went a long way toward eliminating the total inflationary gap estimated at $190 billion. The payroll deduction savings plan initiated in 1942 is of special interest in this regard. Nearly 28 million workers were participating in the plan by June 1944, with monthly deductions totaling $500 million.   This amount represented 10 percent of the total pay of those participating in the plan, resulting in a sizable reduction in their purchasing power.[11]   Furthermore, there were few redemptions of savings bonds during the war, with only 15 percent of savings bonds sold having been redeemed by June 30, 1945.[12]   This low level of redemption meant that purchasers were willing to hold on to bonds as savings, which reduced their demand for goods and services. It also meant that individuals were satisfied with the security of the bonds.   Treasury officials were aware of the propaganda value of the Savings Bond Program in fostering patriotism and national unity, and many of the savings bonds sales campaigns reinforced other patriotic appeals.   The low level of redemptions would indicate that this aspect of the program was also a success.   It is estimated that during the course of the war the sale of Series E, F, and G savings bonds absorbed 6.7 percent of total personal income.[13]

This increased reliance on nonmarketable securities also helped the Treasury attain one of its other goals, widespread ownership of the debt. One reason for paying for a war by borrowing instead of taxing has to do with equity. The government was spending as much as 50 percent of annual national income during World War II, meaning taxes would have had to average 50 percent of individual income for a "pay-as-you-go" plan to work. Even if the income of the wealthy was taxed at higher rates, as was done during the war, people of lower income would still have faced a relatively more severe tax burden. A policy of deficit financing would merely shift this burden into the future if it was not done carefully. As taxes were later collected to pay for the debt or for interest payments on the debt, if ownership of the debt was skewed toward upper income persons or toward banks, payment of debt or interest on it could represent a transfer of income from lower-income to higher-income persons. To offset this possibility, Series E savings bonds carried higher interest rates (2.9 percent if held to maturity) than other securities. In addition, there were limits set on the amount of savings bonds an individual could purchase in a year, so wealthy persons could not receive an unfair share of those higher interest rates.

The high volume of sales of savings bonds indicated that the distribution of ownership of the government debt was fairly broad. While there are no records of government debt ownership by income groups, the Treasury did keep track of individual versus bank holdings of the debt. The record shows that both groups held reasonably constant shares of debt ownership over the years. Individuals held 20 percent of government securities, and commercial banks held 39 percent on June 30, 1941. Both groups had increased their shares slightly by June 30, 1945, with individuals holding 23 percent and banks holding 40 percent. The remainder of the debt in 1945 was held by insurance companies (9 percent), mutual savings banks (4 percent), corporations (12 percent), state and local governments (2 percent), and government agencies and trust funds (10 percent). Additionally, the holdings listed above for banks include those of the Federal Reserve, which amounted to 4 percent of the total debt in 1941 and 8 percent in 1945.[14]

This increase in the Federal Reserve's holdings of government securities was in part caused by the policy of interest rate stabilization. Another goal of the Treasury's debt management plan was the sale of debt at levels of interest that were as low as possible and as steady as possible. This was not achieved during World

War I, when each successive debt offering carried a higher interest rate. This pattern was unsatisfactory for the government for two reasons. First, higher rates of interest meant higher expenses for debt service, and it was one aim of debt policy to keep those costs as low as possible with low interest rates. Second, when interest rates were rising, it became harder to sell bonds, as purchasers were determined to wait until interest rates rose before making their purchase of bonds. This second aspect is complicated and requires some elaboration.

Government securities at that time were all sold with a fixed maturity value (e.g., $1,000) and at a fixed interest rate (e.g., 5 percent). The market in government securities, however, will see to it that the rate of return or yield on all bonds is made equal by adjusting the market price of individual issues to values different from their maturity values. If interest rates rise, the market value of previously sold bonds will fall. For example, if a new issue of government bonds carries an interest rate of 6 percent, the price of previously issued 5 percent bonds will fall to $83.33 to give the bonds an equivalent yield. This process is often referred to as "interest-rate risk," and the rise of interest rates during World War I helps to explain why the value of some issues of Liberty bonds declined. A prudent investor has two choices to avoid facing interest-rate risk. First, he can purchase short-term securities and when interest rates change, wait a short time for the securities to mature and receive the full purchase price for them. As they are not subject to interest-rate risk, short-term securities usually carry a lower interest rate than do long-term securities. Second, if an investor wants the higher return of long-term securities, but anticipates rising interest rates, the investor can decide to wait until interest rates hit their peak before making his purchase(s).

The Treasury determined to maintain interest rates at a constant level throughout the war to avoid this problem. At the time the government began its wartime borrowing, interest rates were still in the low ranges that had persisted throughout the Great Depression of the 1930s. Short-term notes carried rates of less than 1 percent, with long-term issues yielding in the range of 1.25 percent to 2.5 percent. The Treasury needed the cooperation of the Federal Reserve Banks to maintain these rates.

As noted previously, there is an inverse relationship between the market value of a marketable security and its yield. As the interest rates rise or fall, the market price of the security will change inversely to bring the yield on all securities to a constant, adjusting for different dates of maturity. Alternatively, when the market price of a security falls, its yield rises, requiring subsequent issues to have a higher interest rate. Whenever the Treasury sells a new issue of securities, it must be careful that it does not push the price of all securities down and force interest rates up.

One way for the Treasury to do away with this problem would be to sell securities directly to the Federal Reserve, which has the power to print new money that could be used to purchase government securities. However, the Banking Act of 1935 prohibits the Federal Reserve from making direct purchases of securities from the Treasury.[15] Instead, the Federal Reserve is only permitted to purchase government securities on the open market, from banks and individuals, in what are called open market operations. This manner of purchasing government securities enables the Federal Reserve to keep their prices steady and thereby maintain interest rates at a constant rate.

During World War II, the Federal Reserve cooperated with the Treasury in terms of interest-rate management. The interest rate on long-term bonds was set at 2 1/2 percent for the term of the war, and while presidents of some Federal Reserve Banks indicated they would have preferred to see 3 percent, they agreed to support the lower rates. While no official statement to that effect was made, the financial markets assumed that this policy would be followed.[16] There was debate about the amount of interest for the short-term rate, with the Treasury desiring it to be at 1/4 percent, and the Federal Reserve lobbying for 3/8 percent. The Federal Reserve prevailed in this matter. Secretary of the Treasury Henry Morgenthau was able to report, "On April 30, 1942, the Federal Open Market Committee directed the twelve Federal Reserve Banks to purchase for the System Open Market Account at a rate of 3/8 of 1 percent per annum all Treasury bills offered to them."[17] There would be no problem of rising interest rates during the war with the Federal Reserve willing to follow this plan.

The range of interest rates agreed to by the Treasury and the Federal Reserve was maintained successfully throughout the war. As a result, the computed rate of interest on government debt fell during the war, as shown in Table 6.1 (the computed rate of interest is determined by dividing the total debt by the actual amount of interest paid). This decline in computed interest indicated that the Treasury's goal of financing the war at low and steady interest rates was achieved.

There was a cost to accomplishing this goal in terms of increased ownership of government securities by

Table 6.1
Computed Rate of Interest on the Public Debt (1941-45)

Year	1941	1942	1943	1944	1945
Computed Rate	2.52	2.28	1.98	1.93	1.94

Source: Annual Reports of the Secretary of the
          Treasury, 1941-45.

the Federal Reserve.   The pattern of interest rates
agreed to by the Treasury and the Federal Reserve,
namely low short-term rates and higher long-term rates,
would indicate, under a free market, that investors were
anticipating an increase in interest rates.   Investors
would be buying short-term securities (pushing their
interest rates down) and avoiding long-term securities
(forcing their rates up).   The spread between the long-
term and short-term rates would be the premium for being
subjected to interest-rate risk.   There was no interest-
rate risk with the Federal Reserve standing ready to
"peg" the interest rates through open market operations.
Consequently, investors of all classes had no incentive
to purchase short-term securities.

The Treasury was tempted at the same time to do as
much short-term borrowing as possible and take advantage
of the lower interest rates on this class of security.
Long-term bonds constituted 77 percent of marketable
securities in 1940, but only 60 percent in 1945.[18]
Federal Reserve open market operations thus had to be
concentrated in short-term securities, with the result
that by December 31, 1944, the Federal Reserve held 68
percent of all Treasury bills outstanding, 12 percent of
marketable notes and certificates, but only 1.5 percent
of long-term marketable bonds.[19]   While the Federal
Reserve would have held a similar amount of government
debt in any event, this skewing of its portfolio toward
short-term securities meant that the low rates at which
the Treasury financed the war were to some degree at the
expense of the Federal Reserve.

As noted above, the sale of government securities
to the banking system was viewed as being inflationary,
while those sold to individuals who paid out of current
income were noninflationary.   The Treasury hoped to pull
as much of new savings as possible into its securities.
During the five years of the war, sales of government
securities absorbed about $121 billion out of $189
billion of new savings.   Approximately $38 billion of

the remaining $68 billion were put in highly liquid
checking accounts, where they were in the greatest
danger of being spent immediately. But to some extent
these funds represented new accounts opened by persons
who had been so impoverished during the depression that
they had no liquid funds prior to their increases in
income during the war and who were determined to save.
As a result, it was concluded at the Treasury that "only
a relatively small part of the $38 billion increase in
demand deposits is dangerous money in the inflationary
sense," and "the inflationary dollars involved in the
$68 billion in money savings made over the five-year
period represents a small portion of the total."[20] To
be sure, government securities that could be turned into
cash rather easily always presented a threat of
inflation. However, Seymour Harris, a noted economist,
calculated that only a third of government debt holdings
were potentially inflationary.[21]

The wartime debt management plan of the Treasury
was a relative success. In terms of interest rates, the
government fared much better than it had in World War I.
During the first war, the average rate of interest on
the interest-bearing portion of the government debt went
from 2.36 percent in 1914 to 4.22 percent in 1920.
During World War II, that same average interest actually
fell from 2.6 percent in 1939 to 1.94 percent in 1945.[22]

But as often happens, the benefits of that low
interest showed up as a cost elsewhere. The support of
the Treasury's financing by the Federal Reserve did
cause an increase in the money supply, with a resulting
bout of inflation in the economy. Milton Friedman and
Anna Schwartz calculate that 21 percent of the war was
financed by the creation of money and that inflation
imposed a tax that amounted to about 5 percent of total
war expenditures.[23] In comparison to World War I, the
overall rate of inflation during World War II was lower,
with actual rates of inflation totaling slightly less
than 30 percent. Friedman and Schwartz attribute this
positive result to "the much greater increase in
willingness to save in World War II."[24] To the extent
that government policy with regard to savings bond sales
helped foster this higher level of savings, credit for
lower inflation is due to the Treasury. The deficit
caused by the war would have been financed in any event,
but the methods used by the Treasury did help to
eliminate some of the inflationary gap caused by the
government expenditures. It also helped that the level
of inflation was managed by price controls, enforced by
the Office of Price Administration; price limits were
placed on a number of scarce items in 1941, and most
prices came to be controlled in spring 1942, with farm
prices added in 1943. The Treasury's policies made it
an easier fight against inflation, however.

One economist who studied the pattern of price changes during the war, Henry C. Murphy, concluded that there was no correlation to be found between changes in the money supply and changes in government spending and the price level, indicating that in terms of fighting inflation during the war, "the direct controls were all-important and the monetary-fiscal policy was insignificant."[25]

Overall, it can be concluded that the Treasury's plans were successful for managing the debt with a minimal impact on the economy. The rate of inflation was kept within tolerable limits with a large amount of wartime income being absorbed by sales of government securities. A widespread distribution of ownership of the debt securities was achieved and interest rates were kept low and stable. These plans relied heavily on the cooperation of the Federal Reserve Banks, which was readily granted to the Treasury. An effective sales campaign for management of the debt was also required and attained.

The entire promotion of sales of government securities was coordinated by the War Finance Division of the Treasury Department, formed on June 25, 1943, through the consolidation of two separate agencies--the Victory Fund Committee and the War Savings Staff--that had previously performed the same functions independently of each other and often at cross purposes. The organization of this promotional effort replicated that of World War I, by dividing the country into Federal Reserve Bank districts. However, the savings bond sales agencies were not as reliant on volunteer help as had been the case in the first war; a salaried staff of 2,043 persons was in place by July 1, 1944, with a supplemental corps of 938 "dollar-a-year" volunteers.[26] Much of the promotional effort in the area of savings bonds initially fell to the Division of Savings Bonds of the Bureau of the Public Debt, which continued to promote the sale of savings bonds even when that function was consolidated with the War Finance Committee. The Division of Savings Bonds mailed more than 650 million pieces of advertising to schools, banks, newspapers, and various special groups during the war.[27]

WARTIME DEBT ADMINISTRATION PROBLEMS

The Bureau of the Public Debt encountered a host of problems in discharging its administrative function because the sale of government securities went so well. A sixfold increase in the government's debt over a five year period certainly created a massive amount of additional work. The workload was tolerable in the area

of marketable securities, which were sold to banks and
the Federal Reserve, and past procedures for managing
their sale continued to work well. For example, in the
Office of the Register it was noted that the volume of
redemption   in   marketable   securities   increased
considerably between 1941 and 1945. This excess volume
was handled with only a slight increase in personnel,
made possible primarily through such improved procedures
as the elimination of certain operations and records
that were deemed to be unessential to the Register's
function.[28]
     The real test of the Bureau's ability to cope with
the wartime financing activities of the government would
come from the sale of savings bonds, as $50 billion in
these securities sold during the war amounted to 12
times the amount sold during the previous five years.
The Fiscal Assistant Secretary estimated in 1952 that
during the war, 900 million savings bonds were sold to
85 million different persons.[29]
     Sales of the Series E, F, and G bonds commenced on
May 1, 1941. The Series E bonds were intended for the
small investor and were made available at banks and
through payroll deduction plans. Many problems due to
the inexperience of sales agents arose as a result of
this expansion. The savings bond organization--the
Division of Savings Bonds--was already experiencing
difficulties in handling the increased volume of bond
sales by the time of the declaration of war in December
1941. Savings bond issues totaled 1,160,806 pieces in
May 1941; in December 1941 that figure increased
dramatically to 5,100,770 pieces. The peak monthly
figure, 32,665,663 pieces, was reached in August 1943.[30]
     The procedures followed at the time required that
as each bond was sold by an agent, a duplicate stub was
forwarded to the Bureau, where it was first audited and
then delivered to the Machine Accounts Division to be
arranged numerically, filmed in the Microphotographic
Subunit, keypunched, sorted alphabetically to the
seventh letter of the surname and first letter of the
given name, and then turned over to the Stub Files
Subunit for filing.[31] Nearly a billion units of Series
E, F, and G savings bonds were sold and processed during
the war.
     Several changes were implemented to handle this
volume of business. All stubs on bonds issued after
December 1941 were of the punchcard type.[32]
Addressograph equipment was installed in the Division of
Loans and Currency to eliminate the typing involved in
producing 4,000 to 6,000 labels a day for packaging
bonds. The embossing of the impression seal of the
Treasury was omitted from savings bonds in July 1942,
with the seal being printed on the bonds instead. The
size of the bonds was reduced by 50 percent in 1943,

saving paper and storage space. Another modification
was that on January 29, 1942, the positions of Deputy
Commissioner, Budget Officer, and Management Officer
were created in the Office of the Commissioner.[33]
Despite all these changes, by early 1942 there was
a backlog in all phases of work associated with the
Savings Bond Program. Since there was a shortage of
available space and a tight labor market in the
Washington, D.C., area, in April 1942 the Under
Secretary of the Treasury decided that the entire
Savings Bond Program should be moved to Chicago. The
midwest location was chosen for the efficiency of its
central location in terms of the receipt and delivery of
items by mail.[34] Sufficient space was found to be
available in the Merchandise Mart. Eventually, as
volume in the Chicago office expanded to the point where
even corridors were being used as storage sites for
registration stubs for Series E bonds, its operations
would be relocated to five separate buildings, with
almost a million square feet of floor space.[35]
It was initially planned that about 2,100 employees
would be transferred from Washington to Chicago. Many
of the best qualified employees resigned to take other
jobs rather than make the move. Only 1,227 persons
actually were transferred. Those employees transferred
to Chicago received extensive training to prepare them
for the increased responsibility and leadership they
would hold in the new operation. They were also given
assistance in securing housing in the Chicago area.
The workers found, upon arrival in Chicago, that
their work space had not been properly prepared, as the
buildings were still in the process of being converted
from their previous use as furniture display and storage
rooms. Materials and office furniture were scarce, and
as more new employees were added, conditions became
crowded. Due to a faulty heating system, room
temperatures throughout the building ranged from 90
degrees in interior offices to very cold in areas near
windows. Still, the work was accomplished.[36]
The operations for which the Chicago branch assumed
responsibility included transactions concerning
retirement and reissue of savings bonds, maintenance of
accounts for bondholders, issuance of interest checks
for Series G bonds, auditing of sales reports by agents
directly accountable to the Treasury Department, and
operation of the Machine Accounts and Statistical
Section of the Division of Loans and Currency. This
section was formed on January 29, 1942, to provide
mechanical processing of accounting data. The Chicago
office had 5,200 employees by February 1943, less than
one year since its inception.
The Washington office continued to handle the
actual issuing of savings bonds because of its proximity

to the Bureau of Engraving and Printing. The limited
size of the office space, however, made it necessary to
operate the staff on a two-shift basis, with three
shifts being used for a brief time in 1942.
Productivity of employees was also increased through use
of mechanical aids and a better use of idle time by
shifting workers to those operations with the most
pressing needs.

Recruiting personnel had to be sent out to the
Chicago office 30 days before it was to open in order to
hire local staff.   Advertisements were placed in the
newspapers to attract new employees.   When want ads
reached the limit of their effectiveness, direct field
recruiting was used. Visits were made to high schools
to bring in graduating students, and during summer
vacation, schoolchildren above the age of 16 were hired.
A special evening shift and a shortened day shift were
initiated for the convenience of housewives. A special
unit of 25 hearing-impaired persons was formed to cancel
savings stamps in the Stamp Section.   The office
followed a liberal policy of hiring physically
handicapped persons, and this group, which performed
very well, made up about 10 percent of the Chicago
office work force.[37]

The Chicago office employed 9,916 persons at its
peak, June 30, 1945.[38] A total of 26,565 persons were
hired during the course of the war. This turnover
required an extensive training program.[39] Mechanical
preparation of the payroll was begun in 1943 to handle
this volume of personnel work, and autotypist machines
were installed to prepare personnel folders. A branch
office was opened in Danville, Illinois, in 1945. This
was an installation of 150 keypunch machines, which
eliminated a backlog of unpunched registration stubs.[40]
Keypunch operations, used for the registration of
savings bonds, facilitated the processing of such a
large volume of sales, and the register of savings-bond
holders eventually became the largest alphabetical
register in the world.

The Chicago branch of the Chief Counsel's Office of
the Bureau was established on June 15, 1942. Its legal
staff averaged six attorneys during the war. The
transactions conducted by the Bureau are governed by
regulations issued by the Secretary of the Treasury, by
rules set forth for the Federal Reserve Banks, and by
the instructions placed on the forms used by the public
in buying government securities. Generally, these rules
could only be waived by the top officials of the Bureau
and the Treasury, who, during the war, were located in
Washington. However, as a result of a high caseload in
the Chicago Counsel's office, general waivers that
applied to common categories of cases were granted. The
Law Library in Chicago grew from 870 to 4,614 volumes

during the war.[41]

Two further examples of the amount of work done in Chicago can be given. Savings stamps in very small denominations were made available during the war. The Destruction Committee in Chicago destroyed 2,469,808 pounds of stamps with a redemption value of $1.3 billion during the three years of its operation. The number of checks issued in payment of interest on Series G savings bonds grew from 41,866 at the initial mailing on November 1, 1941, to 787,538 in June 1946.[42]

The Federal Reserve Banks were very important in the actual sale of savings bonds. When the Savings Bond Program began in 1936, the Federal Reserve Banks had been granted authority to issue savings bonds, and in 1937 were permitted to redeem certain of them and to enlist the services of member banks to act as issuing agents. Federal Reserve Banks were granted the authority to redeem savings bonds prior to submission to the Treasury during the war. This authority was extended in October 1944 to all banks and trust companies within each Federal Reserve district.[43]

This expansion of the number of issuing and redemption agents provided better service for the purchasers of savings bonds. At the same time, the work of the Registration and Retirement Section of the Chicago office, set up in August 1942, increased in difficulty as the system of processing claims and answering correspondence became more complicated.

In summing up the wartime work of the Bureau, its in-house historian observed:

> The Bureau of the Public Debt encountered most of the major problems that beset other large-scale operations during the war period, such as those created by an unprecedented volume of work increasing at a rate to preclude estimate; lack of space and facilities; and shortages of personnel, equipment and supplies. In the administration of savings bond work, these problems were further complicated by lack of autonomy, caused by decentralization of an activity for which procedures had not had time to become crystallized.
>
> The solutions to these problems were frequently nothing more than stopgaps to tide over an emergency and while not always satisfactory from an efficiency viewpoint, they usually satisfied immediate and pressing needs. As a result a great deal of the refinement of procedure and more satisfactory solutions to administrative problems remained

to be finished at the conclusion of the war.[44]

The operations at the rest of the Bureau were more satisfactory. The removal of the savings bonds activities from Washington facilitated the handling of the administrative duties there.   Outside of the Chicago office, the Bureau employed 2,492 persons on June 30, 1945, indicating that little expansion in personnel had taken place in terms of the prewar employment figures.[45]

NOTES

1. Secretary of the Treasury, <u>Annual Report</u> (Washington, D.C.: 1945), pp. 81-82.

2. Robert A. Gordon, <u>Economic Instability and Growth: The American Record</u> (New York: Harper & Row, 1974), pp. 84-90.

3. Esther R. Taus, <u>The Role of the U.S. Treasury in Stabilizing the Economy</u> (Washington, D.C.: University Press of America, 1981), p. 77.

4. Taus, <u>Role of the U.S. Treasury,</u> pp. 99-100.

5. Secretary of the Treasury, <u>Annual Report</u> (1945), pp. 82-83.

6. Secretary of the Treasury, <u>Annual Report</u> (Washington, D.C.: 1944), p. 40.

7. Henry C. Murphy, <u>National Debt in War and Transition</u> (New York: McGraw-Hill, 1950), pp. 106-107.

8. Taus, <u>Role of the U.S. Treasury,</u> pp. 84-86.

9. Secretary of the Treasury, <u>Annual Report</u> (1945), p. 51.

10. Secretary of the Treasury, <u>Annual Report</u> (Washington, D.C.: 1941), p. 18.

11. Secretary of the Treasury, <u>Annual Report</u> (1944), p. 53.

12. Secretary of the Treasury, <u>Annual Report</u> (1945), p. 57.

13. Murphy, <u>National Debt,</u> p. 196.

14. Secretary of the Treasury, _Annual Report_ (Washington, D.C.: 1946), p. 61.

15. Murphy, _National Debt_, p. 127.

16. Murphy, _National Debt_, pp. 92-93.

17. Secretary of the Treasury, _Annual Report_ (Washington, D.C.: 1942), p. 25.

18. Margaret G. Myers, _A Financial History of the United States_ (New York: Columbia University Press, 1970), pp. 350-352.

19. Murphy, _National Debt_, p. 207.

20. Secretary of the Treasury, _Annual Report_ (1945), pp. 83-86.

21. Seymour E. Harris, _The National Debt and the New Economics_ (New York: McGraw-Hill, 1947), p. 228.

22. Taus, _Role of the U.S. Treasury_, p. 89.

23. Milton Friedman and Anna Schwartz, _A Monetary History of the United States_ (Princeton, N.J.: Princeton University Press, 1963), p. 571.

24. Friedman and Schwartz, _Monetary History_, p. 569.

25. Murphy, _National Debt_, p. 276.

26. Jarvis M. Morse, _Paying for a World War_, (Bureau of the Public Debt Files, undated), pp. 77, 144.

27. U.S. Department of the Treasury, Bureau of Public Debt, _History of War Activities, Bureau of the Public Debt_ (Washington, D.C.: 1949), p. 41.

28. U.S. Dept. of Treasury, _History of War Activities, BPD_, p. 10.

29. U.S. Department of the Treasury, _Report to the Secretary from the Fiscal Assistant Secretary_ (Washington, D.C.: December 1, 1952), p. 3.

30. U.S. Dept. of Treasury, _History of War Activities, BPD_, p. 7.

31. U.S. Department of the Treasury, _Administrative History of War Activities of the Chicago Office of the Bureau of the Public Debt_ (Internal report prepared circa July 1946, copy in Parkersburg, W. Va., office of

the Bureau of the Public Debt), p. 121.

32. U.S. Dept. of Treasury, _History of War Activities, BPD_, p. 3.

33. U.S. Dept. of Treasury, _History of War Activities, BPD_, pp. 6-8.

34. U.S. Dept. of Treasury, _History of War Activities, BPD_, p. 21.

35. U.S. Dept. of Treasury, _Administrative History, Chicago Office, BPD_, p. 75.

36. U.S. Dept. of Treasury, _Administrative History, Chicago Office, BPD_, pp. 27-29.

37. U.S. Dept. of Treasury, _War Activities BPD_, pp. 36-37.

38. Secretary of the Treasury, _Annual Report_ (1945), p. 171.

39. U.S. Dept. of Treasury, _War Activities, BPD_, p. 34.

40. U.S. Dept. of Treasury, _War Activities, BPD_, p. 37.

41. U.S. Dept. of Treasury, _Administrative History, Chicago Office, BPD_, pp. 37-39.

42. U.S. Dept. of Treasury, _Administrative History, Chicago Office, BPD_, pp. 66, 196.

43. U.S. Dept. of Treasury, _War Activities, BPD_, pp. 51-52.

44. U.S. Dept. of Treasury, _Wartime Activities, BPD_, p. 78.

45. Secretary of the Treasury, _Annual Report_ (1946), p. 160.

Stock Certificate dated 1814 issued to John Q. Adams

$50 5 2/5 Note dated 1846

$500 7 3/10 Loan of 1861

$100 Gold Certificate of Act of 1863

$10,000 1878 Issue

$5,000 Note signed by Rosencranz

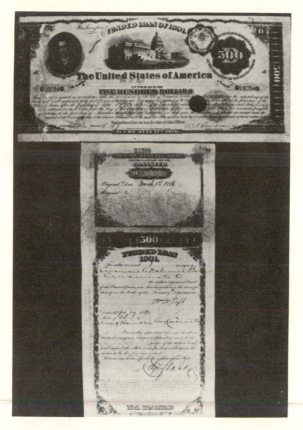

Funded Loan of 1890

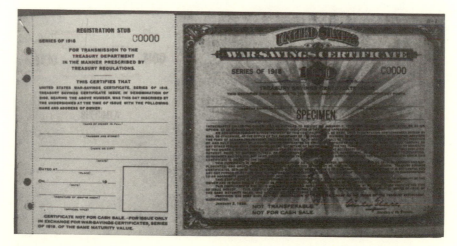

War Savings Certificate (1918)

War Savings Stamp (1918)

Postal Savings Bond (1933)

Series A, B, C, and D Savings Bonds
Issued in Four Successive Series from
1935 to 1941

Series E War Savings Bond

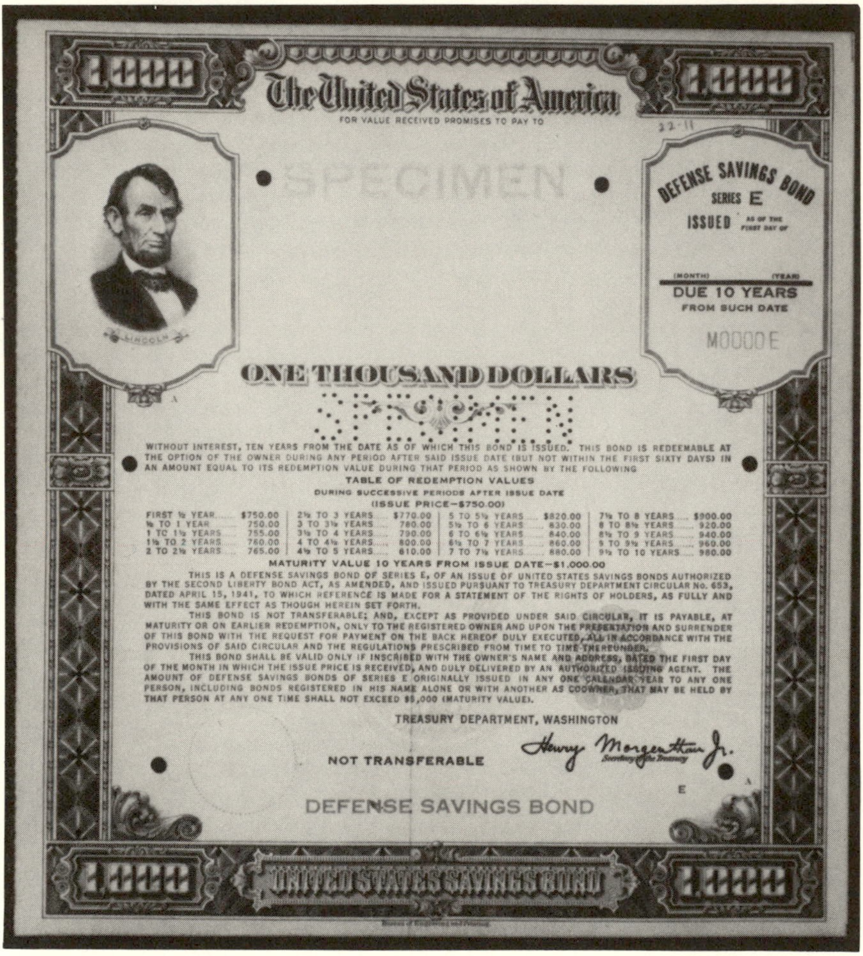

1,000

The United States of America

FOR VALUE RECEIVED PROMISES TO PAY TO

SPECIMEN

DEFENSE SAVINGS BOND

SERIES E

ISSUED AS OF THE FIRST DAY OF

(MONTH) (YEAR)

DUE 10 YEARS FROM SUCH DATE

M0000 E

LINCOLN

ONE THOUSAND DOLLARS

WITHOUT INTEREST, TEN YEARS FROM THE DATE AS OF WHICH THIS BOND IS ISSUED. THIS BOND IS REDEEMABLE AT THE OPTION OF THE OWNER DURING ANY PERIOD AFTER SAID ISSUE DATE (BUT NOT WITHIN THE FIRST SIXTY DAYS) IN AN AMOUNT EQUAL TO ITS REDEMPTION VALUE DURING THAT PERIOD AS SHOWN BY THE FOLLOWING

TABLE OF REDEMPTION VALUES

DURING SUCCESSIVE PERIODS AFTER ISSUE DATE

(ISSUE PRICE—$750.00)

FIRST ½ YEAR	$750.00	2½ TO 3 YEARS	$770.00	5 TO 5½ YEARS	$820.00	7½ TO 8 YEARS	$900.00
½ TO 1 YEAR	750.00	3 TO 3½ YEARS	780.00	5½ TO 6 YEARS	830.00	8 TO 8½ YEARS	920.00
1 TO 1½ YEARS	755.00	3½ TO 4 YEARS	790.00	6 TO 6½ YEARS	840.00	8½ TO 9 YEARS	940.00
1½ TO 2 YEARS	760.00	4 TO 4½ YEARS	800.00	6½ TO 7 YEARS	860.00	9 TO 9½ YEARS	960.00
2 TO 2½ YEARS	765.00	4½ TO 5 YEARS	810.00	7 TO 7½ YEARS	880.00	9½ TO 10 YEARS	980.00

MATURITY VALUE 10 YEARS FROM ISSUE DATE—$1,000.00

THIS IS A DEFENSE SAVINGS BOND OF SERIES E, OF AN ISSUE OF UNITED STATES SAVINGS BONDS AUTHORIZED BY THE SECOND LIBERTY BOND ACT, AS AMENDED, AND ISSUED PURSUANT TO TREASURY DEPARTMENT CIRCULAR No. 653, DATED APRIL 15, 1941, TO WHICH REFERENCE IS MADE FOR A STATEMENT OF THE RIGHTS OF HOLDERS, AS FULLY AND WITH THE SAME EFFECT AS THOUGH HEREIN SET FORTH.

THIS BOND IS NOT TRANSFERABLE; AND, EXCEPT AS PROVIDED UNDER SAID CIRCULAR, IT IS PAYABLE, AT MATURITY OR ON EARLIER REDEMPTION, ONLY TO THE REGISTERED OWNER AND UPON THE PRESENTATION AND SURRENDER OF THIS BOND WITH THE REQUEST FOR PAYMENT ON THE BACK HEREOF DULY EXECUTED, ALL IN ACCORDANCE WITH THE PROVISIONS OF SAID CIRCULAR AND THE REGULATIONS PRESCRIBED FROM TIME TO TIME THEREUNDER.

THIS BOND SHALL BE VALID ONLY IF INSCRIBED WITH THE OWNER'S NAME AND ADDRESS, DATED THE FIRST DAY OF THE MONTH IN WHICH THE ISSUE PRICE IS RECEIVED, AND DULY DELIVERED BY AN AUTHORIZED ISSUING AGENT. THE AMOUNT OF DEFENSE SAVINGS BONDS OF SERIES E ORIGINALLY ISSUED IN ANY ONE CALENDAR YEAR TO ANY ONE PERSON, INCLUDING BONDS REGISTERED IN HIS NAME ALONE OR WITH ANOTHER AS COOWNER, THAT MAY BE HELD BY THAT PERSON AT ANY ONE TIME SHALL NOT EXCEED $5,000 (MATURITY VALUE).

TREASURY DEPARTMENT, WASHINGTON

NOT TRANSFERABLE

Henry Morgenthau Jr.
Secretary of the Treasury

E

DEFENSE SAVINGS BOND

UNITED STATES SAVINGS BOND

Series E Defense Savings Bond

Series F and G Investor-Type Savings Bond

7

Postwar Debt Consolidation (1946–60)

At previous times in the nation's history, as earlier chapters have indicated, the end of a war usually brought about a decrease in government spending and plans for reducing the debt incurred during the war. The period immediately after World War II showed a deviation from this pattern, however. Expenditures fell from $95.2 billion in 1945 to $36.9 billion in 1947, but the prewar level of government budgets of under $10 billion was never again reached. To some extent this same effect took place after the end of the Civil War and World War I, but not to the extent that happened after World War II. Even though the budget was in surplus in each year from 1946 to 1949, total public debt never fell below $250 billion.

There are several reasons why balanced budgets and debt reduction took less of a priority after World War II. One particular difference was in defense spending, which remained high with the inception of the Cold-War era with the Soviet Union. Equally important was the beginning of a changing attitude toward public finance. While not all economists and government leaders uniformly agreed, sound fiscal prudence no longer centered on balancing the budget, but took into account the effect that government spending had on economic growth and stability.

A new fiscal philosophy following the economic ideas of John Maynard Keynes was incorporated into the Employment Act of 1946. The act's Declaration of Policy stated that the federal government was given responsibility for fostering "conditions under which there will be afforded useful employment for those able, willing, and seeking work, and to promote maximum employment, production and purchasing power."[1] The basic idea of the new school of economics was that government spending should be used as a tool for

controlling total demand in the economy. The government
was to increase its spending during periods of
recession, to maintain the sale of goods and services at
a high level. If inflation became a problem, the
government would reduce its spending as a way of cutting
down the inflationary gap. In this way, as Seymour
Harris, a leading proponent of the new economics stated,
"Debt management can be an instrument for keeping our
economy on an even keel."[2]

In effect, this school of economics established a
different set of standards for managing the government's
fiscal affairs. Few persons would object to a
government maintaining a deficit during a national
emergency such as a war, so long as it was paid back
during normal times. There was nothing imprudent about
borrowing money to save the nation. However, the new
program viewed a period of recession in the economy as
important an emergency as a war. Therefore, the same
criteria that applied to wartime spending should apply
in peacetime. A public debt incurred during a recession
was to be reduced when normal times returned. These
economists were indifferent as to whether the public
debt should ever be totally retired. Keynes had stated
the position quite clearly: "I think the argument for
extinguishing the National Debt is partly an aesthetic
argument, that it looks nice to have a clean balance
sheet, and I think it is partly false analogy from
private account keeping; an individual likes to be out
of debt. But for the nation as a whole it is merely a
bookkeeping transaction."[3]

THE POSTWAR ECONOMY

The Keynesians were very fearful of a postwar
recession and urged the government to develop new
spending plans. Paul Samuelson, a follower of Keynes
and later Nobel Prize winner, argued at this time, "We
have reached the present high levels of output and
employment only by means of $100 billion of government
expenditures, of which $50 billion represents deficits."
When that spending stopped, Samuelson continued, private
businesses would not be able to "maintain their present
level of employment or one-half or one-third of it."[4]

Although Keynes's views on fiscal policy and debt
management did not prevail completely in government
circles, officials at the Treasury and the Federal
Reserve did worry about what they would do if the
postwar economy suffered from a recession. For the most
part, however, fiscal policy during this entire period
(1946-60) relied on what economists call automatic
stabilizers. Under this policy, the government aims at
a balanced budget. If a recession develops, tax

collections decline and welfare and unemployment payments rise, causing a deficit. The government's job is then to accept the deficit and do nothing to correct it. During a recovery, tax payments go up and transfer payments decline, generating a surplus, which the government again does nothing to alter. For 15 years this passive policy worked tolerably well in terms of securing the goals of the Employment Act.[5]

The fears of a postwar recession were overblown. A mild recession took place during the process of converting to peacetime activities, but GNP fell by less than the drop in government spending. Recovery came about by the end of 1946, but a period of inflation was ushered in. To a large extent, rapid increases in business purchases of plant and equipment to replace factories that had grown old during the depression and been worn out by the war fostered the recovery. Consumer spending also showed a sharp rise.

Both these sources of demand leveled off, and by 1949 another recession hit the economy. This recession, too, proved to be mild. Its ending was aided by the single-most important fiscal policy of this period. In 1948 the Congress passed a significant tax cut over the veto of President Harry S. Truman. The tax cut was not intended as a Keynesian boost to spending, but it had that effect, and the timing of its implementation was ideal for easing the strain of the 1949 recession when it hit. Truman remained against the tax cut and was still proposing a tax increase six months into the recession.[6] These leaders were not all Keynesians then.

After the recovery, the economy showed rapid growth during the Korean War. During the Eisenhower administrations, there was a mild recession in 1953-54, and another in 1957. These were followed by a sharp recovery in 1955 and a somewhat disappointing level of growth in 1958-60. The Republicans in the 1950s were nowhere close to being Keynesians, with Eisenhower's policy of attaining a budget surplus in the late 1950s being held responsible for the slow growth of that period.[7]

FISCAL MANAGEMENT

Along with concern over the state of the economy in the immediate postwar period, there was doubt at the same time about whether policies that had worked reasonably well to finance the war effort could be continued in the postwar period without damaging the economy. In the autumn of 1945, for example, Secretary of the Treasury Fred Vinson told an audience in Peoria, Illinois, that interest rates "should continue low for a long time to come," a view that was repeated a year

later by Secretary of the Treasury John Snyder.[8] Low
interest rates, it was felt, would help to stimulate the
economy by making it easier for businesses and consumers
to borrow. Since the government pays interest on its
debt as well, low rates would also serve to keep taxes
down.

At the same time the possibility of a period of
postwar inflation was being recognized at the Federal
Reserve. As a result, its officials began pushing for
a different approach to fiscal management, in order to
allow it to use its inflation-fighting tools.

The Federal Reserve uses its open market operations
during normal periods to control the amount of money and
credit in the economy, not to help finance public debt.
When it wants to expand money and credit, the Federal
Reserve purchases government securities, and when it
wants to contract them, it sells government securities.
As long as the Federal Reserve must buy government
securities in support of the Treasury's desire for low
interest rates, it cannot exercise any influence over
the amount of money and credit in the economy.

The situation immediately after the war was very
tricky in terms of the management of money and credit.
As long as the Federal Reserve stood ready to buy
government securities, those securities were extremely
liquid. Savings bonds, because they could be redeemed
at any time, were also liquid. Consequently, a large
proportion of government securities were as good as
money, for they could readily be turned into cash and
spent at any time. Although their existence did not
represent an inflationary gap per se, they had the
potential for causing one. These worries concerning
inflation would become greater after 1947, when consumer
prices rose by 18 percent.[9]

The Treasury tried to offset some of the
inflationary gap through its postwar debt management
program. The program had as a goal, in addition to
reducing the debt, "to reduce bank ownership of Federal
securities and widen the distribution of the debt."[10]
The debt reduction plan was helped by the government
budget surpluses that were run until 1948, when, as
mentioned above, Congress enacted a tax reduction over
the veto of President Truman. Total debt was reduced by
$28.5 billion from February 28, 1946 to June 30, 1949.
Holdings of debt by banks were reduced by $34 billion
during the same period. Since this reduction was funded
in part by the sale of savings bonds, which increased by
$7.5 billion during the same period, the goal of
achieving a wider distribution of debt was attained.[11]
Nonmarketable securities were 22.3 percent of total
public debt outstanding by June 30, 1949.[12]

This increase in the proportion of savings bonds as
a funding source was a continuation of the policy of

fighting inflation by absorbing purchasing power from individuals. However, the Federal Reserve still had concerns over inflation rates and the interest rate structure. The Federal Reserve would have preferred to regain some influence over money and credit by withdrawing its support of interest rates on Treasury securities. They felt that this was especially important as businesses began borrowing funds to reconvert and rebuild their factories in the transition from war production to consumer goods production. The Federal Reserve stopped its support of the 3/8 percent interest rate on Treasury bills in the second half of 1947; later that year the price at which the Federal Reserve would support long-term government securities was also lowered. As a result, the interest rate structure changed from its wartime levels to a range of 1 to 1.5 percent on shorter-term issues and 2.5 percent on longer issues by the end of 1948. This policy meant that long-term rates would actually rise, because in 1946 longer-term issues were selling at prices above par, with their yields falling to as low as 2 percent.

The policy of the Federal Reserve was characterized in early 1948 by Alan Sproul, president of the New York branch, as one of "modest restraints" designed "to prevent bank credit from adding further to inflationary pressures and, if possible, to reduce somewhat the supply of money."[13] The Federal Reserve recognized that its policies allowed the existence of too much liquidity in the banking system, as banks could turn their holdings of government securities into reserves at any time. In fact, the Board of Governors of the Federal Reserve had warned in its annual report for 1945, "The money supply can be increased on the volition of the banks irrespective of national monetary policy."[14]

This combination of tighter credit by the Federal Reserve and the sole use of longer-term issues of higher interest savings bonds by the Treasury resulted in increases in the annual interest rates that the Treasury had to pay, as can be seen from Table 7.1. However, by 1947 conditions in the government securities market stabilized and remained so for the next several years, with the total debt remaining fairly constant. Sales of new issues, and exchanges of maturing and called debt for new securities were accomplished quite smoothly. Since some of these exchanges were for new issues with lower interest rates, the computed rate of interest actually declined slightly in 1950.

OPERATIONS AT THE BUREAU OF THE PUBLIC DEBT

As the debt reduction immediately after the war was small and relied heavily on nonmarketable savings bonds,

Table 7.1
Computed Rate of Interest on the Public Debt (1946-50)

Year	1946	1947	1948	1949	1950
Computed rate	2.00	2.11	2.18	2.24	2.20

Source: Annual Reports of the Secretary of the
          Treasury, 1946-50.

the workload of the Bureau of the Public Debt was not significantly reduced after the war. There was a tremendous backlog of work in the Chicago office by the end of the war. As the Fiscal Assistant Secretary reported several years later, "The condition that impressed us most was what we considered a serious 'bottleneck' of a tremendous mass of work in the Chicago Departmental Office of the Bureau of the Public Debt. Problems which are simple in principle sometimes become almost unmanageable because of sheer volume."[15]
     Much of the volume of work arose through the redemption of Series E savings bonds. Throughout the depression of the 1930s, many Americans had not had sufficient income to purchase the consumer goods they desired. The return of prosperity brought about by the war production caused incomes to rise. But in general, consumer goods were not available for purchase due to the production of materiel and equipment needed for the war. It is important to remember, for example, that no automobiles for sale to the general public were produced during the war. Personal income that was not spent on necessities had to be saved, and savings bonds were an important method for that saving to take place. The Savings Bond Program probably helped to reduce the inflationary pressures that existed during the war by drawing off money from the public. When the war ended, Americans wanted to go on a buying spree. For many, this meant that they had to use at least a part of their savings for this purpose. This meant that they began presenting their savings bonds for redemption.
     Commissioner of the Public Debt E. L. Kilby reported on January 1, 1946, that there were backlogs in the audit operation of 67 million redeemed bonds and in the posting operation of 76 million redeemed bonds. At the same time there was a backlog of 93 million bond stubs in the alphabetic keypunch operation. The keypunch backlog was solved within a year through the use of extra operators and overtime.[16]
     The problem of handling voluminous bond redemptions

required a more complex solution. As part of the trend
that started when operations had been moved to Chicago,
a further decentralization took place. Regional offices
were opened in Cincinnati, St. Louis, Chicago, New York,
and Los Angeles to handle the auditing of the bonds that
were being redeemed in such great numbers by the Federal
Reserve Banks. This plan worked well, with the backlog
of redeemed bonds eliminated early in 1947. The system
proved so effective within two years that it was
possible to close the regional offices in St. Louis and
Los Angeles, and transfer those Federal Reserve
districts being served from those offices to the Chicago
and Cincinnati offices.[17]

It was also during this time that microfilm
recording began to replace the storage of actual bond
stubs as a system of recordkeeping for new issues. All
records were stored in the Chicago office up until this
time, which created a problem due to limited space. A
policy was begun, with the approval of the Comptroller
General on May 7, 1946, of microfilming the registration
record of savings bond holdings and eliminating the
paper records by selling them as wastepaper under proper
supervision by the Bureau. Thousands of square feet of
space in the Chicago office were released for other
use.[18]

Other members of the federal government were also
concerned with bringing some order to the sprawling
bureaucracy brought about by the war. The Hoover
Commission, in 1949, headed by former President Herbert
Hoover, completed an evaluation of the executive branch
and reported to the Congress: "The United States is
paying heavily for a lack of order, a lack of clear
lines of authority and responsibility, and a lack of
effective organization in the executive branch."[19] The
Commission, based on the findings of over 300
economists, management consultants, and organizational
authorities, issued 19 reports with 281 specific
recommendations for improving operations in the
executive branch.[20]

The Hoover Commission made two specific
recommendations with reference to the Fiscal Service and
the Bureau of the Public Debt. First, it recommended
that the Savings Bond Division, the Bureau of the Mint,
the Bureau of Engraving and Printing, and the Secret
Service be made part of a proposed new Department of
Fiscal Service. Those opposed to this argued that these
organizational components had to be located where they
could be most effectively supervised by the Secretary of
the Treasury.[21] However, some reorganization of the
Bureau of the Public Debt was put into place. Functions
of the Division of Savings Bonds of the Bureau were
transferred to a new United States Savings Bond Division
on November 30, 1951, under the authority of

Reorganization Plan No. 26 of 1950, and the duties of the Division of Paper Custody were turned over to the Bureau of Engraving and Printing on July 31, 1950.[22]

The second specific recommendation of the commission concerning the Bureau was that much of the accounting and recordkeeping associated with bond sales be shifted to the Federal Reserve System, with an ultimate potential reduction of 4,000 employees. Responding, Commissioner Kilby pointed out that many such functions had already been shifted to the Federal Reserve, but it was doubtful that many more could be. Therefore, he did not think the projected reduction of 4,000 employees was realistic.[23] Besides, the Bureau had already done well in reducing the total amount of its employees, as can be seen in Table 7.2.

Table 7.2
Employees of the Bureau of the Public Debt
(1945-46, 1948-50)

Year	1945	1946	1948	1949	1950
Number of Employees	12,408	9,753	7,990	5,848	4,670

Source: U.S. Department of the Treasury, Bureau of the Public Debt, Summary of Its History and Principal Functions, etc. (Washington, D.C.: May 1954).

FISCAL MANAGEMENT IN THE 1950s

The opportunity to continue a careful policy of debt management and administration was diminished with the onset of hostilities in Korea. While not a declared war and not conducted with an all-out effort equal to that of World War II, the Korean conflict put new pressure on the Treasury, and for a time strained relations between the Treasury and the Federal Reserve.

Prior to the conflict, the Treasury had refrained from refunding its maturing securities with short-term obligations. Free from the necessity of supporting low short-term interest rates, in the spring of 1950 the Federal Reserve embarked on a moderate policy of selling government securities. Inflationary pressures were being felt at the time as the economy entered into an expansionary phase. Business and consumer borrowing were increasing at this time.[24]

The Treasury became concerned again with the problem of financing a war effort with the outbreak of hostilities in Korea in June 1950. Defense spending jumped from $17.7 billion in 1950 to $46 billion in 1952 and $53 billion in 1953. The Federal Reserve was willing to use open market operations to help secure the funds the Treasury would need, but it did not want to return to the interest rate structure of World War II.[25]

The difference of views came to a head in August 1950, when the Treasury attempted to refund long-term issues of 2 percent to 2 1/2 percent in exchange for 13-month notes carrying interest at 1 1/4 percent. The exchange was effected only after the Federal Reserve carried out some very tricky open market operations by selling issues other than those coming due (pushing their interest rates up), and using the proceeds to purchase large quantities of the issues coming due, which were then exchanged for the new securities. When this was completed, the Federal Reserve held nearly 75 percent of the new issue of short-term securities, and the sale of other short-term issues by the Federal Reserve had pushed their yields from 1 1/4 percent to 1 3/8 percent.[26]

Secretary of the Treasury Snyder disagreed strongly with the stance taken by the Federal Reserve. He was concerned that with the outbreak of hostilities in Korea a war on the scale of World War II might develop. Consequently, he told the chairman of the Board of Governors of the Federal Reserve System, "Every circumstance at the present time calls for steadiness and manifest strength in the Federal security market as a primary measure of economic preparedness."[27] While the Treasury had been willing to go along with interest-rate increases earlier, now it wanted its financing to be at the lowest possible rates.[28] Snyder maintained that the refunding program in August 1950 was in line with the market at the time the new issues were offered. He blamed Federal Reserve open market operations just prior to the date of exchange for the poor showing of the offering, wherein only 6 percent of the new issue was exchanged by private holders.[29]

After several meetings between officials of both agencies, including a series of conferences with the Secretary of the Treasury, the Chairman of the Federal Reserve, and President Truman, on March 3, 1950, the following agreement was announced: "The Treasury and the Federal Reserve System have reached full accord with respect to debt-management and monetary policies to be pursued in furthering their common purpose to assure the successful financing of the government's requirements and, at the same time, to minimize monetization of the public debt."[30]

Accordingly, the Federal Reserve would continue to help the Treasury with its financing, but it would also operate more independently in terms of its efforts to control money and credit. This new arrangement meant that the Federal Reserve would not maintain a specific range of interest rates on government securities. Instead, interest rates would be subject to the influence of market forces. A period of transition was arranged, to allow financial markets time to adjust to this agreement.[31]

Specifically, the Treasury would take some long-term debt off the market by offering to exchange it for a new issue of nonmarketable 29 year 2 3/4 percent bonds that were redeemable prior to maturity only by conversion into a five-year marketable Treasury note at 1 1/2 percent. The idea was to keep liquidations of long-term debt to a minimum. At the same time, the Federal Reserve refrained from purchasing short-term securities, with the result that those interest rates began to rise.[32]

There was still some disagreement over the extent to which the accord would permit the Federal Reserve to control money and credit. Secretary Snyder defined a stable market for government securities as one "in which prices and yields fluctuate within a moderate range over a considerable period, but without exhibiting any pronounced upward or downward trend."[33] As discussed earlier, the need for this stability was to keep confidence in the credit of the government, keep debt service costs as low as possible, and maintain a wide ownership of the debt. At the same time, the Federal Reserve needed to keep control over money and credit and use interest rates as a device for allocating credit. The Federal Reserve also wanted to keep the market for government securities in some sort of balance.

Normally, an accommodation between the two agencies and their separate goals is possible as long as the government's spending program is in line with overall economic conditions. When the government's financing needs are not in concert with economic conditions, as happens when the government runs a deficit while the economy is expanding, the job of the Federal Reserve in controlling the money supply becomes more difficult. In extreme cases, such as World War II, the Federal Reserve is forced to abdicate its control over money and credit to service the Treasury's needs. The Treasury felt the same conditions should prevail during the Korean conflict, but the Federal Reserve did not agree.

A resolution of the disagreement was effected by the change of administration in 1953, when President Eisenhower took office. First, the ending of hostilities in Korea was a top priority with Eisenhower, and an uneasy truce was soon negotiated. The new Secretary of the Treasury, George Humphrey, set forth a debt management program that had three goals: "(1.) Freedom for the Federal Reserve System, with the Treasury financing at 'going market rates.' (2.) Extension of debt maturities. (3.) Reduction of bank-held debt."[34]

There was little initial progress toward meeting these goals. The Federal Reserve consistently followed a policy of credit restraint throughout the 1950s to ensure that inflation did not return. At the same time, government fiscal policies were also only mildly expansionary at best, and several years of budget surplus were experienced. As a result, economic growth remained sluggish and two recessions took place, during which times the Federal Reserve did ease up on credit and government spending increased.

These events hindered the efforts of the Treasury to meet its goal. For example, in 1955 the Secretary of the Treasury reported:

> During the earlier part of the fiscal year, when the Federal Reserve was still emphasizing its policy of credit ease to smooth the readjustment to lower levels of Government spending, the Treasury purposely refrained from putting out any long-term issues which might interfere with the flow of long term money into mortgages, corporate securities and State and municipal bonds.[35]

A year later, the Secretary of the Treasury could report that the debt management program was showing signs of progress, resulting in the Treasury's being able to reduce the number and amount of its offerings. Only four major loans were undertaken in 1956, in comparison to about 12 a year in the early postwar period. This improvement permitted the Federal Reserve more freedom "during the fiscal year 1956 in which to exercise an independent money and credit policy."[36] With an economic recovery in place at this time, no further issues of long-term securities were contemplated.[37]

Economic conditions handicapped the Treasury in meeting its debt management goals after the turmoil of the Korean conflict. The Treasury believed that it would not be able to sell long-term bonds in a weak market, while in periods of recovery it refrained from selling long-term bonds to avoid competing with business for investment funds. As a result, while some initial gain was made in terms of lengthening the maturity of the debt, by the end of the decade there was little overall progress (see Table 7.3). The inability of the

Treasury to lengthen the average maturity of its securities caused bank ownership of public debt, mostly short-term, to decline only slightly during the same time period (see Table 7.4). Finally, because of the independent activity of the Federal Reserve, interest rates drifted up slightly during the 1950s. The rate, in 1959, on long-term bonds reached the ceiling of 4 1/4 percent imposed by the Second Liberty Bond Act of 1917. The Treasury had to sell short-term securities at rates (4.625 percent) above the long-term rate, a very unusual situation. The overall effect on computed interest rates is given in Table 7.5. The total public debt outstanding was $287.5 billion at the end of fiscal year 1960.

Table 7.3
Maturity Distribution of Public Debt (1953, 1956, and 1960)

	1953	1956	1960
Marketable:			
Due within 1 yr.	24.6	23.8	24.5
1-5 yrs.	13.5	13.6	25.3
Over 5 years	17.3	19.4	14.1
Total	55.4	56.8	63.9
Nonmarketable:			
Savings Bonds	21.8	21.1	16.5
Investment Bonds	7.5	5.7	3.5
Gov't. Trust Bonds	15.2	16.5	15.7
Total	44.5	43.3	35.7

Source: Annual Reports of the Secretary of the
          Treasury, 1953, 1956, and 1960.

Table 7.4
Ownership Distribution of the Public Debt (1953, 1956, and 1960)

	1953	1956	1960
Nonbank:			
Gov't. Investment Accounts	17.9	19.6	19.3
Individuals	24.6	24.5	24.1
Other	26.1	26.2	27.8
Total Nonbank	68.6	70.3	71.2
Bank:			
Commercial Banks	22.2	20.9	19.3
Federal Reserve	9.2	8.8	9.3
Total Bank Holdings	31.4	29.7	28.6

Source: Annual Reports of the Secretary of the
          Treasury, 1953, 1956 and 1960.

Table 7.5
Computed Rate of Interest on the Public Debt (1952-56, 1959-60)

Year	1952	1953	1954	1955	1956	1959	1960
Computed Interest	2.27	2.38	2.28	2.35	2.58	2.87	3.30

Source: Annual Reports of the Secretary of the
          Treasury for the given years.

EFFICIENCY IN ADMINISTRATION

Meanwhile, progress was being shown in making the operations of the Bureau of the Public Debt more efficient. The total number of employees at the Bureau had been reduced by October 1, 1952, to 3,806, with an annual payroll of $13.5 million.[38] This was a considerable decrease from the more than 12,000 employed during World War II and closer to the figures given for 1936. The number of employees continued to decline in the early 1950s, as can be seen in Table 7.6. Administrative expenses for fiscal year 1952 were $50.9 million, a reduction of nearly $35 million from fiscal year 1945.

Despite these improvements in operations, there were still troublesome areas. It was calculated that on June 30, 1952, the $25 Series E bonds represented 68.4 percent of Series E bond sales and 73.6 percent of redemptions, but only 16.8 percent of the total amount of Series E bonds outstanding.[39] Reviewing the same situation during the Korean War, Commissioner Kilby concluded, "On the present volume of sales, over $6,000,000 of administrative costs could be saved annually if this denomination were discontinued."[40] The savings Kilby projected would have amounted to more than 10 percent of the administrative expenses of the Bureau at that time. However, the sale of $25 denomination savings bonds was not discontinued, and in order to handle the high volume of bonds that this policy made necessary, the Bureau had to find better ways of performing all the tasks associated with a bond sale at a reduced cost. The predominant method of choice was use of electronic data processing through the installation of a new computer facility in Parkersburg, West Virginia.

Table 7.6
Employees of the Bureau of the Public Debt (1951–53, 1955)

Year Ending June 30	1951	1952	1953	1955
Employees	4,494	3,888	3,522	3,411

Source: Annual Reports of the Secretary of the
           Treasury for the given years.

The move to Parkersburg and to the use of computers was begun in May 1955 when Commissioner Kilby wrote to the major manufacturers of electronic data processing equipment advising them that the Bureau wanted to determine if any of its work could "be performed more economically and expeditiously on electronic data processing which is now or may in the near future become available for use." To help make this determination, Kilby invited these manufacturers to attend a symposium to be held in July of that year. At the symposium, exhibits were presented outlining the flow of operations that was required in every bond transaction. The symposium was hosted by a "Public Debt Electronic Committee," whose members ended the meetings with the belief that the savings bond area seemed "to be the most fertile one, from the standpoint of further mechanization of a large volume job and the realization of large-scale savings."[41]

In early 1957, the final decision to use electronic data processing in the savings bond operation was made. Parkersburg was chosen as the location for the computer operations installation; the primary advantage of that area was its available labor pool, central location between the Bureau's offices in Washington and Chicago, and its rural isolation, which made it less likely to be the target of an enemy attack.

The operations transferred from Chicago--constituting about half of the operations of the savings bond function--included the auditing, accounting, and recordkeeping functions pertinent to the Series E bonds. Operations concerned with claims, correspondence, and current income bond interest remained in Chicago, along with the records of all bonds other than the new Series E punchcard bonds that were adopted for handling by computer.

The Parkersburg office opened in August 1957, with a staff composed of about 30 persons who had been employed in Chicago. About 100 members of the local community began training programs for employment at the office, with their first date of work being August 25, 1957. Several of the staff joined a group of 40 being trained in data processing methods and Bureau operations at a special workshop held in Boston. The choice of Parkersburg as location for these operations proved to be very wise. The local labor force provided many loyal and efficient workers, mostly female. Of the original group of employees, several have remained on the staff of the Parkersburg office for all of their subsequent working years and have risen from their original entry-level jobs to top management positions.[42] On October 1, 1957, the Series E punchcard bond was first introduced. The stubs and redemption cards associated with these bonds were sent to the Parkersburg office to

be processed.   Because the computer equipment had not
yet been installed, conventional equipment was used to
audit sales and redemptions, and the new system began
with a backlog.
     By December 1958, the computer system was in place,
taking up one floor of space in an old department store
building in downtown Parkersburg.   The computer used was
a Minneapolis-Honeywell Datamatic D-1000.   Under the
system, each bond was reproduced on microfilm by serial
number and alphabetically by purchaser's name and
geographic location.   The cards were keypunched and fed
through the computer for recording the location of the
microfilm file on tape.   The D-1000 used three-inch-wide
tape, and the tape reels weighed about 35 pounds each.
One employee characterized them as looking like
Volkswagen wheels.   By the end of 1957, the Parkersburg
office employed 125 persons, with the employment figure
reaching 500 by the end of the decade.   Included in this
total were several hundred keypunch operators.   Once in
full operation, the computer system processed enough
bonds to require destruction of paper records in the
amount of one rail carload per week.[43]
     The new system also provided for further
organizational change.   In 1956, the Division of Retired
Securities was formed to take over functions that had
been performed by the regional offices and the
Washington Office of the Register of the Treasury; this
change reflected an allocation of the actual tasks being
performed.[44]   The regional offices in New York and
Chicago were closed in September 1957.   In 1958,
Commissioner Kilby recommended that since the functions
of the Register of the Treasury had been transferred to
the Division of Retired Securities, the position of
Register should be dropped from the Bureau's
organizational structure.[45]   In 1960, the Secretary of
the Treasury could report that "the electronic data
processing operations in the Parkersburg Office were
current in all respects."[46]   The Bureau of the Public
Debt had completely recovered from and adjusted to the
large volume of debt that had resulted from financing
World War II.
     The use of new technology helped prepare the Bureau
for its new responsibilities.   Although the Bureau was
not a leader in the development of new technology, it
was quick to learn about the new methods and to apply
them to its work.   Punchcards were first used by the
Census Bureau for the 1890 census, but their application
in other areas did not become widespread until the
1930s.   The initial electronic digital computer was
built during World War II, yet the first generation of
computers applied to administrative work only appeared
in the 1950s.[47]   With just a short time lag, the Bureau
was using punchcards to handle its savings bond records.

Its computer facility represented one of the earliest adaptations of computers by an agency of the federal government. These usages of new technology were signs of a forward-looking attitude on the part of Bureau personnel.   By 1960, techniques, organizations, equipment, and expertise were all available to enable the Bureau to enter into the computer age.

NOTES

1. Robert Lekachman, The Age of Keynes (New York: Random House, 1966), pp. 170-171.

2. Seymour E. Harris, The National Debt and the New Economics (New York: McGraw-Hill, 1947), p. 271.

3. Harris, National Debt, p. 70.

4. Lekachman, Keynes, pp. 160-161.

5. Herbert Stein, Presidential Economics (New York: Simon & Schuster, 1984), p. 80.

6. Robert A. Gordon, Economic Instability and Growth: The American Record (New York: Harper & Row, 1974), pp. 101-106.

7. Gordon, Economic Instability and Growth, pp. 133-134.

8. Charles C. Abbott, The Federal Debt: Structure and Impact (New York: Twentieth Century Fund, 1953), pp. 39-41.

9. Henry C. Murphy, National Debt in War and Transition (New York: McGraw-Hill, 1950), p. 275.

10. Secretary of the Treasury, Annual Report (Washington, D.C.: 1949), p. 15.

11. Secretary of the Treasury, Annual Report (1949), pp. 15-17.

12. Secretary of the Treasury, Annual Report (1949), p. 78.

13. Abbott, Federal Debt, p. 63.

14. Abbott, Federal Debt, p. 67.

15. U.S. Department of the Treasury, _Report of the Fiscal Assistant Secretary to the Secretary of the Treasury_ (Washington, D.C.: December 1, 1952), p. 7.

16. E.L. Kilby, _Report of Commissioner E.L. Kilby to the Secretary of the Treasury_ (Washington, D.C.: December 1, 1952), p. 2.

17. Kilby, _Report,_ pp. 3, 5-6.

18. Kilby, _Report,_ p. 3.

19. U.S. Congress (82nd), _Reorganization of the Federal Government_ (Washington, D.C.: Senate Document No. 91, 1952), p. 1.

20. U.S. Congress (82nd), _Reorganization,_ p. 1.

21. John L. Snyder, _Letter from John L. Snyder, Secretary of the Treasury, to Senator John L. McClellan_ (Washington, D.C.: August 2, 1949), p. 17.

22. U.S. Department of the Treasury, _Bureau of the Public Debt, Summary of Its History and Principal Functions, etc._ (Washington, D.C.: May 1954), p. 1.

23. E.L. Kilby, Memorandum (Washington, D.C.: March 19, 1949), copy in Bureau of the Public Debt Files.

24. Abbott, _Federal Debt,_ pp. 93-95.

25. Tilford C. Gaines, _Techniques of Treasury Debt Management_ (New York: Free Press of Glencoe, 1962), p. 62.

26. Abbott, _Federal Debt,_ pp. 95-98.

27. Secretary of the Treasury, _Annual Report_ (Washington, D.C.: 1951), p. 265.

28. Secretary of the Treasury, _Annual Report_ (1951), p. 265.

29. Secretary of the Treasury, _Annual Report_ (1951), p. 267.

30. Secretary of the Treasury, _Annual Report_ (1951), p. 271.

31. Gaines, _Treasury Debt Management,_ p. 66.

32. Secretary of the Treasury, _Annual Report_ (1951), pp. 272-275.

33. Secretary of the Treasury, Annual Report (1951), p. 296.

34. Gaines, Treasury Debt Management, p. 70.

35. Secretary of the Treasury, Annual Report (Washington, D.C.: 1955), p. 25.

36. Secretary of the Treasury, Annual Report (Washington, D.C.: 1956), p. 23.

37. Secretary of the Treasury, Annual Report (1956), p. 23.

38. U.S. Department of the Treasury, Bureau of the Public Debt, Document contained in Important Data File D-120, History of the Public Debt Organization (Washington, D.C.: 1952).

39. U.S. Department of the Treasury, Fiscal Assistant Secretary, Report, p. 21.

40. Kilby, Report, p. 9.

41. U.S. Department of the Treasury, Bureau of the Public Debt, Savings Bond Symposium (Parkersburg, W.Va.: July 11, 1955), bound manual in Parkersburg Office Files.

42. U.S. Department of the Treasury, Bureau of the Public Debt, History of the U.S. Savings Bond Office (Copy circa 1975 in Parkersburg Office Files). Additional information based on conversations with employees of Parkersburg office held August 24, 1987.

43. Conversations with Parkersburg employees, August 1987.

44. Secretary of the Treasury, Annual Report (1956), p. 7.

45. E.L. Kilby, Memorandum to William W. Parsons (Washington, D.C.: November 17, 1958), copy in Bureau files.

46. Secretary of the Treasury, Annual Report (Washington, D.C.: 1960), p. 119.

47. Donald H. Sanders, Computers in Society (New York: McGraw-Hill, 1981), pp. 23-33.

8

A New View
on the Debt (1960–69)

In the 1960s, the notion that anything was possible in terms of public policy and public behavior came to pervade the country, and social change seemed to be the only constant. It was a decade marked by civil rights marches, student protests, and urban riots. In response to the problems underlying these upheavals, the federal government increased its activities in the social arena. This was the era of the "Great Society" of President Lyndon Johnson, which saw the rise of new government agencies designed to help the poor and the uneducated. It was also a period of war, as the U.S. involvement in Vietnam escalated. The war abroad and the fight against poverty at home would prove costly to finance, leading to increased borrowing by the federal government.

After the turbulence of the period died down, a new view on the public debt in terms of government policy remained. At the beginning of the decade a revolution in economic policy took place, one that had been building in the minds of economists for nearly two decades. As part of that revolution the taboo was broken in terms of the intrinsic desirability of balanced budgets and a reduced public debt. Instead, the ideas of functional finance were given free play. This new attitude toward fiscal prudence combined with government expansion and the war in Vietnam would produce a steady stream of federal government deficits during the 1960s. By the end of the decade, the Treasury Department and the Bureau of the Public Debt would be facing greater pressures in their joint efforts to manage and administer the government's debt. It should be noted here that the Treasury and especially the Bureau of the Public Debt have little influence on the amount of spending and debt that government operations entail. Rather, they must operationalize the government's fiscal policies and manage the debt with

the best of their experience.
    It is doubtful that anyone could have forecast this
increase of government activity and debt at the
beginning of the 1960s. Up to that time, the post-World
War II period had seen seven years of government
deficits, largely associated with the Korean War or
economic recessions, mixed with seven years of budgetary
surplus. The total debt rose by a modest $30 billion,
from $260 billion to $290 billion.[1]
    If inflation were taken into account, the real
value of the debt would have fallen during this time
period.[2] As a percent of GNP, the total federal
government debt had fallen from its high of 116 percent
in 1946 to 56 percent in 1961.[3]

THE ECONOMY AND FISCAL POLICY

    The era of the 1960s can be conveniently marked off
by the inauguration of John F. Kennedy as President in
1961. Just prior to Kennedy's election, the economy had
been mired in a sluggish period of mild recession. The
recession ended in February 1961 and was followed by the
longest period of expansion in U.S. history, as the peak
of the recovery was not reached until November 1969.
Unemployment fell from a 7 percent rate at the beginning
of the period to 3.5 percent in December 1969. The
first half of the expansion saw prices remain fairly
steady at an annual rate of 1.4 percent. As the
expansion continued, and especially after government
spending in Vietnam began increasing in 1965, inflation
increased to an annual rate of 3 to 4 percent.[4]
    Despite his campaign promise to "get America moving
again" with appropriate government policies, Kennedy
could not take credit for a recovery that started within
a month of his taking the oath of office. Moreover,
when he took office, Kennedy had fairly conservative
views about fiscal policy, remaining "skeptical about
the capacity of budget deficits to stimulate economic
expansions."[5] In 1961, when military spending went up
because of the crises in Cuba and Berlin, Kennedy
actually favored a tax increase.
    But Kennedy's economic advisors had been influenced
by Keynesian ideas, and the chairman of his Council of
Economic Advisors, Walter Heller, schooled the President
in the "new economics." With his education complete, by
1963 Kennedy presented to Congress his view that, "in
today's economy, fiscal prudence and responsibility call
for tax reduction even if it temporarily enlarges the
federal deficit." The choice, he went on, was not
between "tax reduction and a deficit on the one hand and
a budget easily balanced by prudent management on the

other." If the budget were balanced by cutting spending, that "would so depress demand, production and unemployment that tax revenues would fall and leave the government budget still in deficit."[6]

Support for this new point of view was not unanimous by any means. Former President Eisenhower, for example, maintained that "the time-tested rules of financial policy still apply. Spending for spending's sake is patently a false theory . . . . Imagine how much better the country would feel if it had no debt at all but a healthy surplus."[7] But the country might not feel better off if it suffered a bout of high unemployment.

The economy began to falter in 1962, so Kennedy's economic advisors started urging him to take action. Their recommendation was for a series of tax cuts that would force the government's budget into a bigger deficit than it was already running. Since a tax reduction when there already was a deficit was indeed a novel prescription, a new definition for fiscal prudence had to be designed.

The result was the concept of the high-employment or full-employment budget. As previously noted, the government's budget depends partly on the state of the economy. A recession will push the government's budget toward a deficit. But the new economics was concerned with planning a budget deficit in order to have an expansionary impact on the economy. To gauge whether a deficit was expansionary, it was necessary to factor out the recessionary part of the budget deficit to determine whether the planned part was large enough to have an impact on the economy. As a way of factoring out the effect of a recession, the budget was recalculated to show what it would have been had the economy been at full employment. Whether this full-employment budget showed a deficit or surplus would determine whether or not it had an expansionary effect on the economy. As the Kennedy Council of Economic Advisors put it in their Annual Report of January 1962, "The full-employment surplus is a measure of the restrictive or expansionary impact of a budget program on over-all demand. Generally speaking, one budget program is more expansionary than another if it has a smaller full employment surplus."[8]

According to this way of thinking, fiscal prudence came to mean that budget deficits were acceptable as long as the budget would have been balanced if the economy were at full employment. Proponents of this view were aware that this new policy might lead to more deficits and a larger public debt, but they minimized the problems a larger debt might create. As the Council of Economic Advisors stated the case in the Economic Report of the President for 1963,

> there is no reason to fear such increases in
> the public debt as tax reduction may entail.
> The ratio of interest payments on the debt is
> small and likely to fall, not rise. Nor is
> there any danger that the increase in the
> federal debt will be a burden on future
> generations. Tax reduction will increase
> investment, and hence the wealth we will
> bequeath.[9]

Concern over the level of the public debt would not be
allowed to vitiate the effectiveness of the full-
employment budget.

When the full-employment budget concept was applied
to the government budget deficit of 1963, as Walter
Heller later reported, it was found to show a surplus of
$12 to $13 billion.[10] To eliminate the drag that this
"surplus" was having on the economy, tax reductions had
been proposed by Kennedy in 1962. An initial reduction
in the form of an investment tax credit for business and
a change in regulation regarding depreciation went into
effect in 1962.

The major part of the program was passed by
Congress as the Revenue Act of 1964. It was the largest
tax cut in U.S. history up to that time, and was the
country's first attempt to stimulate the economy by an
intentional budget deficit. The tax cut appeared as a
great success to its proponents, for the economy, fueled
by large jumps in investment and consumption,
experienced a sharp increase in growth. In fact, total
income in the economy rose rapidly enough to enable tax
collections by the government to increase.[11] With the
economy functioning well, government deficits during the
Kennedy administration were about the same size as had
been incurred in any single deficit year during the
previous decade.

However, there was one significant difference.
Whereas the previous decade had seen four years of
budget surplus, the 1960s would have only one year of
surplus. This new pattern of government finance had its
beginning in the shift in emphasis to direct spending on
welfare by the federal government that began in the
administration of President Lyndon Johnson. In the
Kennedy administration it had been hoped that economic
growth would pull individuals' incomes above the poverty
level. When this hope was perceived as not having been
achieved, more specific programs designed to end poverty
were enacted. By 1965, social programs were about 25
percent of the government budget. A typical agency in
the antipoverty program was the Office of Economic
Opportunity, but over 150 new agencies were created.
During the 1960s, 400,000 new jobs were added to the
federal government, bringing the total number of federal

employees to about 3 million by 1970, a 15 percent increase.[12]

The war in Vietnam required greater intervention by the United States from 1965 onward, with military spending rising at an annual rate of $3 billion in the second half of 1965 and $13 billion in 1966 and reaching a total of $30 billion by the end of 1968.[13] As had been the case in previous wars and certainly should have been true under the new economics, the appropriate policy would have been an increase in taxes. In fact, the Council of Economic Advisors advised President Johnson to raise taxes in 1966.[14] Due to Johnson's concern over how a tax increase might affect the economy, and because of the growing unpopularity of the war, taxes were not raised until 1968,[15] when Congress passed a 10 percent tax surcharge on incomes. As a result, the budget deficit reached $25.2 billion in 1968, the most it had been since World War II. With the tax increase, the budget for 1969 actually showed a surplus of $3.2 billion, marking the last time the federal government's finances were in the black. In 1970, total debt was $382.6 billion, an increase of about $92 billion over the past decade.[16] It should be noted that on an inflation adjusted basis, however, the real debt remained nearly constant for the decade.[17]

The Federal Reserve, by pursuing an expansionary money policy for most of the 1960s, helped the Treasury to manage the continual stream of deficits. In the fiscal year beginning the decade, the Federal Reserve purchased on the open market $0.7 billion in government securities, bringing its total holdings of debt to $25.5 billion (9 percent of the total).[18] At the end of the decade the Federal Reserve was running a tight money policy by purchasing $1.9 billion in 1969, down from the $5.5 billion purchased the previous year; this policy was an effort to fight inflation, which had reached over 5 percent by then. The Federal Reserve's holdings of federal government debt had grown to $54.1 billion in 1969 (15 percent of the total).[19]

DEBT MANAGEMENT POLICIES

In 1961 more than one-fourth of the debt had to be replaced or paid off during the year. This fact combined with the constant stream of deficits created debt management problems for the Treasury. During the 1960s, the Treasury continued to improve its ability to manage the debt by lengthening the maturity of the debt, thus providing for fewer issues coming due during a year. One method by which this was accomplished, advance refunding, was introduced in 1960. Under advance refunding, holders of outstanding debt were

given the option of exchanging their securities for
issues with a longer maturity and higher interest rate.
This plan enabled the Treasury to market more
intermediate and long-term securities, decreasing the
problem of frequent sales.[20] For example, in September
1961, holders of $3.75 billion in bonds maturing in 1970
and 1971 exchanged their holdings for longer-term issues
that were due in 1980 and 1998.[21]

Advance refunding was employed quite usefully for
the next several years, resulting in the average
maturity of the debt being lengthened from 4 years 6
months on June 30, 1961,[22] to 5 years and 4 months on
June 30, 1965.[23] By the end of the decade, the larger
deficits combined with the Federal Reserve's pursuit of
a tight money policy sent interest rates soaring from
the 2.5 to 4 percent range in 1961, and to the 7 to 7.5
percent range in 1969. As Congress was still imposing
a ceiling of 4.25 percent on securities with maturities
longer than seven years, the Treasury was unable to
offer any long-term debt for sale. As a result, the
average maturity of the debt fell to 4 years on June 30,
1969.[24] Table 8.1 shows computed interest on the total
debt for fiscal years 1963 through 1970.

Table 8.1
Computed Interest on Total Debt (1963-70)

Fiscal Year by percent

1963	1964	1965	1966	1967	1968	1969	1970
3.36	3.56	3.68	3.99	4.04	4.50	4.89	5.56

Source: U.S. Department of the Treasury, Treasury
          Bulletin, February 1972, Table FD-2.

Another method by which the Treasury's debt
management problems could be reduced would be through
the increased sale of savings bonds. Since the owners
of savings bonds held them for an average of 7.5 years,
their continued sale helped restructure the debt toward
a longer maturity. In 1961, to encourage continued
ownership of savings bonds, the Treasury made a second
ten-year extension of Series E bonds that had been
purchased in the period from May 1941 to May 1949; the
interest on the bonds was raised to 3.75 percent per
year for the period of the extension. Series H bonds
sold from June 1952 to January 1957 were also given a
ten-year extension. On June 30, 1961, Series E and H

savings bonds were 15 percent of the total public
debt.[25]

Sales of savings bonds remained fairly steady in
the early 1960s, and they were still 15 percent of the
total debt in 1963. To further encourage the sale of
savings bonds, the Treasury in September 1962 had
announced that taxpayers would be given the choice of
accepting Series E savings bonds as payment for their
tax refunds; by June 30, 1963, $19 million in Series E
bonds had been issued in this way.[26] Effective December
1, 1965, the interest rate on old and new Series E and
H savings bonds was raised to 4.15 percent. This
increase was made after it was discovered that sales of
savings bonds were lagging due to higher rates of
interest being offered on other forms of savings
available to individuals.[27] Series E and H savings
bonds still constituted about 15 percent of total debt
in 1966.

In 1967, the Treasury began the most intensive
sales campaign for its savings-type instruments since
World War II; a U.S. savings note referred to as a
"Freedom Share," which carried a return of 4.74 percent
when held to maturity (4 and 1/2 years), was introduced
on May 1. During 1967, $4.6 billion in Series E bonds
were sold, the highest sale of this series since 1946.[28]
By June 30, 1969, U.S. savings bonds and notes totaled
$52.2 billion, still about 15 percent of the debt.[29]

As a result of these debt management policies and
Federal Reserve open market operations, the ownership
composition of the debt changed during the 1960s. The
portion held by the Federal Reserve and by government
accounts increased, while that of individuals remained
steady (see Table 8.2).

At this time, the Federal Reserve, as part of its
duties as fiscal agent for the Treasury, gave
considerable assistance in the process of selling new
issues of securities. Federal Reserve Banks would print
announcements of the new issues and distribute them to
organizations that were usually interested in purchasing
new issues. The Banks would then accept subscriptions
for the new issues and transmit them to the Treasury.
In cases of oversubscription, the Treasury would make
percentage allotments to various classes of subscribers.
The Federal Reserve would also handle the exchange of
securities involved in a refunding.

For the purpose of facilitating secondary market
transactions of outstanding Treasury securities, the
Federal Reserve also provided useful services. To
permit a wire transfer of securities, each of the
Federal Reserve Banks kept a supply of unissued
securities in its vault. A person selling a government
security in one part of the country to someone in
another part would deliver the security to the Federal

Table 8.2
Ownership of Federal Securities (1961, 1965, and 1969)

	1961	1965	1969
Individuals	22%	23%	22%
Savings Banks, Corporations, etc.	28%	27%	23%
Commercial Banks	22%	18%	16%
Federal Government Accounts	19%	20%	24%
Federal Reserve Bank	9%	12%	15%

Source: Annual Reports of the Secretary of the
         Treasury for 1961 (p. 98), 1965 (p. 30),
         and 1969 (p. 13).

Reserve Bank in his home area, requesting that it be sold in another Federal Reserve district. A new security would be issued in the second district and given to that purchaser on receipt of payment; thus the security in the first district would be retired and payment given to the seller.

In this way, a national market for government securities was established. Buyers and sellers of government securities could buy or sell in whatever area of the country gave them the best price, and the entire transaction could take place in an hour. As part of this process, a national market for government securities would be maintained. The Federal Reserve Banks were also keeping many of the records of sales and redemptions of securities for the Treasury. The Federal Reserve Banks also continued to coordinate the Savings Bond Program, designating issuing and paying agents, keeping issuing agents supplied with unissued bonds and stocks, reimbursing paying agents, and keeping the records involved with the program.[30]

DEBT ADMINISTRATION

Despite the assistance of the Federal Reserve Banks in administering the debt, the trends in the size of the public debt and the program of managing it as adopted by the Treasury had a great impact on the workload of the Bureau of the Public Debt. This impact can be seen in the increase in the number of accounts of each type of security that had to be administered. One of the Bureau's functions, for example, involved keeping

accounts of registered securities issued by the
Treasury. In 1961, 34,581 individual accounts were
opened, 30,530 closed, with the total number of accounts
outstanding at the end of the year at 248,678.[31] In
1963, the Bureau opened 19,011 such accounts and closed
22,363; the total number of accounts had declined to
242,184.[32] By 1966, 24,453 accounts were opened and
26,293 closed, and the total number of accounts declined
further to 213,180.[33] In 1969, however, continuing a
trend of the previous two years, outstanding accounts
increased to 227,642.[34]

     This increase in the number of accounts of
registered securities was matched by the growth of
issues of bearer securities. In 1961, 4.1 million
bearer bonds were redeemed and audited.[35] The
comparable figure for 1969 had risen to 7.4 million.[36]

     The workload in the savings bond area also became
greater during this time. Because of the promise to
replace any U.S. savings bonds that have been lost,
stolen, or destroyed, all accounts for savings bonds are
permanent. Since none of the savings bond accounts
maintained by the Bureau can ever be eliminated, the
total number of accounts in the savings bond register
can only increase. From 1961 to 1969, the total number
of savings bond accounts increased by 900 million to a
total in 1969 of 3.2 billion, with about 750,000 claims
of lost, stolen, or destroyed bonds being adjudicated
during that same time.[37],[38]

     Despite this increased workload, total employment
at the Bureau of the Public Debt actually declined
during the 1960s. By January 31, 1960, the Bureau
employed 2,317 persons; by January 31, 1970, the number
of employees was down to 1,915. This means that while
total employment by the federal government was
increasing by 15 percent, the Bureau of the Public Debt
was reducing its level of employment by 17 percent.
Historians and critics of government bureaucracy often
make much of "empire building" taking place at
government agencies during the 1960s. But this charge
could hardly be leveled at the Bureau of the Public
Debt. For a detailed listing of the employment record
at the Bureau during the 1960s, see Table 8.3.

     The Bureau was able to attain the impressive result
of handling an increased workload with fewer employees
through the introduction of a variety of managerial and
technological improvements. Foremost among these was
the continued adoption of automatic data processing
equipment, which greatly enhanced the Bureau's ability
to process increasing amounts of paperwork.

     Some advances in the use of automated data
processing had already been made by the Bureau. The
sale of Series E savings bonds in punchcard form had

Table 8.3
Employees at the Bureau of the Public Debt (1960, 1966, and 1970)

	1960	1966	1970
Washington	674	602	627
Female	483	414	434
Male	191	188	193
Chicago	959	708	616
Female	772	562	500
Male	187	146	116
Parkersburg	460	578	672
Female	378	493	584
Male	82	85	88
TOTAL	2,317*	1,888	1,915
Female	1,836	1,469	1,518

*Includes two employees remaining at the Cincinnati office.

Source: Personnel Reports of Full-Time Employees, Bureau of the Public Debt File, D-200.5.

started in 1957, for example. The Datamatic D-1000 computer installed in 1958 was found to be saving the Bureau approximately $6 million annually by 1962.[39]

The 1960s would see further progress. In 1961, the computer system was upgraded with the installation of a Honeywell H-800 computer. The new system made several improvements. The large tape reels needed for the older system had become costly to purchase and store; the new system used smaller size tapes, which reduced much of that expense. The new equipment was faster than the old system, enabling the Bureau to process more data and to centralize its savings bonds records. It was estimated that the speed and efficiencies provided by the new equipment would permit the Bureau to close the Cincinnati office.[40] It was further estimated that by fiscal year 1963 the new system would result in annual savings of $3.6 million.[41]

At this time, all bond stubs and redeemed bonds were sent to Parkersburg, where they were microfilmed by a bank of 16 machines, at the rate of 450 per minute for each machine. The microfilm was then duplicated by a diazo process, with one copy being sent to archives in Wisconsin for security purposes.[42]

In 1962, the Cincinnati regional office was closed by the transfer of the function of auditing retired paper bonds to Parkersburg, increasing the number of employees at Parkersburg to 600.[43] In 1964, the Bureau microfilmed the numerical registers containing the manually posted records of retirements of Series E paper issues. The film could be used in high-speed information systems, thus helping to reduce the space and employees needed in the Chicago office.[44]

After the introduction of punchcard bonds, several large issuing agents began using computers to print new issues. A study was made to determine if the magnetic tapes used in the process could be employed in reporting bond sales. In 1964, the Army Finance Center in Indianapolis became the first issuing agent to report its sales in this manner.[45] The Navy Bureau of Supplies and Accounts and the Air Force Accounting and Finance Center began reporting in the same way in 1966.[46] Within ten years, ten Federal Reserve Banks, six Treasury Disbursing Offices, seven military installations, and eleven private companies were using automated reporting equipment, accounting for about 26 percent of total Series E bond sales.[47]

Efforts to improve the computer operations continued throughout the 1960s. In 1964, a second H-800 computer was acquired, along with a Honeywell H-200 computer. Some typical improvements made during this time (with their annual savings) were:

- Programming of various housekeeping operations from manual to computer handling ($20,910) (June 1963);
- Electronic printing of Adjustment Advice Form PD 2792 ($34,000) (July 1965);
- Automation of Series H interest accounts and check writing ($132,000) (April 1967); and
- Installation of NCR 735 Encoders that allowed for direct entry of data to magnetic tape, replacing the keypunch and verifying machines in Retired Paper Bond Subunit ($40,069) (January 1968).[48]

In 1967, with computer operations at Parkersburg running smoothly, it was decided that some operations in Washington could be converted to electronic data

processing methods.   Several computers were being
evaluated by the end of the year.[49] Whenever automation
takes place, there is always a fear on the part of
employees that their jobs might be lost. But changes in
technology can create new jobs even as they eliminate
old ones.   The Bureau was committed to seeing that
employees were able to take advantage of the new careers
opening up in automated data processing.   As H.J.
Hintgen,   then   Deputy   Commissioner,   informed   all
employees at the Bureau:

> We foresee no cause for concern about
> continued employment on the part of an
> employee.   In fact the introduction of the
> EDP system will open opportunities in a new
> and challenging field for employees who are
> interested and qualified. We expect to fill
> most, if not all, of the positions related to
> the   EDP   system   through   training   and
> reassignment of present Bureau employees.[50]

The system was fully operable by 1969 and was used to
perform public debt accounting and other operations that
had used conventional tabulating equipment.[51]
    Automated data processing also improved operations
at the Chicago office. In 1968, through the purchase of
a used computer from the Federal Reserve at a savings of
$450,000, the Bureau was able to automate the interest
accounts of Series H and K bonds, which required the
servicing of 1.6 million current interest payment
accounts. Labor time to handle the accounts was reduced
by half, 89 employees could be used elsewhere, and
13,000 square feet of prime Chicago office space was
released--giving   a   combined   annual   savings   of
$600,000.[52]

OPERATIONAL IMPROVEMENT

    In addition to the administrative efficiency gained
through the changes just mentioned, the Bureau responded
to the pressures it faced with a number of small changes
in its operations that added up to further improvement.
While many of these changes were related, they can be
better gauged by considering them in separate categories
of Employee Suggestions, Service, Book-Entry, and
Organizational Changes.

Employee Suggestions

    Some of the operational improvements made at the
Bureau during the 1960s came from employee suggestions.

In 1961, an employee incentive awards program encouraged
204 suggestions from employees; the Bureau adopted 103
of these for an estimated savings of $23,010, paying
$1,745 in cash awards.[53]   During 1963, 45 employee
suggestions resulting in savings of $19,963 were put
into place.[54]   In 1968, Golden Skeen of the Parkersburg
office was specially cited for suggesting a way to
automate the printing of shipping dates on bond stubs
received each day at the Parkersburg office. Since over
2.5 million stubs were being received annually, this was
a significant improvement that saved over $6,300 per
year.[55]

Service

Service to the public was also improved during the
1960s. In 1961, a new procedure was devised for direct
submission of requests for replacement of savings bonds
to the Parkersburg office on a special form. The new
procedure eliminated paperwork and reduced the time it
took to issue a replacement bond.[56]   In 1962, the
procedure for replacing savings bonds was changed to
allow for the issuance of a check for the redemption
value of the bond when the owner requested it.
Previously, a duplicate savings bond was first issued
and then redeemed for payment. Elimination of this step
also saved bond owners time in receiving their
replacements.[57]

Book Entry

On January 1, 1968, regulations were put into place
for the use of book-entry Treasury securities.
Securities in book-entry form would consist of
transferable Treasury bonds, notes, bills, and
certificates of indebtedness. Under the new system,
these securities would be recorded as entries in the
accounts of the Federal Reserve Bank that issued them,
instead of as definitive securities issued in the form
of printed pieces of paper. The system, which had been
the subject of a four-year joint study by the Treasury
and the Federal Reserve, had as its purpose the
reduction of the amount of paperwork involved with
government securities transactions. Initially, the
system was only available for transferable Treasury
securities deposited with a Federal Reserve Bank as
collateral for Treasury tax and loan accounts, as
collateral for the deposit of public money, or for
safekeeping or collateral by a member bank. All
transferable Treasury securities held for Government
Investment Accounts were deposited with the Federal

Reserve Bank of New York to be held in book-entry form. Special Treasury issues held by Government Trust Funds were also established into book-entry form, with their accounts being maintained by the Bureau of the Public Debt. Studies were also being made of how feasible it would be to convert other classes of securities to book-entry form.[58]

In 1969, the book-entry system was expanded to include U.S. savings bonds issued to trustees of certain employees' thrift and savings plans. In this case, the system would allow for the change of securities from book-entry to definitive form and reverse, as the need arose. Still, the Bureau gained the advantage of a reduced number of securities to process.[59]

Organizational Changes

Several organizational changes also took place at the Bureau during the 1960s. In 1962, three subunits in the Division of Loans and Currency branch in the Chicago office were reorganized; the Numerical Register Section of the Division of Retired Savings Bonds was abolished; and in the Washington office, the Securities Transactions and the Claims sections of the Division of Loans and Currency were merged.[60]

An important step was taken in June 1963 with the formation of the Management Analysis Office. The new office replaced the Methods and Procedures Office, but its responsibilities had evolved greatly over the years. At this point, the Management Analysis Office would provide all parts of the Bureau with management counseling and advisory service, identify projects for management improvement, analyze organizational effectiveness, revise methods and procedures of operation, conduct management surveys, and undertake research into new managerial ideas and techniques.[61]

On July 1, 1969, a Division of Data Processing was put in place to operate the Washington office computer facility; the new Division would also serve as advisor to the Commissioner on automated data processing, interact with other Treasury bureaus and government agencies in terms of joint data processing, and would act as a resource center for the Bureau in continually monitoring changes in data processing methods and equipment.[62]

NOTES

1. Gary M. Anderson, "The U.S. Federal Deficit and National Debt: A Political and Economic History," in James M. Buchanan, Charles K. Rowley, and Robert D.

Tollinson, eds., Deficits (New York: Basil Blackwell, 1987), pp. 13-14.

2. Robert Eisner and Paul J. Pieper, "How to Make Sense of the Deficit," in Robert H. Fink and Jack C. High, A Nation in Debt (Frederick, Md.: University Publications of America, 1987), p. 93.

3. Secretary of the Treasury, Annual Report (Washington, D.C.: 1961), p. 83.

4. Robert A. Gordon, Economic Instability and Growth: The American Record (New York: Harper & Row, 1974), pp. 137-155.

5. Robert Lekachman, The Age of Keynes (New York: Random House, 1966), p. 271.

6. Michael G. Rukstad, Macroeconomic Decision Making in the World Economy (Chicago: Dryden Press, 1986), pp. 204-205.

7. Rukstad, Macroeconomic Decision Making, p. 204.

8. The Council of Economic Advisors, "The Full Employment Surplus Concept," in Warren L. Smith and Ronald L. Teigen, eds., Readings in Money, National Income and Stabilization Policy (Homewood, Ill.: Richard D. Irwin, 1970), p. 332.

9. Quoted in David J. Ott and Attiat F. Ott, "Fiscal Policy and The National Debt," in Warren J. Smith and Ronald L. Teigen, eds., Readings in Money, National Income and Stabilization Policy (Homewood, Ill.: Richard D. Irwin, 1970), p. 377.

10. Milton Friedman and Walter Heller, Monetary vs Fiscal Policy (New York: W.W. Norton, 1969), p. 67.

11. Herbert Stein, Presidential Economics (New York: Simon & Schuster, 1984), pp. 101-111.

12. Matthew A. Crenson and Francis E. Rourke," By Way of Conclusion: American Bureaucracy since World War II," in Louis Galombos, ed., The New American State (Baltimore: The Johns Hopkins University Press, 1987), pp. 148-151.

13. Gordon, Economic Instability and Growth, p. 155.

14. Friedman and Heller, Monetary vs Fiscal Policy, p. 35.

15. Stein, *Presidential Economics,* pp. 116-122.

16. Anderson, "*U.S. Federal Deficit,*" pp. 13-14.

17. Eisner and Pieper, "*Deficit,*" p. 93.

18. Secretary of the Treasury, *Annual Report* (1961), p. 98.

19. Secretary of the Treasury, *Annual Report* (Washington, D.C.: 1969), p. 13.

20. William H. Anderson, *Financing Modern Government* (Boston: Houghton Mifflin, 1973), p. 254.

21. Secretary of the Treasury, *Annual Report* (1961), p. 17.

22. Secretary of the Treasury, *Annual Report* (1961), p. 84.

23. Secretary of the Treasury, *Annual Report* (Washington, D.C.: 1965), p. 28.

24. Secretary of the Treasury, *Annual Report* (1969), p. 12.

25. Secretary of the Treasury, *Annual Report* (1961), pp. 15, 18.

26. Secretary of the Treasury, *Annual Report* (Washington, D.C.: 1963), p. 35.

27. Secretary of the Treasury, *Annual Report* (Washington, D.C.: 1966), pp. 30-31.

28. Secretary of the Treasury, *Annual Report* (Washington, D.C.: 1967), pp. 14, 23.

29. Secretary of the Treasury, *Annual Report* (1969), p. 14.

30. Thomas O. Waage, "Service and Supervisory Functions of the Federal Reserve System," in Herbert V. Prochnow, ed., *The Federal Reserve System* (New York: Harper & Row, 1960), pp. 241-242.

31. Secretary of the Treasury, *Annual Report* (1961), p. 185.

32. Secretary of the Treasury, *Annual Report* (1963), p. 119.

33. Secretary of the Treasury, Annual Report (1966), p. 109.

34. Secretary of the Treasury, Annual Report (1969), p. 98.

35. Secretary of the Treasury, Annual Report (1961), p. 185.

36. Secretary of the Treasury, Annual Report (1969), p. 98.

37. Secretary of the Treasury, Annual Report (1961), pp. 183-184.

38. Secretary of the Treasury, Annual Report (1969), p. 98.

39. M.P. Heckman, Memorandum (Bureau of the Public Debt files: February 19, 1962), pp. 3-4.

40. U.S. Department of the Treasury, Bureau of the Public Debt, Summary of Decisions Made and Action Taken to Upgrade the EDP System in Parkersburg, West Virginia (Parkersburg, W.Va.: Memo dated September 28, 1962).

41. Heckman, Memorandum, p. 4.

42. Author Unknown, "A Record Home for Millions," Business Automation, June 1963, p. 29.

43. U.S. Department of the Treasury, Bureau of the Public Debt, Untitled and undated (circa 1976) report in BPD files.

44. Secretary of the Treasury, Annual Report (1964), p. 107.

45. Secretary of the Treasury, Annual Report (1964), p. 107.

46. Secretary of the Treasury, Annual Report (1966), p. 108.

47. U.S. Department of the Treasury, Bureau of the Public Debt, Description of Parkersburg Office Responsibilities and Functions (Washington, D.C.: October 18, 1974).

48. U.S. Department of the Treasury, Bureau of the Public Debt, Draft Memo P.D. 2694 (8.57) (Washington, D.C.: April 1976), pp. 3-6.

49. Secretary of the Treasury, Annual Report (1967), p. 88.

50. H.J. Hintgen, Memorandum to all employees (Washington, D.C.: BPD, June 16, 1967).

51. Secretary of the Treasury, Annual Report (1969), pp. 96-97.

52. U.S. Department of the Treasury, Progress in Management Improvement (Washington, D.C.: FY 1968), p. 9.

53. Secretary of the Treasury, Annual Report (1961), p. 179.

54. Secretary of the Treasury, Annual Report (1963), p. 118.

55. U.S. Dept. of Treasury, Progress in Management Improvement, p. 16.

56. Secretary of the Treasury, Annual Report (1961), p. 179.

57. Secretary of the Treasury, Annual Report (Washington, D.C.: 1962), p. 143.

58. Secretary of the Treasury, Annual Report (Washington, D.C.: 1968), p. 93.

59. Secretary of the Treasury, Annual Report (1969), p. 97.

60. Secretary of the Treasury, Annual Report (1963), p. 118.

61. H.J. Hintgen, Memorandum to D.M. Merritt (Washington, D.C.: Bureau of the Public Debt File D-120.9, June 26, 1963).

62. Secretary of the Treasury, Annual Report (1969), p. 97.

9

Debt Growth in a Stagnant Economy (1970–80)

The 1970s will be remembered as a disappointing decade in terms of the performance of the economy. The causes of that poor performance are still being debated by economists. Included are the negative impact of the Vietnam War on monetary and fiscal policy, two energy crises engineered by OPEC, and a decline in productivity. But the poor performance itself cannot be denied. From 1960 to 1964, real GNP grew at a 3.9 percent annual rate and inflation averaged 1.2 percent per year, with the comparable figures for 1965-69 being 4.2 percent GNP growth and 3.4 percent average inflation--all in all a fairly respectable showing. The economy would not do nearly as well during the next decade. In the years 1970-74, real GNP grew annually at 2.4 percent and prices rose by 6.1 percent per year, while for the second half of the decade real GNP growth averaged 2.7 percent and inflation 7.7 percent.[1]

After the 1960s, a decade during which the business cycle seemed to have been banished and the unemployment rate averaged 4 percent, the next ten years saw three recessions and unemployment rates averaging over 6 percent. In government finance, the robust economy of the 1960s produced a successful experience in terms of small passive automatic deficits, and active Keynesian deficits to stimulate the economy seemed to pay for themselves. With a decade of stagnant growth in the economy, however, it is no surprise that the federal government budget was in deficit for all of the 1970s. The only surprise was in their size, for record peacetime deficits would become the norm during this period.

A part of the blame for this period of deficits could be placed on the formation of a variety of new agencies, such as the Environmental Protection Agency, the Occupational Safety and Health Administration, and the Consumer Product Safety Commission. Expenditures in these areas would also add to the increasing annual budget deficit. The key to explaining the deficit remains economic conditions, for despite the creation of these new agencies, total federal government employment leveled off during the 1970s, increasing from 2,928,000 persons in 1970 to 2,987,000 persons in 1980--a rise of only 2 percent.[2]

THE NIXON YEARS

When the administration of President Richard M. Nixon took office in 1969, the policies set in place during the Kennedy-Johnson years were continued. In part this was because Nixon did not consider himself an expert on economics and did not want to upset the economy. In the short-term he had no other choice, as these programs had built up a momentum of their own. Besides, the economy was doing quite well, with the unemployment rate at 3.3 percent at the beginning of 1969 and inflation running at 5 percent. To be sure, this level of inflation was high by previous standards, but moderate compared to what the next decade would bring.[3] The economy did experience a mild recession in 1969-70, caused by the Federal Reserve's tight money policy intended to fight that inflation. At the same time, in part to ease the strain of the recession, the 10 percent tax surcharge of 1968, which had been extended to 1970, was allowed to expire.[4]

One of the hallmarks of Keynesian policy is a willingness to incur budget deficits during a recession. To some extent, this happens automatically. When the economy experiences unemployment, government expenditures for welfare and unemployment programs increase while tax collections decline, resulting in an increase in the deficit. Economist James Tobin has estimated that for each percentage increase in the unemployment rate, the government deficit will grow by $25 to $30 billion.[5] Pre-Keynesian fiscal prudence would call for a tax increase to reduce this deficit, whereas Keynesian policy encourages a deficit. Expiration of the tax surcharge, basically a tax cut, was in keeping with Keynesian views. Nixon admitted as much when he announced in 1971, "I am now a Keynesian."[6]

The economy began a slow recovery in 1971, which must have confirmed Nixon's beliefs in Keynesian economics. His attitude toward deficits certainly indicated that he followed the notion of the full-employment budget. He noted, "The full-employment budget principle permits fiscal stimulation when stimulation is appropriate and calls for restraint when restraint is appropriate. But it is not self-enforcing.

It signals us what course to steer, but requires us to take actions necessary to keep on course."[7] Nixon was apparently willing to pin his hopes on discretionary fiscal policy. With the economy heading for a recession in 1971, Nixon pushed for tax reductions to take place in 1972.[8] Deficits thereafter began rising to levels previously unheard of except during wartime. In 1973, for example, the budget deficit was $14.3 billion.[9]

The Nixon years also saw the beginning of inflationary pressures coming to bear on the economy. In addition to the fiscal stimulus of Nixon's policies, the Federal Reserve began easing up on credit. As part of that policy of easy money, for example, the Federal Reserve purchased on the open market $7.8 billion in government securities in 1971 and $5.8 billion in 1972.[10] As a result of all this stimulation of the economy, recovery accelerated in 1972 and inflationary pressures began building. As Nixon's statement just cited indicates, the full-employment budget principle would call for fiscal restraint to keep the economy from overheating and bringing about higher inflation. Nixon, however, surprised the country by imposing wage and price controls--in force from August 1971 to April 1974.[11] In this way a lid was put on inflationary pressures and the economic expansion could continue. Keynesians would not care to have Nixon in their camp.

Whatever his economic leaning, Nixon still had to conduct the war in Vietnam, and the government had to find the means to pay for it. But Nixon had also inherited many of the welfare programs that had continuing built-in increases. To bring the budget more in line with his own priorities, after his landslide reelection in 1972, Nixon began impounding funds authorized for spending by Congress. During the election campaign, Nixon had chastised Congress for creating deficits due to the "hoary and traditional procedure of the Congress, which now permits action on the various spending programs as if they were unrelated and independent actions."[12]

Nixon had a point. At this time, Congress did not have an overall approach to budgeting. Control over the budget presumably rested with the Appropriations Committees of the House and Senate, but other committees could also approve funds for areas that came under their jurisdiction. This made fiscal policy difficult to achieve, because there was no correlation established between the various spending proposals that were set forth nor were those proposals linked in any way with tax policy. Nixon lost his fight over the impounding of funds in the courts. But his raising of the issue did result in the Congressional Budget and Impoundment Control Act, which he signed on July 12, 1974. This measure established a Budget Committee in both the House

and Senate and created the Congressional Budget Office
to give Congress the data and analysis it needed to make
up its own budget.[13]   The new plan was intended to
provide for a better application of the full-employment
budget principle to fiscal policy.

With the sharp rise in price of petroleum products
due to the OPEC-engineered shortage of 1973, and with
the lifting of price controls, inflation had increased
dramatically by 1974. It should be noted, however, that
to the extent that individuals experience inflationary
income increases, those increases raise their taxes (by
boosting them into higher tax brackets), thus helping to
keep government deficits lower.

The potential gain in tax receipts due to inflation
did not materialize, however, because the economy
entered into a recession late in 1973, at that time the
longest and most severe since World War II.   The
unemployment rate rose to 9.2 percent in early 1975.
The immediate cause of the recession was tight money
policy on the part of the Federal Reserve, which drove
interest rates to double-digit levels, with the prime
rate hitting 12 percent on July 3, 1974.   Despite this
recession, which ended early in 1975, the rate of
inflation did not level off.[14]   But by this time Nixon
had made his wrenching exit from office and a new
administration was in charge.

THE FORD YEARS

The administration of President Gerald Ford took
office with restrictive monetary and fiscal policies
already in place.   To continue the fight against
inflation, Ford followed a policy of cutting back on
government spending while the Federal Reserve put a
tighter rein on the growth of the money supply and
credit. As the economy continued in a recession through
1974-75, these cutbacks turned counterproductive. They
were offset by the impact of the recession on the
government's finances, so budget deficits continued to
rise.   But in 1974, the full-employment principle
actually showed a surplus.[15]

Ford recognized the problem and proposed a $15
billion tax cut and an increase in spending.   In
following this policy Ford may be called a reluctant
Keynesian. As he expressed his position, "I regret that
my budget and tax proposals will mean bigger deficits,
temporarily, for I have always opposed deficits.   We
must recognize, however, that if economic recovery does
not begin soon, the Treasury will . . . incur even
larger deficits in the future."[16]   In terms of the
immediate impact of his program, Ford's assessment was
proven correct, because in 1975 the deficit climbed to

$59 billion, the largest it had been since the $61.8 billion deficit in 1944, during a period of all-out war.[17] The budget deficit for 1976 surpassed both these figures, hitting $87.2 billion.[18] In order to help with Ford's policy for economy growth, in 1975 and 1976 the Federal Reserve boosted the money supply, purchasing $4.3 billion in government securities in the former year and $9.7 billion in the latter year.[19] The economy recovered and showed a rapid expansion in 1976 and 1977, but that would come as no solace to Ford, whose attempt to win office on his own did not succeed.

THE CARTER YEARS

In the presidential election campaign of 1976, Jimmy Carter voiced his concern over the large deficits being run by the Ford administration. As he put it, "Mr. Ford's budgets will account for the largest single deficit and more than one-third of the public debt incurred during our 200-year history. The increase in the public debt during the Nixon-Ford years will be greater than the total public debt incurred under all other presidents in our history."[20] In keeping with this attack, Carter maintained an attitude toward fiscal policy similar to that of the other engineer who resided in the White House, Herbert Hoover. Carter felt that the government should get its budget in order, arguing, "I have never known an unbalanced budget--in my business, on my farm, as Governor of Georgia. And I've set a goal for myself, which I intend to meet: that before my administration is over, the budget of the United States will be balanced."[21]

When he took office, however, Carter continued with an expansionary fiscal policy. Taxes were cut during 1977 in an effort to stimulate spending. Carter justified this program by telling the public, "I'm unalterably opposed to fighting inflation by keeping unemployment high and factories idle."[22] Along with this expansionary fiscal policy, the Federal Reserve increased the growth of the money supply, acquiring $8.3 billion in government securities in 1977 and $10.6 billion in 1978.[23] The economy responded, and after several years of growth, the size of the deficit declined to $27.3 billion in 1979. However, inflation, fueled by the energy crisis of 1979, began rising, reaching 11.3 percent in 1979 and 13.5 percent in 1980.

To fight inflation, monetary policy was tightened in 1979. The Federal Reserve, in October 1979, made a dramatic shift in its policy by placing less emphasis on control of interest rates and more on the growth of the money supply. In keeping with this policy, in 1979 it purchased a mere $0.7 billion in government

securities.[24] Interest rates hit new highs, with market
yields on Treasury securities reaching the 14 to 16
percent range. The economy entered into a recession in
January 1980, which caused the deficit to rise again,
reaching $59 billion in 1980.[25]

The recession lasted for only six months, as the
Federal Reserve soon relaxed its tight money policy.
Carter persisted in his efforts to fight inflation by
keeping his fiscal policy contractionary. Even though
his proposed budget for fiscal year 1981 showed a
deficit, under the full-employment budget principle it
was in surplus. The economy remained sluggish, and
Carter was turned out of office. By 1980, the total
debt of the federal government stood at $914 billion, an
increase of $532 billion since 1970.[26] Even if the debt
were adjusted for the high levels of inflation that took
place during the decade, there was still a significant
increase in the total.[27] Interest rates on the total
debt showed an upward trend during the 1970s, as can be
seen in Table 9.1.

DEBT MANAGEMENT POLICIES

As had happened in the past when the workload
increased, measures were taken to enable the Treasury
authorities to manage the rapid increase in debt that
took place during the 1970s. When interest rates
reached the 7 to 8 percent range in early 1970, Congress
eased away from the 4 1/4 percent ceiling imposed on the
sale of bonds by the Second Liberty Loan Act, by
allowing the Treasury to issue up to $10 billion in
bonds to the public at any interest rate. In addition
to gaining greater flexibility on interest rates, the
Treasury improved its policies with regard to Treasury
auctions, savings bonds, and foreign sales. The
following discussion will highlight each of these.

Table 9.1
Computed Interest on Total Debt (fiscal years 1972-80)

1972	1973	1974	1975	1976	1977	1978	1979	1980
5.09	5.98	6.56	6.35	6.44	6.43	7.13	8.06	9.03

Source: U.S. Department of the Treasury, Treasury
          Bulletin, December 1980, Table FD-2.

Treasury Auctions

In 1971, the Treasury also began selling new issues of Treasury notes for cash at competitive auctions, instead of employing its longtime policy of offering securities for subscription at fixed prices and interest rates announced in advance. This practice left it to the financial markets to set prices and rates of interest on the securities, thereby ensuring that each offering could be sold with minimal intervention in financial markets by the Federal Reserve. In addition, the Federal Reserve continued to assist the Treasury by administering the auctions in each Reserve Bank by receiving tenders, tabulating bid data, and reporting same to the Bureau's financing staff for immediate calculations of the auction results (high, low, and average prices, "split" percentage, etc.) and determination of the accepted amounts to be allotted in each Reserve district.

In January 1973, the Treasury conducted the first of several auctions using the uniform-price method, in which all tenders accepted in the auction are awarded at the price of the lowest accepted tender. In this way investors, wary of buying long-term securities in a normal auction, given a substantial range of prices, would be provided an incentive to bid at prices sufficiently high to be sure of awards. They would also be assured that if they bid at prices within the accepted range, they would be awarded the bonds at the same price as every other bidder.[28]

Under the debt administration policy then in place, when a sale of a marketable Treasury issue was conducted, a public notice was prepared at the Bureau and released to the press. It was then disseminated to each of the Federal Reserve Banks. The public notice gave a brief description of the security being offered, terms of the offering, method of allotment and payment, the action provisions, and other general terms. Usually, a few days later, a second press release would be prepared by the Bureau that provided the interest rate to be set on the security (if it had not been announced in the original press release), if the auction was on a price basis. During this time, as in most previous periods, the Bureau of Engraving and Printing would print the new issues of securities.

In offerings of securities at auction, competitive bids would be made in terms of price on the basis of 100 (with not more than three decimal places) or yield (to two decimal places). In a yield basis auction, when the accepted range of bids to complete the amount of the offering was determined, an interest coupon rate based on the average of accepted bids would be established to the nearest 1/8 percent to make the average accepted price $100.00 or less. Noncompetitive tenders (up to the stated dollar limit) and the competitive tenders at the lowest yields would be accepted until the amount offered was covered. Tenders received at the Federal Reserve Banks and the Treasury were all reported to the Office of the Commissioner of the Bureau of the Public Debt, where final acceptance of offers would be determined. Successful bidders would be informed through the Federal Reserve Banks or the Treasury. When payment for the securities was received by the Treasury, either directly or through the Federal Reserve Banks, the Commissioner of the Public Debt would be authorized by the Fiscal Assistant Secretary to issue the securities.[29]

In September 1972, the Treasury converted its end-of-the-month, one-year cycle bill to a 52-week bill cycle with offerings made every four weeks. The previously offered nine-month bill was discontinued.[30] By 1976, it could be reported that the Treasury's financing activities were becoming increasingly regularized, with a schedule of weekly auctions of 13- and 26-week bills, the auction of 52-week bills every four weeks, traditional quarterly refunding, end-of-the-month two-year note offerings, end-of-the-quarter four-year note sales, a cycle of five-year notes sold in the first month of each quarter, and regular offerings of long-term bonds.[31]

Negatively, during 1971, after nearly six years of being unable to issue long-term bonds with interest rates more than 4-1/4 percent, the average length of the debt held by the public had fallen to three years six months.[32] In 1972, the policy of competitive auctions was extended to longer-term issues, including offerings of ten-year and 12-year bonds. Those issues, totaling $4.7 billion, were made under the newly authorized exception Congress had granted in terms of exceeding the interest rate ceiling on long-term bonds.[33] Despite these changes, the average maturity length of the outstanding debt continued to fall, reaching a record low of two years four months in February 1976.[34]

Savings Bonds

Sales of savings bonds continued to rise, but did not keep pace with the increase in the total debt. In 1970, the total Series E and H savings bonds and savings notes outstanding was $52 billion, 14 percent of the total public debt. At the end of the decade, in 1980, the total of $72.7 billion in savings bonds and notes was only 8 percent of the public debt.[35],[36],[37] In 1979, it was decided that there would be no further extensions of the maturity of the Series E and H savings bonds issued between May 1941 and April 1952. Two new series of EE and HH savings bonds were first offered for sale in the early part of 1980.[38]

The limit on the value of the new Series EE and HH that could be purchased during one year was raised from the $10,000 that had been in place on the Series E and H to $30,000 for Series EE and $20,000 for Series HH. Series EE bonds could not be redeemed until after six months from their purchase, which cut down somewhat on the workload at the Bureau. Equally important in terms of saving the Bureau administrative costs, time limits were established for servicing claims on lost or stolen bonds. If a claim was filed more than ten years after the recorded date of redemption, the Bureau would not have to provide the claimant with a copy of the paid bond. A claim filed six years or more after the maturity date of the bond would have to be accompanied by the serial number of the bond.[39]

Foreign Sales

During this period, there was an increase in the amount of public debt securities owned by foreign governments. In 1962, for the first time since 1918, the Treasury had begun borrowing directly from foreign official agencies by selling them special issues of nonmarketable securities. During the 1960s, the total of these issues stayed in the $1 to $2 billion range. In 1971, however, they rose from $4.8 billion to $9.3 billion, with an even more dramatic increase to $19 billion coming in 1972. Sales of these securities continued to climb, reaching $28.5 billion in 1973.[40] They then leveled off to about $21 billion in 1976.[41]

The sale of Treasury securities to foreign citizens also increased during the 1970s. While no separate accounting of these sales was given by the Treasury, their rise can be seen in the overall rise of foreign holdings of debt, which includes the sales to foreign governments. Total foreign holdings of public debt securities reached $60.2 billion in 1973 and $70.6 billion in 1976.[42] Foreign holdings continued to rise, totaling $95.1 billion in 1977, $121 billion in 1978, $125.2 in 1979, and $126 billion in 1980.[43,44,45,46] Since sales to foreign governments and agencies had leveled off by 1976, the increases after that year represent sales made mainly to foreign citizens. By 1978, foreign governments and agencies and foreign citizens held 16 percent of the total of public debt securities and the Treasury began including this fact in its annual table of estimated public debt ownership.[47] For a comparison of the shifting composition of public debt ownership during the 1970s, see Table 9.2.

Table 9.2
Public Debt Ownership
(fiscal years* 1970, 1975, and 1980)

	1970	1975	1980
Individual	22%	16%	14%
Savings Banks, Corporations, etc.	22%	28%	26%
Commercial Banks	14%	13%	11%
Federal Reserve Banks	16%	16%	13%
Government Accounts	26%	27%	22%
Foreign & International			14%#

* The government's fiscal year end was changed from June 30 to September 30 in 1976.
# These holdings were included in other categories for prior years.

Sources: Annual Reports of the Secretary of the Treasury, 1970 (p. 14), 1975 (p. 14), and 1980 (p. 13).

DEBT ADMINISTRATION

Operations at the Bureau of the Public Debt continued to keep pace with the expansion of the debt, but the pace was not always even. A statistical measure of the workload at the Bureau can be seen again in the number of accounts being handled. During 1970, 78,883 accounts for registered marketable securities were opened and 40,530 were closed, with the total number of open accounts at 261,686 at the end of the year. In 1975, about 180,000 accounts were opened and 70,000 were closed, with the total then at 383,175. By 1980, the figures had risen sharply, with opened accounts hitting 1,269,000 and closed accounts at 1,001,000--with a total of 1,171,000 accounts at year end.[48,49,50] The total of savings bond accounts reached 4.7 billion in 1980, an increase of 1.4 billion since 1970.[51]

Because of this extremely large growth in its workload, the Bureau had to expand its employment from 1,915 persons in 1970 to 2,200 in 1980. Although this 15 percent increase during the decade may appear to compare unfavorably with the 2 percent rise in total federal government employment during the same period, it is important to note that during the 1970s the total dollar value of the public debt nearly tripled, and the average maturity of the debt was approximately half of its level in the 1960s, pointing up the extensive use of more frequent offerings of shorter-term issues during the period. The Bureau's capability to administer this increased workload was enhanced by expansion of the book-entry system, increased use of automated data processing equipment, and continued improvements in management and organization. Table 9.3 contains information about employment levels during the 1970s.

Table 9.3
Employees at the Bureau of the Public Debt
(1974, 1976, and 1980)

	1974	1976	1980
Washington	646	795	984
Chicago	500	---	---
Parkersburg	885	1,282	1,216
TOTAL	2,031	2,077	2,200

Source: Personnel Reports of Full-Time
          Employees, Bureau of the Public Debt, File
          D-200.5.

THE BOOK-ENTRY SYSTEM

As previously noted, a trend had started in the late 1960s to a system of keeping Treasury securities as entries in ledger books. This book-entry system for registering securities was extended in 1970 to include securities deposited with Federal Reserve Banks stemming from deposits of securities at commercial banks by political subdivisions, or from performance obligations in connection with legal cases. Treasury securities held by the New York Federal Reserve Bank as part of its open market operations or for most of its official foreign accounts were also converted into book-entry form. The total of marketable book-entry securities was $100 billion. In addition, eight industrial savings plans using U.S. savings bonds were put into book-entry form. Book-entry transactions were simply recorded in account books of the Federal Reserve Banks, eliminating the need to issue, reissue, or retire physical securities. The use of book-entry thus greatly reduced administrative costs.[52]

In 1971, a large study of records relating to the processing of claims for lost or stolen marketable securities was undertaken; the total of losses and thefts of securities had risen dramatically to $30 million in 1969 and 1970. As a result of this study, on May 27, 1971, Congress approved a law permitting the Bureau to speed up the replacement of stolen or lost securities. Previously, the person or corporation with the missing securities had to wait until maturity to recover the value of their securities. The new procedure aimed at better service to the financial community.[53] The total number of cases of lost or stolen securities that the Bureau was able to settle within six months nearly doubled.[54]

As the book-entry system was expanded, the problems of loss or theft of securities would become less of a concern since they were only records at a Federal Reserve Bank--there were no physical securities to lose. In 1971, the Federal Reserve Banks were legally permitted to convert Treasury securities held by banks for their own accounts, in customers' accounts, and in dealers' trading inventories into book-entry form. These were the most important and voluminous types of holdings in the Treasury securities market. In 1971 that market involved about $230 billion in negotiable securities, of which $125 billion were in book-entry form.[55]

COMPUTER OPERATIONS

In 1970, all operations in the Washington office that had previously been done on manual tabulating machines were fully converted to computer operations.[56] In 1971, the Parkersburg office leased an additional Honeywell H-1250 computer to handle the increased workload from savings bond sales. It was also reported that the use of new encoders for entering data directly to tape had increased productivity by 12 percent.[57] In 1973, the Division of ADP Services oversaw the installation of a Univac 1108 computer system in the Washington office. Although the plans called for turning the system's operation over to the Office of the Secretary, it would serve the needs of the Bureau and several other Treasury agencies. Indeed, the Office of Tax Policy was asking to use the system as a backup while it was still being tested, citing "the urgent nature of the President's tax program."[58] The new system would have much greater speed and storage capacity compared to the Honeywell system. Because of better use of tapes, card readers, and disk drives, the Univac system would be 24 times larger in capacity and 16 times faster than the older computer.[59] ADP Services also converted programs of the Washington office to the new system.[60]

After the installation of the automatic data processing equipment in the 1960s, the time and effort required to search records for evidence of lost or stolen savings bonds was quickly reduced. But as more bonds were added to the register, the search time greatly increased. By 1969, an inquiry that would have necessitated six electronic searches in 1960 required 15 searches. At this time, the register was compiled on the basis of bond serial number and by issuee's last name (first six letters), first initial, and city of issue. The problem was that for each year the number of entries could expand by one to 12 purchases for each of seven denominations, for a total of 84 entries. Additional computer equipment was requested to handle this extra work.[61]

This situation was eased in 1974 when bond purchasers were required to provide their social security numbers for inscription on bonds. In addition to the social security number, each bond record contained the bond serial number, date of issue, and four characters of the purchaser's surname. Bond searches became much more efficient; a purchaser's entire holdings could be located with a single inquiry, although care was taken to restrict the search to the requested denomination and date.[62]

ORGANIZATIONAL CHANGES

Several important organizational changes took place at the Bureau in the early 1970s. In 1970, the internal audit activity was reformed as the Internal Audit Service and given greater centralized responsibility.[63] Early in 1972, Commissioner H.J. Hintgen reported the ending of the nearly 100-year-old Division of Loans and Currency. In reviewing the need for the change, Hintgen said, "The use of the word "Loans" in this connection has been out-of-date for many years, and all of the "Currency" functions have been transferred elsewhere."[64] As part of this change, the registered accounts function was moved from the old Division of Loans and Currency to the Division of Public Debt Accounts; at the same time, the remaining work of the Division of Loans and Currency was added to the activities of the Division of Retired Securities to create a new entity named the Division of Securities Operations.[65]

Major changes were also taking place at the Parkersburg and Chicago offices at this time. In April 1970, the Fiscal Assistant Secretary sought permission to determine the feasibility of consolidating the Public Debt field offices in order to correlate the activities taking place in Parkersburg and Chicago, to improve efficiency, and to take advantage of the favorable labor market in Parkersburg. Plans to move the Chicago office to Parkersburg were realized on June 30, 1971, when Congress passed a bill that contained an appropriation to underwrite the project.[66]

The first phase of the consolidation took place in 1972, when the claims adjudication function was moved to Parkersburg.[67]   In addition, a significant "new beginning" occurred on June 9, 1973, when ground was broken for a new building in Parkersburg.[68] The phasing out of operations in the Chicago office continued in 1974, with several additional functions being moved to Parkersburg. A special storage warehouse was built in Ravenswood, West Virginia not far from Parkersburg; this facility was used to store the microfilm records of savings bonds that had been kept in an older building in Wisconsin.[69]

The new savings bond operations center in Parkersburg was to be a 285,000-square-foot, six-floor building of modern design overlooking the Ohio River. It would utilize an advanced heating system that operated on the warmth generated by the sun, lighting and machinery, and the occupants of the building. A backup boiler system was included in the structure and sensors would put it into operation whenever the intensity of the sun became too low. The plans also permitted the movement of the interior walls, so individual departments could expand or contract their floorspace as need arose.[70]

The move from Chicago was a very large undertaking, affecting a large number of employees. To some extent, the problem of moving a long distance that was faced by longtime employees was alleviated by a staff reduction through attrition. Remaining employees in Chicago were given the opportunity to transfer to Parkersburg. Those who chose not to move were given assistance in finding jobs with other federal agencies in the Chicago area. Job fairs were held and employment officers of several agencies were contacted on behalf of employees.[71]

Overall responsibility for coordinating the move was placed in the hands of Michael E. McGeoghegan, Assistant Commissioner in charge of the Chicago office, and later head of the consolidated operation in Parkersburg. McGeoghegan expressed his concern over the problem faced by employees in the Chicago office in a letter to government officials in the Chicago region. After describing the details of the transfer, he noted, "The effect of the transfer of functions is of great concern to the Department of the Treasury, to the Bureau of the Public Debt, and to me personally. It is unfortunate that many of our fine employees are unable to relocate and are forced to seek other employment."[72] Enclosed with the letter was a booklet containing qualification briefs of all employees of the Chicago office who were seeking employment with other federal agencies in the Chicago area.

The important task of arranging for the smooth transfer of Chicago personnel to Parkersburg or to other jobs in the government was given to Mary K. Rose. Her records show that a total of 148 employees elected to move to Parkersburg, 176 took jobs at other agencies, 224 retired from government service, and 68 discontinued service.[73] In recognition of her effective performance of this difficult task, Rose was awarded a Meritorious Service Award at the Department of the Treasury's 1976 Annual Awards Ceremony. In presenting the award, George H. Dixon, Deputy Secretary of the Treasury, cited Rose for "her major contributions to the consolidation of two field offices of the Bureau of the Public Debt, which exemplify a career marked by dedication, loyalty and integrity."[74]

As part of the consolidation plan, with a new building being built in Parkersburg, it was decided to upgrade the computer operations there. Plans were made for replacing the old computer system, assuring greater use of third-generation software and equipment and creating a communications network among Washington, Parkersburg, and the Federal Reserve Banks.[75] The new building also allowed for operations that had been scattered in several old buildings in the downtown area of Parkersburg to be brought together in one facility. At the same time, the computer that had been used in Chicago was added to the Parkersburg operation. The new building in Parkersburg was opened at a dedication ceremony on February 10, 1975. The office was officially designated as the Savings Bond Operations Office.[76] As can be seen from Table 9.3, the number of employees in Parkersburg represented a decline of about 100 persons from the combined total that had previously worked in Parkersburg and Chicago.

The new office in Parkersburg began smooth operations almost immediately, with several employees getting awards from the Secretary of the Treasury in 1976. In addition to Mary K. Rose, as noted above, Marianne P. Heckman, a management analysis officer, was given a Meritorious Service Award in honor of her "consistently outstanding contributions which markedly increased productivity and reduced costs." She was the first woman at the Bureau to be given this award. Other awards went to Charles I. Gardner, director of the Division of Transactions, Richard F. Merz, deputy director of that division and Wilburn French, manager of the Records Storage Branch, Division of Management Services.[77]

As happened in many government agencies, the Bureau of the Public Debt itself was affected by the social changes that were taking place during the 1960s and

1970s. The Bureau had always had a high proportion of women among its employees. By 1975, it had a Federal Women's Program Coordinator, Terry Tucker, who was making plans for the observance of the International Women's Year. Commissioner Hintgen was on record as a strong supporter of an affirmative action approach to the employment of women, their promotion to higher levels of responsibility, and their participation in career development training.[78]

As part of this commitment to equal employment opportunity, at the Parkersburg field office, Kathy Moran was appointed as both Federal Women's Program Coordinator and Spanish-Speaking Program Coordinator on May 1, 1977.[79]

OPERATIONAL IMPROVEMENT

Even though it was coming under increasingly heavy pressure due to social changes as well as from continual increase in its workload, the Bureau continued making those small changes that added up to further improvement in its operations. Notable among the changes instituted were those made in the areas of computers, book-entry, service, employee suggestions, organization, and savings bonds. The following discussion highlights each of these areas.

Computers

In 1976, a Univac 1110 computer system was put into operation in the Parkersburg office. This new system replaced a burgeoning older system that used five computers and three different computer languages. The new system also included a communications link with the Washington office, which allowed the Washington office to begin phasing out its use of the computer system previously installed in the Office of the Secretary.[80]

The new system was a great advance over the previous one. It established COBOL as the standard language for the Bureau, reduced the number of savings bond computer programs from 660 to 394, cut down the number of reels of tape for the savings bond master files from 2,840 to 369, and improved computer planning throughout the Bureau. Leo Zajac, Director of the Division of ADP Management, was given an award for his leadership in implementing the new system by the Interagency Committee on ADP.[81]

Book Entry

Even with the use of book-entry recording of certain securities, the accounting procedures associated with new marketable issues remained complex. For definitive securities, accountability started when printed issues were delivered from the Bureau of Engraving and Printing to the Division of Securities Operations, which then reported the receipt of the securities for examination and storage to the Principal Accounts branch. When a security was paid for, a definitive security would be sent to the purchaser by the Federal Reserve Banks from their stock. In a book-entry transaction, upon payment for the security, the Federal Reserve Bank included a purchaser's amount of securities with a collective total for that issue in the account of the bank or dealer that had submitted the tender. The Federal Reserve Bank then reported the issue to the Principal Accounts branch as an original issue (OI) book-entry transaction. Purchases and sales of securities between individuals could still be made via wire transfer through the Federal Reserve Banks.[82]

To provide for the greatest possible service to purchasers, conversion of securities from book-entry to definitive form or the reverse was permitted. In going from a definitive security to book-entry, the definitive security would be treated as a retired security reported as a conversion to book-entry, with the book-entry issue being recorded as a book-entry issue on conversion. A similar but reversed type of recording would take place when book-entry issues were converted to definitive form. All such transactions would be reported to the Principal Accounts branch.[83]

To eliminate much of the paperwork involved with the issuance of securities in definitive form and the conversions taking place between definitive and book-entry forms, a Treasury-Federal Reserve task force was formed in 1976 to plan for the expansion of the book-entry system for issuing Treasury securities. The goal of the task force was to eliminate the issuance of definitive securities in all new Treasury offerings, with an overall purpose of reducing paperwork, protecting against loss, theft, and counterfeiting, and eliminating printing costs.[84]

By 1977, the task force was planning for a timed phaseout of definitive securities starting in 1977. A 52-week-bill issue in December 1976 became the first offering of securities in book-entry form only. Use of book-entry was expanded to include 26-week bills in June 1977 and 13-week bills in September 1977. For the first time, the Treasury provided book-entry accounts for investors who did not buy securities through financial institutions or dealers. As of September 30, 1977, the

Treasury had 6,690 book-entry accounts for a total of
$182 million.[85]   Table 9.4   outlines the growth of
book-entry accounts for the rest of the decade.

Table 9.4
Book-Entry Accounts as of December (1976-80)

	Number of Accounts	Face Value
		(billion)
1976	102	----
1977	19,429	0.5
1978	58,164	1.2
1979	291,169	5.1
1980	515,000	8.5

Source: Bette B. Anderson, Internal memorandum
          December 24, 1980, BPD File D-120.9.

Service

     Other areas of management improvement included
having several banks and branches of the Federal Reserve
System begin to report daily securities transactions on
magnetic tape.   In its continuing effort to serve the
public, in 1976 the Bureau formed the Issues Branch of
the Division of Transactions and Rulings at the
Parkersburg office.   The new branch was able to reduce
by three weeks the time needed to process claims for
bonds lost, stolen, or destroyed.[86]   In 1977, a Division
of Financial Management was formed to handle the
Bureau's budget and administrative accounting functions,
and a Division of Financing was established to act as
liaison with department-level officials who were
involved with debt financing policy, and to organize the
financing staff concerned with offerings and the conduct
of auctions into a separate entity, no longer part of
the Commissioner's immediate staff.[87]
     As one way of measuring the impact of all these
changes, it can be noted that in 1957 the staff at the
Chicago, New York, and Cincinnati offices totaled 2,349;
at that time the total of savings bonds outstanding was
$53.2 billion.   In February 1976, when savings bonds
outstanding totaled $68.1 billion, the number of
employees in the Savings Bond Operations Office was
1,248.   The installation of computers had reduced the
manpower needs in savings bond operations by nearly
half.[88]

Employee Suggestions

Employee assistance in improving operations continued to prove effective. Lewis W. Emrick, supervisory computer specialist at the Parkersburg office, in February 1978 was the first Bureau employee to be given an award under the Presidential Recognition Program started by President Carter in 1977. President Carter had asked that he be made aware of any suggestions made under an incentive awards program that produced first-year savings of $5,000. Emrick's suggestion that shipments of savings notes and retirement securities from Federal Reserve Banks be cut down to twice monthly produced first-year savings of $7,500.[89]

Savings Bonds

With the transition to the new Series EE and HH savings bonds taking place in early 1980, two new conditions governing the sale of these issues helped to reduce administrative costs at the Bureau. First, the minimum time required of holders before redemption of their securities was extended from two months to six months. Second, the $25 denomination was eliminated and the accrual rate at which bonds were sold was changed. These changes served to reduce the number of bonds that had to be sold for equivalent dollar volume when comparing Series E with Series EE.[90]

The program of reporting savings bond sales on tape also increased. By 1977 major issuers of savings bonds were reporting $67.7 million sales on tape, 13 percent of E bond sales and 50 percent of payroll deduction sales. The handling of daily summary reports from Federal Reserve Banks was placed completely on a computerized basis during 1979.[91]

LOOKING AHEAD

As the decade of the 1970s ended, the Bureau continued its search for new and innovative management methods and computer applications. Starting in 1980, the Bureau began preparing a series of five-year plans. During the same year, an experiment was undertaken that permitted employees to work under a system of flexi-time.[92]

There is one final project that deserves mention, for it is a harbinger of things to come in the next decade. Because of the growth in book-entry accounts, which in many cases were still kept on a manual recording system, problems were arising in ensuring a timely processing of the issue and redemption of 13 and 26-week bills. In fact, unusual circumstances in April and May 1979 had resulted in 4,000 redemption checks being mailed out after the due date of the securities.[93]

The delay resulted in lost interest of about $125,000 to the debt holders. Since there was no legal authority to enable the Bureau to compensate these debt holders for their loss, a bill to authorize payment of this lost interest and to extend the authority of the Bureau to make payments for such future losses was recommended by the House and Senate. At the same time, a suit was filed on behalf of the debt holders to compel the interest payments, and the Justice Department was in the process of settling those claims.[94]

This problem occurred despite automation. During fiscal year 1979, a first phase of selected automation of book-entry accounts maintained by the Treasury was completed. This system made it possible for the Treasury to service accounts with computer-generated statements of account and to issue checks for discount and redemption payments. Faster service and more timely issuance of payments were thereby provided to investors.[95] To avoid the type of delays in payment just mentioned, however, the system would have to be expanded. Over the next several years, this expansion would take place, generating a revolution in the sale of marketable government securities.

NOTES

1. Rudolph G. Penner and Alan J. Abramson, Broken Purse Strings (Washington, D.C.: Urban Institute Press, 1988), pp. 9, 25.

2. U.S. Government, Statistical Abstract of the United States (Washington, D.C.: 1985), p. 322.

3. Herbert Stein, Presidential Economics (New York: Simon & Schuster, 1984), pp. 133-134.

4. Wallace C. Peterson, Income, Employment and Economic Growth 6th ed. (New York: W.W. Norton, 1988), p. 605.

5. James Tobin, "A Keynesian View of the Budget Deficit," in Robert H. Fink and James C. High, eds., A Nation in Debt (Frederick, Md.: University Publications of America, 1987), p. 79.

6. Stein, Presidential Economics, p. 134.

7. James D. Savage, _Balanced Budgets and American Politics_ (Ithaca, N.Y.:   Cornell University Press, 1988), p. 183.

8. Stein, _Presidential Economics_, pp. 200-204.

9. Secretary of the Treasury, _Annual Report_ (Washington, D.C.:   1973), p. 11.

10. Secretary of the Treasury, _Annual Report_ (Washington, D.C.:   1972), p. 18.

11. Douglas A. Hibbs, Jr., _The American Political Economy_ (Cambridge, Mass.:   Harvard University Press, 1987), p. 271.

12. Penner and Abramson, _Broken Purse Strings_, p. 9.

13. Penner and Abramson, _Broken Purse Strings_, p. 5.

14. Alan L. Sorkin, _Monetary and Fiscal Policy and Business Cycles in the Modern Era_ (Lexington, Mass.: Lexington Books, 1988), pp. 66-67.

15. Peterson, _Income_, p. 609.

16. Savage, _Balanced Budgets_, p. 183.

17. Secretary of the Treasury, _Annual Report_ (Washington, D.C.:   1975), p. 9.

18. Secretary of the Treasury, _Annual Report_ (Washington, D.C.:   1976), p. 11.

19. Secretary of the Treasury, _Annual Report_ (1976), p. 33.

20. Savage, _Balanced Budgets_, p. 190.

21. Savage, _Balanced Budgets_, p. 223.

22. Savage, _Balanced Budgets_, p. 190.

23. Secretary of the Treasury, _Annual Report_ (Washington, D.C.:   1978), p. 15.

24. Secretary of the Treasury, _Annual Report_ (Washington, D.C.:   1979), p. 15.

25. Secretary of the Treasury, _Annual Report_ (Washington, D.C.:   1980), p. 9.

26. William H. Anderson, _Financing Modern Government_ (Boston: Houghton Mifflin, 1973), p. 14.

27. Robert Eisner and Paul J. Pieper, " How to Make Sense of the Deficit," in Robert H. Fink and Jack C. High, eds., _A Nation in Debt_ (Frederick, Md.: University Publications of America, 1987), p. 93.

28. Secretary of the Treasury, _Annual Report_ (1973), p. 12.

29. U.S. Department of the Treasury, _Public Debt Accounting_ (Washington, D.C.: 1976), pp. 7-13.

30. Secretary of the Treasury, _Annual Report_ (1973), p. 12.

31. U.S. Department of the Treasury, "Wrestling with Leviathan--How Treasury Manages the Debt," _Treasury Papers_, October 1976, p. 14.

32. Secretary of the Treasury, _Annual Report_ (Washington, D.C.: 1971), pp. 10-11.

33. Secretary of the Treasury, _Annual Report_ (1972), p. 14.

34. Secretary of the Treasury, _Annual Report_ (1976), p. 12.

35. Secretary of the Treasury, _Annual Report_ (Washington, D.C.: 1970), p. 13.

36. Secretary of the Treasury, _Annual Report_ (1975), p. 11.

37. Secretary of the Treasury, _Annual Report_ (Washington, D.C.: 1980), p. 11.

38. Secretary of the Treasury, _Annual Report_ (1979), p. 160.

39. U.S. Government Printing Office, Regulations Governing United States Savings Bonds, Series EE and HH, _Federal Register,_ December 26, 1979.

40. Secretary of the Treasury, _Annual Report_ (1973), pp. 13-15.

41. Secretary of the Treasury, _Annual Report_ (1976), pp. 30, 33.

42. Secretary of the Treasury, _Annual Report_ (1973), pp. 13-14, and (1976), p. 33.

43. Secretary of the Treasury, _Annual Report_ (Washington, D.C.: 1977), p. 14.

44. Secretary of the Treasury, _Annual Report_ (1978), p. 15.

45. Secretary of the Treasury, _Annual Report_ (1979), p. 14.

46. Secretary of the Treasury, _Annual Report_ (1980), p. 13.

47. Secretary of the Treasury, _Annual Report_ (1978), p. 14.

48. Secretary of the Treasury, _Annual Report_ (1970), p. 103.

49. Secretary of the Treasury, _Annual Report_ (1975), p. 178.

50. Secretary of the Treasury, _Annual Report_ (1980), p. 163.

51. Secretary of the Treasury, _Annual Report_ (1980), p. 161.

52. Secretary of the Treasury, _Annual Report_ (1970), p. 102.

53. Secretary of the Treasury, _Annual Report_ (1971), p. 109.

54. U.S. Department of the Treasury, Bureau of the Public Debt, _Public Debt News,_ First Quarter, 1972, p. 5.

55. Secretary of the Treasury, _Annual Report_ (1970), pp. 110-111.

56. Secretary of the Treasury, _Annual Report_ (1970), p. 102.

57. Secretary of the Treasury, _Annual Report_ (1971), p. 110.

58. Frederick W. Hickman, Memorandum to H. J. Hintgen (Washington, D.C.: Bureau of the Public Debt File 120.611, April 3, 1973).

59. U.S. Department of the Treasury, Bureau of the Public Debt, <u>Public Debt News,</u> First Quarter, 1973, p. 4.

60. Secretary of the Treasury, <u>Annual Report</u> (1973), p. 116.

61. U.S. Department of the Treasury, Bureau of the Public Debt, <u>Request for Purchase of Computer Equipment</u> (Parkersburg W.Va.: September 1969), pp. 10-12.

62. U.S. Department of the Treasury, Bureau of the Public Debt, Internal Memorandum (Washington, D.C.: October 18, 1974).

63. Secretary of the Treasury, <u>Annual Report</u> (1970), p. 103.

64. H.J. Hintgen, <u>Circular letter,</u> BPD File D-120.9 (Washington, D.C.: March 20, 1972).

65. Secretary of the Treasury, <u>Annual Report</u> (1972), p. 119.

66. U.S. Department of the Treasury, Bureau of the Public Debt, Internal Memorandum, Undated, located in BPD files, 5.

67. Secretary of the Treasury, <u>Annual Report</u> (1972), p. 121.

68. Secretary of the Treasury, <u>Annual Report</u> (1973), p. 117.

69. Secretary of the Treasury, <u>Annual Report</u> (1974), p. 131.

70. U.S. Department of the Treasury, Bureau of the Public Debt, <u>Public Debt News,</u> October 1982, pp. 1-3.

71. U.S. Department of the Treasury, Bureau of the Public Debt, <u>Schedule for Assisting Displaced Employees Find Jobs</u> (Chicago Office Memorandum,   November 11, 1974), located in Parkersburg office files.

72. Michael McGeoghegan, Letter, Public Debt Files, November 20, 1974.

73. Mary K. Rose, Memorandum (Parkersburg, W.Va.: February 21, 1975), pp. 3-4.

74. U.S. Department of the Treasury, Bureau of the
Public Debt Field Office, Newsletter, March 1, 1977,
p. 1.

75. Secretary of the Treasury, Annual Report (1974),
p. 131.

76. Secretary of the Treasury, Annual Report (1975),
p. 176.

77. U.S. Department of the Treasury, Bureau of the
Public Debt Field Office, Newsletter, March 1977,
p. 1.

78. U.S. Department of the Treasury, Bureau of the
Public Debt, Public Debt News, Spring Issue, 1975, p. 7.

79. U.S. Department of the Treasury, Bureau of the
Public Debt, Field Notes, 1978, Issue 2, p. 3.

80. Secretary of the Treasury, Annual Report (1976),
p. 181.

81. U.S. Department of the Treasury, Bureau of the
Public Debt, Public Debt News, June 1979, p. 2.

82. U.S. Department of the Treasury, Public Debt
Accounting, 1976, pp. 24-32.

83. U.S. Department of the Treasury, Public Debt
Accounting, 1976, pp. 40-45.

84. Secretary of the Treasury, Annual Report (1976),
p. 181.

85. Secretary of the Treasury, Annual Report (1977),
p. 167.

86. Secretary of the Treasury, Annual Report (1976),
p. 182.

87. Secretary of the Treasury, Annual Report (1977),
p. 168.

88. U.S. Department of the Treasury, Bureau of the
Public Debt, Draft Memo, P.D. 2994 (88.57), 1976, insert
to p. 1.

89. U.S. Department of the Treasury, Bureau of the
Public Debt, Field Notes, 1978, No. 1, p. 1.

90. Secretary of the Treasury, Annual Report (1980),
p. 162.

91. Secretary of the Treasury, <u>Annual Report</u> (1979), p. 161.

92. Secretary of the Treasury, <u>Annual Report</u> (1980), p. 161.

93. Bette B. Anderson, Internal Memorandum, Washington, D.C.: BPD File D-120.9, December 20, 1980.

94. H.J. Hintgen, Draft Memorandum, Washington, D.C.: in BPD files, undated.

95. Secretary of the Treasury, <u>Annual Report</u> (1979), p. 160.

10

Economic Experimentation and Debt Expansion (1981–88)

If the contents of this book were written in the same proportion as the growth of the public debt, this would not only be the longest chapter, it would also be longer than the previous nine chapters combined. In the 1980s, more debt would be added to the federal government's account than had been incurred during the previous 200 years. The explosion of debt would come as part of an experiment in fiscal policy that took place in the early years of the decade. That part of the story is readily told, however, and does not take up much of this chapter. Instead, the length of this chapter is attributable to the many new programs the Treasury and the Bureau of the Public Debt had to undertake to manage and administer the large debt increase the decade saw.

As the 1980s began, the U.S. economy was going through a difficult period. Despite the brief recession of 1980, inflation had not abated. When the recovery came, the level of price increases accelerated to a pace that reached 13.5 percent for the year. At the same time, the unemployment rate, which had been as high as 7.5 percent, showed little sign of great improvement. To many economists this combination of continued high unemployment and high inflation signalled the end of Keynesian economics because this combination was not supposed to take place. President Carter had tacitly abandoned Keynesian ideas when he ran a full-employment budget surplus during his last years in office.

THE REAGAN REVOLUTION

With a change of administration in 1981, however, the government's policy for dealing with the economy underwent what came to be known as a revolution. The economic plan proposed by President Ronald Reagan

represented a sharp break with trends over the last
decade; it included a tax cut, a reduction in federal
government expenditures for nondefense items, slower
growth in the money supply, and reduction of government
regulation.   It was anticipated that these measures
would enable the government to increase defense spending
and balance its budget.[1]

The key ingredient to the Reagan program was its
emphasis on supply-side economics. For over 100 years,
economists had been aware of the importance of both
supply and demand in determining the state of the
economy. One difference among schools of economics was
in their imputation as to which of these two forces was
the leading factor. During the Great Depression of the
1930s, when there was no doubt as to the ability of
business to produce and supply goods, Keynes identified
declines in consumer and investment demand as most
important in determining why the economy faltered. Thus
he advocated policies to compensate for increases and
decreases in private sector demand as important for
returning the economy to full employment.

During the 1970s, the combination of high prices
and high unemployment called into question the ability
of business to supply all the goods and services that
were being demanded, especially since measures of annual
increases in productivity showed a decline in growth.
For this reason, the attention of economists began
focusing on the area of supply. Programs to enhance the
productive capability of business were being devised by
a group of economic thinkers who called themselves
supply-siders.

The main villain in causing the decline in
productivity, according to the supply-siders, was the
high tax rates imposed by the federal government. These
rates, it was argued, acted as a negative influence on
individual decisions to work, save, and invest.   To
support this argument, supply-side proponents relied on
the "Laffer curve," an economic model generally
attributed to economist Arthur Laffer. Laffer had
argued that when tax rates were zero percent, the
government took in zero dollars in tax collections; when
the tax rate was 100 percent, the government would also
take in zero dollars, because individuals would not
bother to work if they had to pay all their income to
the government. It followed from this logic that there
was a point where an increase in taxes would so stifle
the desire to work and produce that tax collections
would decline. When the economy was at this point it
was better to reduce taxes to encourage individuals to
work harder, earn more income, and increase tax
collections.

To be sure, the Laffer curve did not take into
account the fact that individuals also receive benefits

from the government, something that would greatly expand at a 100 percent tax rate; some work might still be forthcoming. More to the point, Laffer did not present any evidence that the economy was above his critical point where tax reductions would bring about increased tax collections. Rather, he and other supply-siders implicitly assumed that it was, and pushed for tax cuts. As George Gilder, a leading advocate, put it, the proposed tax cuts would work "by increasing the incentives of workers and investors to supply additional goods and services to the market."[2]

There was not total agreement to this plan. Walter Heller, Chairman of the Council of Economic Advisors during the Kennedy-Johnson years, pointed out that the tax cuts would have minimal impact on human behavior. He noted, "The eager beavers will work harder, and the laid-back people will work less."[3] Here was the crux of the issue. Supply-siders believed that tax cuts would improve the income position of workers and investors by giving them more take-home pay. In response to being able to keep more of their pay, they would be willing to work more hours or invest more of their money in productive ventures.

It was just as likely that they would take advantage of their improved conditions by taking more leisure time. If that was the case, since the psychic income of greater leisure is not taxable, individuals would be better off but tax collections would not increase. The question boils down to whether or not humans are industrious by nature. As noted in chapter 2, for example, Alexander Hamilton took a dim view of the native industry of the masses and believed that high taxes were needed to make them work harder in order to maintain their standard of living.

Perhaps because of his experiences as a film-actor during and following World War II, when high marginal tax rates took a large portion of incomes above $100,000, Reagan disagreed with Hamilton on this issue. He also disagreed with Hamilton, in principle, on the size and role of the federal government. Reagan even went so far as to cite the notion of Hamilton's foe, Jefferson, "A wise and frugal government . . . shall restrain men from injuring one another" in support of his views.[4] The Reagan program aimed also at reducing the size of the federal government.

The overall Reagan program would involve planned tax cuts to stimulate the supply-side of the economy and cuts in government spending to lessen the role of the federal government in the economy and the nation. The intended effect would be to reduce the size of the government budget deficit and to achieve a balanced budget. Reagan found deficits to be an unsettling influence on the economy. As he put it, "The

<u>uncontrolled</u> growth of government spending has been a primary cause of the sustained high inflation experienced by the American economy."[5]

Reagan seemed to have overlooked the fact that the Carter budgets actually violated the full-employment budget principle by showing a full-employment surplus even during a recession; in fact, during the three nonrecession years of the Carter administration, government deficits as a percent of GNP fell. Reagan did follow Carter in one respect. As had Carter, Reagan blithely projected that his program would balance the federal government's budget by the end of his initial term of office in 1984.[6] His confidence was based on government budget cuts taking place along with the increased revenue that would result from the supply-side tax cuts.

In more specific terms, the Reagan program was achieved through passage of the Economic Recovery Tax Act of 1981, the largest tax cut in U.S. history, which reduced individual income taxes by 25 percent over a three-year period and cut certain business income taxes. It was estimated that the individual tax reductions would cost the government $626 billion in tax collections over the first five years of the program and the business tax cuts would cost $188 billion.[7] As part of the plan, a portion of these revenue losses was to be offset by the proposed cuts in the federal government's budget, which were targeted at $471 billion over the same five-year period.[8]

The tax cuts were designed to promote economic growth, but something still had to be done about inflation. Here the new plan enlisted the aid of the Federal Reserve in its role of controlling monetary policy. There is a theory in economics that establishes, under certain conditions, a strong, direct relationship between the rate of growth in the money supply and changes in prices of goods and services, that is, inflation. Using this theory as a guide in its efforts to reduce the potential for inflation that existed in the early 1980s, the Federal Reserve continued the policy it had started in 1979 by lowering its target rate of growth in the money supply (M-1 in technical terms) by 3 percent, aiming for an annual growth rate of 2.5 to 5.5 percent.[9] Advocates of this policy felt that if the Federal Reserve clearly stated its tight money policy, the public, recognizing that inflation was ending, would quickly adjust its behavior to the new policy, and thus a recession could be avoided.

The new policy also took into account the rising government debt. The total public debt broke the $1 trillion mark on October 22, 1981.[10] President Reagan had already tried to put that figure into perspective.

In his state of the union speech on February 19, 1981, he pointed out, "A trillion dollars would be a stack of $1,000 bills 67 miles high."[11]   The President in that speech outlined his plan for balancing the budget by cutting spending in nondefense areas and bringing in more tax revenues as the economy began to grow.   Once the budget was balanced, a debt reduction program could take place.

THE ECONOMY IN THE 1980s

The economy did not grow, however; it went into a recession. Much of the blame for the recession has been put on the Federal Reserve, whose monetary policy reduced the money supply much faster than the Reagan plan had intended. Along with the slowdown of the money supply came higher interest rates, with the prime rate hitting 20 percent and yields on ten-year Treasury securities surpassing 14 percent. The negative impact of the high interest rates on economic activity more than offset the positive stimulation of the tax reduction package. The recession officially started in July 1981, with the unemployment rate reaching 10.8 percent in November 1982. The usual expectation is that a recession will cause the government's budget deficit to grow. This expectation was fulfilled in an extreme way during the 1981-82 recession, when the deficit jumped from $79 billion in fiscal year 1981 to $128 billion in fiscal year 1982 and $208 billion in fiscal year 1983.

As a result of the recession and the ensuing deficits, the projected balanced budget for 1984 never came close to materializing. For the period 1981-86, the Reagan administration's prediction of tax receipts fell short of actual collections by $538.5 billion, and the anticipated $471.2 billion in budget cuts never came close to being realized.

The economy began its recovery in November 1982, and total output in the economy (GNP) has continued to expand through the last quarter of 1989. The inflation rate fell rapidly to the range of an annual rate of 4 to 5 percent, and the unemployment rate hit a 15-year low of 5 percent early in 1989. This economic growth has caused some reductions in the size of the deficit, as did corrections of loopholes in the tax cut plan that were enacted in 1982 and minor tax increases in 1983-84.[12]   On the expenditure side of the government's ledger, defense spending has continued to increase and the cuts in nondefense spending have not materialized.

Assessment of the overall success of the Reagan program is difficult to make at this early time. It is true that economic growth has been healthy for over six

years.   But many economists would not ascribe that
growth to supply-side effects.   The level of work
remains an elusive concept to measure, while saving and
investment levels have not shown any startling changes
from their long-term trends.   Keynesian economists,
looking at the deficits of the last eight years in light
of the full-employment budget principle of a balanced
budget at full employment, would find that the economic
growth of the 1980s is based more on demand growth than
on any supply-side effects. As one writer has expressed
this point of view, "When the recovery did occur, it was
due to consumption spending, which is a decidedly
Keynesian policy.   Incurring deficits to stimulate
demand is far removed from Laffer's Curve or supply-side
scenarios."[13]

     There is as yet little evidence in support of any
interpretation of the efficacy of the supply-side
experiment. Economists are well aware that it takes
much longer for supply to change than for demand.   The
present recovery may well be dominated by demand, while
the supply-side effects may be longer in coming.

     Viewed in historical perspective, the Reagan
program has much in common with the old-time Republican
program of trickle down installed by Andrew Mellon in
the 1920s.   In both cases, tax cuts to the wealthy were
expected to lead to economic expansion, the benefits of
which would trickle down to the rest of society.   Nobel
laureate and prominent Keynesian James Tobin argued that
this was the intent of the experiment when the program
was being installed; and in his famous interview in
Atlantic Monthly David Stockman, the budget expert of
the Reagan administration, admitted the supply-side
policies were a "Trojan horse" for a trickle-down
approach.[14]   But there was a difference between the
Reagan and Mellon plans.

     Mellon had made up for the revenue loss from lower
tax rates for the wealthy by raising tariffs.   His
program resulted in budget surpluses for most of the
1920s.   As a committed free trader, Reagan could not
support this option. His program instead resulted in a
situation where the government gave tax cuts to the rich
only to borrow them back again.   In any event, Reagan
put the tax cuts above any need to balance the budget.
As he explained it, "The deficits we propose are much
larger than I would like, but they're a necessary evil
in the real world today."[15]   Then Congressman Jack Kemp
was more direct in setting forth a new political view on
deficits: "The Republican Party no longer worships at
the altar of a balanced budget."[16]   Fiscal prudence now
seemed to advise that the government budget be run with
an eye toward maximizing the potential for tax cuts.

     This period also saw improvement in the budgetary
process. The centralization of budgeting in the Budget

Committees of the House and Senate created a more public process for compiling the budget, which often led to an acrimonious debate over the budget between Congress and the President. At the same time, however, the increased use of professional economists in the Congressional Budget Office added a conservative bias to spending programs; one of the tasks of the Office is to make five-year projections of spending on every bill proposed in Congress, which cuts down on the number of bills that have a small initial funding request that balloons in later years.[17]

The Gramm-Rudman-Hollings Act, passed in 1985, was designed to reduce the government's budget deficit to zero by 1991 by mandating across-the-board budget cuts if specific goals are not met in the annual budget; but its impact has yet to be felt. As a result, federal government budget deficits considerably above the historical average have continued throughout the 1980s (see Table 10.1).

Table 10.1
Federal Government Deficits, Fiscal Year Basis
(1980-88) (in billions of dollars)

1980	1981	1982	1983	1984	1985	1986	1987	1988
73.8	78.9	127.9	207.8	185.3	212.3	220.7	173.2	155.0

Source: A. Sorkin, Monetary and Fiscal Policy & Business Cycles in the Modern Era (Lexington, Mass.: Lexington Books, 1988), p. 112.

There is still debate among economists over whether these deficits have been detrimental to the economy. As noted above, Keynesians would argue that they have created the long recovery of the 1980s. But they and other economists might also point out that the deficit has resulted in high interest rates that have actually stifled investment. In addition, high interest rates increase the amount the government must spend for interest payments, which will then add to the deficit. Table 10.2 gives a measure of the interest rate paid on the debt during the 1980s.

With interest payments on the public debt constantly adding to the deficit, it seems unlikely that deficits and the debt will be reduced. As of September 30, 1989, the total public debt outstanding was $2.88 trillion,[18] an increase of more than twofold over eight years. Whether that debt has become too large is not at issue here, although that question will be considered in

the next chapter. The point to be made here is that the
debt has increased tremendously during the 1980s, and
the increase has had to be managed by the Treasury
Department and administered by the Bureau of the Public
Debt.

Table 10.2
Composite Yield on Treasury Bonds of over Ten Years
Maturity (Yearly Average)

1980	1981	1982	1983	1984	1985	1986	1987	1988	1989
10.8	12.9	12.2	10.8	12.0	10.8	8.1	8.6	9.0	8.6

Source: Cambridge Planning and Analytics, Inc.
         Datadisk (Cambridge, Mass.: 1989).

GENERAL TREASURY ACTIVITIES

The large size of the debt resulted in an increased
market for government securities. As interest rates
rose, more individuals were drawn into investing in
government securities and away from other securities
they had previously purchased. To handle this large
volume of purchases by many new customers, the Treasury
Department and the Bureau of the Public Debt produced
several innovations in the products they offered and the
methods of serving the public that purchased them.
Specific changes were made by conducting auctions on a
regular schedule, offering a new class of "stripped
securities," and putting variable rates of interest on
savings bonds. Each of these changes will be considered
in turn.

Auctions

The Treasury continued previously established
procedures by selling the bulk of its marketable
securities at auction; the auction method had first been
used for Treasury bills in 1929 and had been extended to
include notes and bonds in the early 1970s.
During the 1980s, the auction of government
securities was managed by the Office of Financing of the
Bureau of the Public Debt using the following methods.
The usual practice was that once high-level officials at
the Treasury Department decided how much was to be
borrowed in a given offering, the Office of Financing

took over responsibility for most of the initial administrative aspects of the offering. It prepared the announcement to the press giving the details of the types of securities to be offered for sale. Since this information is very important to potential purchasers of the securities, and since prior knowledge of specific details could be used to unfair advantage by unscrupulous parties, the planning for, and conduct of auctions has always taken place under the strictest security.

Once the auction date was announced, investors submitted their bids, either to the Federal Reserve Banks and branches or directly to the Bureau. The Division of Investor Accounts at the Bureau maintained a "bank window" at the main Treasury Building for the receipt of bids.[19] In 1985 that facility was moved to the Bureau's part of the Bureau of Engraving and Printing Annex. All bids received by the Federal Reserve Banks and branches and the Accounting Control/Securities Transactions branches of the Division of Investor Accounts were compiled and then sent by wire report to the Office of Financing, where the auction took place. In the auction process, each bid report was independently added twice to make sure the details added up to the total as stated by the reporting office, and at the same time each competitive bid price was verified against wire code words. An auditor from the Bureau's Division of Internal Audit was present throughout the auction to verify that the auction results were accurate.

The auctioneer (one member of the two-person auction team), also known as the "wire person," accepted all noncompetitive amounts reported (it was the job of the Federal Reserve Banks to ensure that no noncompetitive tenders exceeded the legal maximum of $1 million each). Then, the competitive bid totals already arranged in order from the highest to the lowest price offered on each bank report were accepted, starting with the highest price, until the total of accepted bids equalled the amount announced for sale. When the amounts at the various accepted prices were determined, calculations of the weighted average price to be paid by noncompetitive bidders were made. All of these calculations would be made by both members of the auction team and would also be checked by the auditor as well as by a third person (the "verifier") in the Office of Financing who had not taken part in the previous verifications or calculations. Once the final results were confirmed, a press release would be prepared announcing the results of the auction to the public. On the issue date, normally three days after the auction, the auction wires would be adjusted by each of the reporting offices to include timely postmarked noncompetitive tenders that had been received after the auction deadline but on or prior to the issue date. Then the new securities would be issued, ending the Office of Financing's involvement with that particular issue, but just starting work for other components of the Bureau.[20]

The auction process was also helped by the Treasury's emerging practice of conducting its sales on a regularly scheduled basis. As one commentator noted in the early 1980s, "When the market is able to anticipate approximately what the Treasury is likely to offer, and to some extent prepare for it, market participants are likely to have a better appetite for the Treasury's offerings."[21]

By 1987, the Treasury's offering cycle had been routinized as follows: A series of 13-week bills and a series of 26-week bills are offered each week, with the announcement coming on Tuesday, the auction taking place on the next Monday, and the bills issued on the Thursday after the auction; 52-week bills are offered every four weeks, with the announcement every fourth Friday, the auction taking place on the following Thursday, and the securities being issued on the Thursday following the auction; two-year notes are issued at the end of each month; four-year notes are sold near the end of March, June, September, and December; five-year two-month notes are issued in early January, March, July, and October; seven-year notes are issued in early January, April, July, and October; and three-year notes, ten-year notes, and 30-year bonds are issued on the 15th of February, May, August, and November.[22] Even though these regular offerings did not reduce the workload at the Bureau, their predictability did make it more manageable.

Stripped Securities

To make marketable government securities more attractive to the investing public, some changes were made in the handling of securities. Starting in 1982, for example, two prominent dealers in government securities, Merrill Lynch and Salomon Brothers, began a practice of separating interest payments from bearer securities in order to sell the parts separately. This process, known as stripping, often made it possible, especially in terms of the high interest rates that existed at that time, to separately sell the interest coupons and principal portion of a government security for more than it would sell for as a whole.

The idea behind stripped securities was to reduce both the principal and interest coupon portions of a security to a "zero-coupon security." (A zero-coupon security is one that bears no interest payment per se, but is sold at a discount from its face value, with the discount being large enough to equal the yield on the security if it were held to maturity.) The benefit to a securities dealer firm is that it could buy long-term securities earning a high yield and then sell stripped coupons as short-term securities earning a lower yield. To create stripped securities, the dealers would buy a government security, deposit it in a bank custody account, and then issue receipts representing ownership claims on the face value and coupons of the security.[23]

The process of stripping in this way was cumbersome, so the Treasury acknowledged and accommodated that market when in August 1984 it began offering "STRIPS," Separate Trading of Registered Interest and Principal of Treasury Securities. STRIPS represented a new form of book-entry security in which principal and interest payments could be separated and sold independently on the open market. Following the allotment of new securities to successful bidders in auctions of selected issues, buyers would be allowed to request that their securities be issued under STRIPS.[24]

By 1987, as interest rates declined, investors often found it advantageous to recombine their previously stripped book-entry securities; at that point, the total security might be sold for more than its separated parts. In the spring of 1987, the Treasury began allowing investors to reconstitute the book-entry components that had been previously issued as STRIPS.[25] By September 30, 1988, $61 billion out of $289 billion in eligible securities were in stripped form and $13 billion had been reconstituted.[26]

In addition to financial gains from recombining stripped securities in either book-entry or bearer form there was also a problem of safety concerning the latter. Stripped coupons or principal (corpus) components of bearer securities are, of course, negotiable by bearer when they become due, so holders of such instruments must safeguard them against loss or theft. The previously mentioned substantial stripping of physical securities in the 1980s had now produced problems for institutional holders, such as the need for fairly elaborate accounting/control procedures for literally thousands of small, detached, unmatured coupons, and the continually increasing costs for insurance and vault storage fees. In the spring of 1985, a Federal Reserve-Treasury task force was formed to consider a way to establish a book-entry system for these stripped coupons; Robert ("Bob") Reed of the Division of Securities Operations and Tom Minter of the Division of Public Debt Accounts were the Treasury's representatives in the group. The system devised by the group, CUBES (Coupons Under Book-Entry Safekeeping), allowed participating depository institutions and their customers to make a onetime conversion of their stripped coupons to a book-entry form in a system operated by the New York Federal Reserve Bank. During the authorized period, January 5 through April 30, 1987, about 87 institutions submitted 410,000 coupons for conversion.[27] The total value of the coupons was over $13 billion, representing nearly two-thirds of the total face amount of all coupons on outstanding Treasury bearer securities at the time.

Savings Bonds

On the savings bond side of securities issues, the high interest rates of the early 1980s were highly detrimental in terms of sales and redemption of bonds. Because interest rates on savings bonds could not be changed quickly, they lagged behind the increased rates of return available on other forms of investment. As a result, investors began putting their money in those alternate forms of investment, such as certificates of deposit and money market funds. The total value of savings bonds outstanding fell from $79.9 billion in 1979 to $68 billion in 1982.[28]

To spur sales, the Treasury placed a variable interest rate on Series EE bonds; after November 1, 1982, Series EE bonds held for at least five years would earn interest at a market-based rate (roughly equal to 85 percent of the average yield on five-year Treasury marketable securities), or a minimum rate established at the time of sale. In this way, interest rates on the Series EE bonds would remain competitive with other investment instruments available to the public.[29] As a result, sales of savings bonds increased by 26 percent during the first year of variable rates[30] and continued on an upward trend that has prevailed throughout the 1980s, as shown in Table 10.3.

Sales of savings bonds, nevertheless, did not keep pace with the growth of the total public debt. With the percentage of the total debt being held as savings bonds declining (see Table 10.3), other financing vehicles were considered and each used briefly to try to find a stable source of funding for government securities. In 1984, for example, the Treasury offered some foreign-targeted securities that were not available to U.S. citizens; the purpose of these securities was to attract funds from foreign investors.[31] By 1988, with the advent of TREASURY DIRECT, the Treasury was also able to offer investors a program of automatic reinvestment in Treasury bills for a period of up to two years. For the impact of all these changes on the ownership of the total debt, see Table 10.4. As a result of its debt

---

Table 10.3
Savings Bonds Outstanding at Year's End (1982-88)

1982	1983	1984	1985	1986	1987	1988
68.0	70.7	73.1	78.1	90.6	99.2	106.2

(In Billion Dollars)

5.7	5.0	4.4	4.0	4.1	4.1	4.1

(Percent of Total Debt)

Source: U.S. Department of the Treasury, _Federal Reserve Bulletin,_ January 1986 (for years 1982-83); _Federal Reserve Bulletin,_ January 1989 (for years 1984-88).

---

management operations, the Treasury was able to extend the average length of maturity of the total debt from four years one month at the end of 1983 to five years nine months at the end of 1987.[32]

The impact of these funding efforts and changes on the operations of the Bureau of the Public Debt, while serious, was kept within bounds. The large number and amount of offerings added to the recordkeeping tasks of the Bureau. In addition, the new types of securities or subsystems, such as STRIPS and CUBES, sales to foreigners, and planned reinvestment, complicated that recordkeeping. But the Bureau had been amply prepared for these tasks. During the 1970s, marketable government securities had nearly all been transformed into manual book-entry accounts. The next logical step was to convert those handwritten accounts to electronic form, using the methods of modern automatic data processing equipment and systems to create an automated book-entry system. This was a step that the Bureau was well equipped to take, both in terms of the equipment it had available and in the expertise and experience of its staff.

THE BUREAU OF THE PUBLIC DEBT KEEPS PACE

In the 1980s, the overall debt administration work of the Bureau was still organized by product. The sale and redemption of marketable securities took place in the Office of Washington Operations, located in the Engraving and Printing Annex where about 700 people were employed, and Savings Bond Operations were housed in Parkersburg, West Virginia, with a staff of 1,150 employees. About 200 people worked in the Office of Administration in Washington; this office had been

reorganized on November 1, 1981, when the Division of
Management and Support Services had been replaced by
three new divisions: Management Analysis, Personnel
Management, and Administrative Services. The ADP
Management Division performed computer systems design

Table 10.4
Ownership of Gross Debt, End of Period
(1984, 1986, and 1988)

	1984	1986	1988
U.S. Govt. Agencies & Trust Funds	16.8	17.9	21.2
Federal Reserve Banks	10.8	9.3	8.8
Individuals	9.4	7.9	6.9
Commercial Banks	13.4	11.8	7.8
Foreign and International	11.8	10.9	12.8
Other*	37.8	42.2	42.5

*Includes State and Local Treasuries, Insurance
Companies, Savings and Loans, Corporations, Pension
Funds, etc.

Source: Calculated from data in Federal Reserve
          Bulletin, January 1989.

---

work with a staff divided between Washington (50 people)
and Parkersburg (30 people). The Office of Financing
with its staff of 12 had charge of the auctioning of
marketable securities. The Division of Internal Audit
and the Office of Chief Counsel rounded out operations
with staffs of 25 and 13, respectively. Additional
office space was contained in the main Treasury Building
and three office buildings in Washington. The total
number of employees was about 2,200.[33]
     In 1981 a T-bill Systems Development Group had been
formed to implement automation of the T-bill book-entry
system. The group was composed of about 30 system
accountants, computer specialists, and support staff.
As the high interest rates of the period enticed more
individual investors into the purchase of marketable
government securities, the workload at the Bureau had
continued to expand. In the area of Treasury bills, for
example, the number of accounts had grown from 20,000 in
1977 to over 800,000 accounts in 1981.[34] The number of
open Treasury bill accounts would moderate over the rest
of the 1980s, reaching 915,463 in July 1982, 924,764 in
July 1984,[35] and leveling off thereafter to 772,000 in
August 1986 as interest rates declined to their lowest

level in nine years.[36]   Registered bond and note
accounts also showed a sharp increase of 211,000 in one
year, as their total went to 853,539 in July 1984.[37]   By
February 1985, the Bureau was paying interest on
1,047,593 open accounts of registered bonds and notes.[38]
Automation of these accounts under the TREASURY DIRECT
system in 1986, to be more fully described below, would
be a significant event at the Bureau during the 1980s.

Meanwhile, other measures were being taken to
improve the efficiency of operations.   By July 1984, 24
of the Federal Reserve Banks and branches were reporting
auction tender information (for entry into accounts in
Washington) for Treasury bills on magnetic tape, making
up 92 percent of the total tenders submitted through the
Federal Reserve that month.   In addition, 84 percent of
the Treasury bills maturing on July 5, 1984, had been
reinvested, the highest rate in the history of the book-
entry system.[39]

Several reorganizations took place in the 1980s.
In October 1984, the establishment of a new Office of
Automated Information Systems (OAIS) was approved,
indicative of the growing importance of computer
operations at the Bureau.   The OAIS included the
Division of ADP Management and the Data Processing
Branch from the Division of Administrative Services,
Office of Administration.   The purpose of OAIS was to
give the Bureau better capability in improving the
automation of office activities, administering data,
planning for long-range applications of ADP, and
enhancing the electronic communications that existed
between the Bureau and the Federal Reserve Banks.   The
new office also carried with it a new position of
Assistant Commissioner.[40]

The first major project undertaken by OAIS was
planning the acquisition of a new computer for the
Bureau's own operations, when it was determined that
future systems being planned could not be maintained on
the Bureau's Univac 1110 computer.   Additional upgrading
of the Univac was deemed impractical because its
operating system was obsolete and could not use more up-
to-date hardware and software components.   An important
aspect of future computer information needs was the
desire to have on-line access to both the computer
system at the Bureau and the one that linked together
the Federal Reserve System.   Under the old system, which
was almost all of such information, the transaction and
accounting data pertaining to the public debt was
handled by telephone, on paper, on punched cards, or
submitted by magnetic tape.   The data often had to be
reworked to be entered in the Bureau's system.[41]

The new system, named Project NEW (Nineteen-ninety
Electronic Workplace), also entailed a great deal of
automation in the Bureau's offices.   With its on-line

capability giving users direct access to information, the new system would speed up inquiries as workers would no longer have to wait for the result of inquiries done with batches of computer punchcards. The correction of errors directly would also be possible, and there would be a drastic reduction in the amount of paperwork that employees would have to handle.[42]

On July 17, 1986, the new computer, an IBM mainframe, was installed. During the testing of the new system and the phase-in of its operations, the Bureau would actually operate two systems. As part of the plan implementing the system, Bureau personnel were given training on similar systems at the Federal Reserve Banks of Chicago, Richmond, and Cleveland. Thus, they were well prepared to handle the transition to the new system, as well as to meet the challenge of hooking up the new system to the one maintained by the Federal Reserve Banks.[43]

The 1980s were a very busy time for ADP at the Bureau. In addition to improvements in internal operations, the Bureau also sought to find better ways to serve the large number of investors who had been drawn into the government securities market. In culmination of a trend that had been going on for over a decade, wherein definitive securities were being eliminated and replaced by manual book-entry accounts, it was decided to apply computer technology to the automation of all accounts held by the Bureau for the investing public.

TREASURY DIRECT

When increased sales of Treasury securities began in the late 1960s, a movement to convert those securities to book-entry form was started. The movement was fueled by an increase in the recordkeeping ("backroom") problems in the financial industry, including thefts of substantial amounts of bearer securities, which prompted the Association of Primary Dealers in U.S. Government Securities to urge expansion of the book-entry system, which was being operated for depository institutions by the Federal Reserve Banks. By 1973, book-entry procedures had been extended to include all customers of member banks of the Federal Reserve System. In 1976, plans were in place for the elimination of all definitive securities and their replacement by book-entry form; the plan also called for a small book-entry system to be created at the Treasury to serve investors who would hold their securities to maturity.[44]

As part of the plan, it was also decided to convert the book-entry system to fully automated electronic accounts. It should be noted that a book-entry system does not require computer technology to function; a book-entry system with manual entry could have been implemented at any time in the Treasury's history, but it is doubtful that purchasers of Treasury securities would have gained any services from such a conversion. The merging of a book-entry system with computer technology would enable investors to gain better service, because the automated system would permit the use of the network of electronic fund transfer (EFT).

EFT in commercial form is as old as the telephone and telegraph. In the public sector of banking, the Federal Reserve set up the first Morse code wire transfer network for transfer of funds among reserve accounts of its member banks in 1918. As long as the technology remained telegraphic, however, the costs of EFT remained high. By the 1960s, improvement in computers and in telecommunications made the costs of EFT low enough to permit its use by nearly all consumers.[45]

The first major component of EFT in the financial community was the creation of automated clearinghouses wherein banks could handle check-clearing transfers by use of data tapes. The first such system was organized starting in 1968 by the Los Angeles and San Francisco Clearing House Associations. By 1974, automated clearinghouses were operated in San Francisco, Los Angeles, Minneapolis, Atlanta, and Boston, and a National Automated Clearing House Association was formed. By the mid-1980s, about 50 automated clearinghouses were in operation, with the Federal Reserve serving as the central agency for the national transfer of data.[46]

The federal government had also been a long-time user of EFT, although initially on a small scale. In the 1920s, Treasury securities were made transferable by telegraph within the Federal Reserve System, but all transfers required the specific approval of the Commissioner of the Public Debt and had to be delivered by hand between the Federal Reserve Bank office and the bank that had ordered the transfer.[47] Large sales of savings bonds by some government agencies were being reported on tape to the Bureau in the early 1960s. In April 1974, the Treasury and the Social Security Administration started a direct deposit system for recipients of social security checks; the U.S. Air Force followed in November of the same year with its own direct deposit program.[48] In December 1982, 18 million of the 49 million payments of salaries and benefits made by the federal government were made by EFT--representing a respectable 36 percent.[49]

A big advantage of EFT over paper transactions is its lower cost. In 1979, the Federal Reserve estimated that it cost the banking system about $.50 per check to operate its check-clearing mechanism.   EFT had the potential to bring that cost down.   For example, a Treasury-sponsored study conducted in 1981 showed that social security checks disbursed by mail cost about $.59 each to process, while direct deposit processing reduced that cost to $.07 per payment. As long as these savings were passed on to consumers, they should be willing to make greater use of EFT.[50] In addition, consumers would receive better servicing and faster availability of funds in their accounts.

Given this background, the development of a system of electronic transfer for Treasury securities seemed an obvious step.   In fact, the development of the system was made difficult for several years by just the sort of problem it would help to resolve.   The large volume of sales of Treasury securities in the early 1980s so strained the resources at the Bureau that planning for automated book-entry had to be delayed.   Finally, in 1983 a plan was approved for the development of the system of automated handling of transactions in Treasury securities.   The system eventually was named "TREASURY DIRECT" and was implemented through the combined efforts of the Bureau of the Public Debt and the Federal Reserve Bank of Philadelphia.[51]

The TREASURY DIRECT system was designed to replace two investor account systems at the Treasury and to integrate with a third system maintained by the Federal Reserve.   At this time, the Treasury was maintaining a Selective Automation System for bills and a Registered Accounts System for notes and bonds. As the new system came into operation, both of these older systems would be phased out, although all registered securities in definitive form could not be eliminated until the year 2015.[52]

The overall intent behind the TREASURY DIRECT system was to service individual investors who bought securities directly from the Treasury and wanted their accounts maintained by the Treasury; these investors primarily would hold their securities until maturity. For investors who purchased government securities through the Federal Reserve or in the secondary government securities market from a dealer, especially with the idea of reselling that security before it matured, the Federal Reserve maintained a separate commercial book-entry system, so-called because it served mainly institutional investors and commercial banks.

Transfer of securities between the Federal Reserve's commercial system and the Treasury's two systems had previously been possible but cumbersome. After the implementation of TREASURY DIRECT, this process, which had taken up to three days, could take place in a few minutes.[53]   While the commercial book-entry system would handle a large volume in terms of dollars, TREASURY DIRECT would involve most of the accounts in terms of numbers. Maintenance of accounts in both systems was also possible.

The main feature of the new system was that it would set up a central file of information that could be reached through the Treasury or from any Federal Reserve Bank or branch. The accounts for all investors choosing to use TREASURY DIRECT would be maintained on a single computer at the Philadelphia Federal Reserve Bank, with the Bureau and all Federal Reserve Banks and branches being connected to that computer by a nationwide telecommunications network.[54]

Design of the TREASURY DIRECT system was extremely complicated, as it involved the integration of over 500 computer software programs. A task force was set up to design and implement the system under the direction of Jon Davis, vice president of the Oklahoma City Federal Reserve Branch. The actual development required the formation of a 20-member project team selected from employees of the Philadelphia Reserve Bank under the leadership of Ed Coia, assistant vice president at Philadelphia. The Bureau members of the task force included Van Zeck, Assistant Commissioner of Financing, Andy Tracy, of the Office of Securities and Accounting Services, and Mark Schurmeier, from the Division of Investor Accounts.[55]

It was anticipated that the new system would provide many advantages in addition to increasing the speed involved in conducting transactions. By using automated clearinghouse procedures, it would be possible to cut down on the number of checks issued. Investors would have the benefit of dealing directly with Federal Reserve Banks and branches for most of their needs. The system would allow for increased security and control over all payments and transfers of securities. It was estimated that the system would save the Treasury $46 million.[56]

There were also some risks and problems involved with implementation of the new system. The big risk was that the system would not work reliably. As project leader Ed Coia put it, "Once the switch goes on, there is no turning back. We are here to stay and highly visible. If TDAB [the original abbreviated name for TREASURY DIRECT] goes down, people will know right away because terminals at the Treasury and in all the Banks will be idle."[57]

In its first real operation in July 1986, the system did indeed cause problems. As described by officials,

> Parts of the complicated program refused to
> "talk" to each other, and the proposed book-
> entry auction of $10 billion of two-year
> notes on July 23 was scrubbed. The program
> managers rushed back to their drafting
> boards, found the errors, and rescheduled the
> first all-book-entry auction to coincide with
> the Treasury's quarterly refunding of August
> 15.[58]

The auction of notes on July 23 was conducted using
previous methods. In the August 25 refunding, the
system worked perfectly and has continued to operate
smoothly ever since. By the end of fiscal year 1987,
811,200 TREASURY DIRECT accounts had been established,
representing 5 percent of the total public debt.[59]

Once in operation, TREASURY DIRECT provided
investors with an automated service for purchase and
transfer of securities at any of the 36 banks and
branches of the Federal Reserve; in addition, the Bureau
would continue to operate its Securities Transactions
branch window, located at the Engraving and Printing
Annex. More than 700 users at 240 computer terminals
throughout the country would be connected with TREASURY
DIRECT. Investors would be able to set up a single
account for all their holdings of Treasury securities,
and transactions involving that account could be handled
at any of the 37 service locations, regardless of where
the account was opened. Investors would be able to
reinvest their holdings of bills automatically for up to
two years. Payments from investments made via TREASURY
DIRECT would be made by direct deposit to an account at
a financial institution designated by the investor.[60]

Implementation of the TREASURY DIRECT system
encompassed a lot more than setting up a computer
system, however. At the Federal Reserve, the commercial
book-entry system was integrated with TREASURY DIRECT to
the extent that securities could be transferred between
the systems. "TRADES" (Treasury/Reserve Automated Data-
Entry System) was the name given to the overall system
of electronic book-entry securities. The TRADES network
handled the relatively few, but large volume accounts of
commercial banks and dealers who make up the government
securities market. When a small investor with a
TREASURY DIRECT account wishes to sell a security, it
must be transferred to the TRADES network, something now
easily done.

With completion of the TREASURY DIRECT project, the
Bureau and the Federal Reserve Banks began development
of a fully integrated automated accounting system, the
Public Debt Accounting and Reporting System (PARS), to
efficiently report and account for government securities
activities. The Treasury and Agencies Securities

Accounting System keeps track of all securities, from printing and issuance to destruction. The "cash system" provides information on the amount of debt outstanding, and the "interest system" records all interest on the debt. Under PARS all the above information will be reported directly from the Federal Reserve to the Bureau. The records will be kept on the Bureau's new IBM mainframe computer, with the personnel from the Cleveland FRB lending their expertise in conjunction with IBM in designing the programs.[61]

A very large portion of the expansion of the public debt in the 1980s took the form of marketable securities, so that many of the innovations in administering the debt, such as TREASURY DIRECT, took place in that portion of the Bureau's operations. But that does not mean that no improvements were made in the nonmarketable securities area. The sale of savings bonds, too, saw changes in the form and recording of the related transactions.

THE SAVINGS BOND OPERATIONS OFFICE

As the 1980s began, the Bureau of the Public Debt's Savings Bond Operations Office (SBOO) had responsibility for all administrative activities associated with savings bonds, operating through five divisions: Data Recording and Search, Data Processing, Accounts and Reconcilement, Transactions and Rulings, and Management Services. These divisions were supported by the three staff branches: Management Analysis, Financial Management, and Personnel.

The initial entry point for the processing of savings bonds during this time was the Division of Data Recording and Search. Bonds were received in a variety of forms: batched punchcard stubs or magnetic tape for new issues, and batched punchcards or paper bonds for redemptions. All bonds received, in no matter what form, were transferred to a microfilm record, with duplicates made for storage outside of the Parkersburg office. In addition, a computer tape record was made of the microfilm location of issued bonds, using a master file based on the purchaser's social security number.[62] Under the system, information concerning the bond's denomination, serial number, and series was prepunched on the stub and could be handled by automatic card readers; transmittal data, issue data, and social security number had to be entered by keypunch operators. Data search to provide photos of bonds took place using high-speed microfilm readers that also had photographic capability. At this time, the SBOO files contained 1.2 million reels of microfilm.[63]

Whenever a bond owner had an account-related problem, such as a lost or destroyed bond, employees of the Division of Transactions and Rulings dealt with it. More than 200,000 cases a year were being processed by this division. The letter writing involved with processing claims of bond owners was typed by employees in the Correspondence Processing branch using word processing equipment hooked up to the central computer and linked to high speed printers.[64]

The processing system for savings bonds worked well. It should be noted, for example, that by the end of fiscal year 1983, 100 issuing agents were reporting sales of savings bonds by tape, accounting for 37.4 million items or approximately 52 percent of total transactions and 60 percent of payroll sales.[65]

In April 1985, Commissioner William Gregg told of plans to automate the processing of savings bonds by using the technology of Optical Character Recognition (OCR) and Magnetic Ink Character Recognition (MICR). Under this system, information relating to each individual savings bond is printed on the bond itself and translated into computer storage by special readers. The new system would permit the elimination of the punchcard savings bond and its replacement with a paper bond.[66] In December 1987, Commissioner Richard Gregg was able to announce the completion of the project to convert from a punchcard to a paper bond, at an estimated annual saving in bond stock costs of $1.2 million.[67]

The transformation of bonds to paper and the use of OCR/MICR technology had other advantages. On December 16, 1987, the Bureau announced a new system that would allow authorized paying agents for savings bonds to process bonds in a way similar to that in which they process checks. Under the new system, called E-Z CLEAR, paying agents would be able to encode their own MICR information on the bonds for forwarding to the Federal Reserve Bank in their area. Previously, bonds had to be sent to the Federal Reserve Banks separately from other items. Based on pilot tests, the new system was found to reduce costs for the Bureau and the Federal Reserve System and was widely accepted by financial institutions.[68]

The pilot test included 67 financial institutions with 813 separate branch operations.[69] When the system started, the number of bonds processed reached 13,215 per day from 144 financial institutions during January 1988.[70] By April 1988, a daily average of 20,458 bonds from 302 participating institutions were going through the E-Z CLEAR system.[71] At the end of fiscal year 1988, the system was judged a success and the decision was made to extend and expand its use. Regulations to make E-Z CLEAR available to all financial institutions were put into place in October 1988.

Another pilot project for handling bond sales was announced in July 1987. Under this program, bond purchasers in the Cleveland district of the Federal Reserve System would have their savings bonds delivered to them by mail. Starting on October 1, 1987, bond purchasers at over 3,000 financial institutions in Ohio would still order and pay for their bonds at their financial institutions as they had in the past. But they would not have to wait for their applications to be processed and their bonds prepared for them. Under the new system, the application would be sent to the Pittsburgh branch of the Cleveland Federal Reserve Bank. There the applications would be processed and the bonds issued and mailed to the purchaser, with receipt within three weeks.[72]

In the first month of operation of the Ohio pilot, about 36,000 applications were sent to the Pittsburgh branch, 40 percent more than had been expected. The applications averaged 1.5 bonds each, and 39,000 bonds were inscribed and mailed during the month.[73] In December 1987, 113,000 applications were received at Pittsburgh, three times the original estimate; many of these applications were for gifts of low-denomination bonds during the Christmas season, and the actual dollar amount rose only slightly, from $15.4 million in November (63,000 applications) to $16.7 million. In January 1988, the number of applications fell to 46,000 but the dollar amount went up to $20.5 million.[74] During March and April 1988, the number of applications seemed to stabilize when the Pittsburgh branch handled about 2,200 applications daily ($900,000 in sales).[75] The program was very cost effective by eliminating the stocks of unissued bonds held at banks and by cutting down on the time bank employees had to spend in preparing bonds for issue. At the end of fiscal year 1988, this program was also considered successful by the Bureau and the decision was made to expand it nationwide in phases.

Innovations were made in areas of consumer service. The Bureau had already been making information about savings bonds, including the current interest rate, available to consumers by an 800-number toll-free telephone service. Starting May 3, 1988, that service was supplemented by the first telephone sales of Series EE bonds. Within the first six days of operation, 1,200 orders for bond purchases were taken; of those orders, 1,137 totaling $372,000 were approved.[76] The costs of handling those orders were so high in terms of manpower, however, it was doubtful that telemarketing would continue after 1988.

From the telemarketing of savings bonds to the TREASURY DIRECT system for selling marketable securities, the Bureau of the Public Debt came a long way during the 1980s in terms of providing service to holders of the public debt. But there was one other area in which individual purchasers of government securities needed assistance. The expansion of the public debt in the 1980s coincided with a period of deregulation and change in the financial industry. Some holders of government securities had made their purchases through many of the financial institutions that had sprung up at this time. While their bonds were backed by the "full faith and credit of the United States," it was not always clear what maintained the security of the financial institutions that purchased those bonds and held on to them. Because this system caused problems for investors in government securities, the Bureau of the Public Debt was called upon to find ways to make it safer.

THE GOVERNMENT SECURITIES ACT

The market for government securities is one of the largest financial markets in existence, with about $1.7 trillion in Treasury-issued bills, notes, and bonds held by the public at the end of 1987, making up 26 percent of the bond market in the United States. (including mortgages).[77] The main actors in the market are the Treasury Department, which authorizes and accounts for the securities, and the Federal Reserve Banks, which handle the sale of most of the issues, acting as fiscal agent for the Treasury. The Federal Reserve Bank of New York is responsible for open market operations wherein the money supply of the country is influenced by the purchase or sale of government securities.

In the private sector there exists a variety of dealers in government securities. Foremost among them are firms designated by the Federal Reserve as primary dealers; these firms take an active part in Treasury auctions and in the Federal Reserve's open market operations. In 1985 there were 36 primary dealers. Of those, 15 were banks or subsidiaries of banks that came under the regulatory jurisdiction of the Federal Reserve and other government agencies, 11 were broker-dealers who were regulated by the Securities and Exchange Commission (SEC), and 10 were not officially regulated, but were monitored by the Federal Reserve to ensure that its dealings with them in open market operations were sound.

In addition, there is a group of secondary security dealers who deal more directly with the public. In 1985 it was estimated that there were 400 to 500 of those dealers. Many of them were banks or broker-dealers, so they came under some form of regulation. But about 100 of these secondary dealers did not come under any form of federal regulation.[78]

The problems that could be caused by these unregulated firms were brought to light by the failure of Drysdale Government Securities, Inc., in May 1982, and E.M.S. Government Securities, Inc., in March 1985. A total of six firms failed in the first half of 1985. The failure of E.S.M., which was an unregulated firm, was especially important for it set off a domino effect by causing the bankruptcy of Home State Savings Bank, Cincinnati, Ohio, which in turn set off a panic that culminated in temporary suspension of savings and loan operations throughout Ohio.

In its analysis of the situation, the Federal Reserve found that these smaller securities firms had issued misleading statements about their finances, had hidden affiliate companies that were sources of trouble, and had not maintained secure capital. A large problem concerned repurchase agreements, for under these a securities firm would sell a government security to a bank with a promise to buy it back at a specified time. In this way the firm could gain short-term loans using securities as collateral.

These repurchase agreements caused two problems. First, the maturity dates of the securities might not match the due date of the repurchase, so the securities firm might not be able to make good on its agreement. Second, the other parties to the repurchase agreement did not always take control over their securities, which made them more susceptible to loss. As a result of these problems, many banks and municipalities were tempted into special deals by the securities firms, believing that they were involved with riskless government securities. But the situation had evolved to the point where, as Gerald Corrigan, president of the New York Federal Reserve Bank, stated, "the security may be risk-free while the transaction can be quite risky."[79]

In recognition of these problems, and as a result of these failures, legislation was introduced in the House and Senate in 1985 to begin federal regulation of the government securities market. A group composed of members from the Treasury Department, the Federal Reserve Board, and the SEC was formed to consider what form the regulation of the government securities market should take. It was agreed that the Federal Reserve would continue its monitoring of the primary securities dealers. While it was desirable that self-regulation among the secondary dealers, as takes place with activities among stock brokerage firms who are members of the New York or other stock exchanges, be considered, this approach was not found feasible. Paul Volcker, Chairman of the Board of Governors of the Federal

Reserve System, stated the case against self-regulation: "Developments also suggest the limitation of such a voluntary approach. The Federal Reserve has no authority over the 'fringe' dealers, cannot examine them, and does not have a business relationship with them. Under those conditions, a dealer wishing to avoid official scrutiny or surveillance can do so."[80]

The Bureau of the Public Debt was involved with the proposed regulations from the beginning of the problems in the government securities market. As part of the move to a full book-entry system, the Bureau's Chief Counsel Calvin Ninomiya had identified the importance of new rules for handling book-entry transactions. With the failure of E.M.S., the rules being set forth for book-entry were considered to see if they could be applicable in the process of protecting investors.[81] The Bureau personnel assigned to the Government Securities Act included Van Zeck, Deputy Commissioner, Anne Meister from the Commissioner's office, and Cynthia Langweisner and Cindy Reese (both from the Chief Counsel's office).[82]

The Government Securities Act passed both houses of Congress in October 1986 as an amendment to the Securities and Exchange Act of 1933. The basic feature of the new act was the requirement that brokers and dealers who only handled government securities had to register with an appropriate regulatory agency. The Securities and Exchange Act had previously excluded them from any registration on the grounds that their dealings were risk-free. Agencies with which firms have registered have included the SEC and the National Association of Securities Dealers. In addition, the new act carried rules requiring firms to maintain adequate capital, describing how customer accounts were to be maintained, and specifying how repurchase agreements would be controlled.

The Government Securities Act went into effect on July 25, 1987, with only very basic regulations. It designated the Secretary of the Treasury as being responsible for making the actual rules. Ultimate responsibility for setting up the new system of rules under the Government Securities Act was given to the Bureau of the Public Debt. The Bureau would have the job of keeping track of the regulations and changing them as needed; it would also have the task of issuing interpretive rulings to brokers and dealers who have registered under the act.[83]

The authority to issue regulations was limited by the act in two ways. First, the Treasury and the Bureau have no enforcement powers; those were accorded to the SEC and bank regulators. As a result, the Bureau must keep track of how that enforcement has taken place as part of its job of changing regulations when needed.

Second, a time limit was placed on the Treasury's authority to issue regulations. In 1990, the Treasury, the Federal Reserve, and the SEC are required to consider how well the regulations have worked, and to tell Congress whether they believe the Treasury's power to regulate should run past 1991, when it is scheduled to expire under a "sunset" provision of the act.

All three agencies were involved in the regulatory process because the Treasury and the Bureau did not have adequate knowledge about the functioning of financial markets in general, and it was important to avoid making regulations in government securities that were already in existence for corporate bonds and stocks.   In addition, it is the other two agencies that would enforce the regulations, so their input was crucial. The interagency effort succeeded. As Ellen Seidman, special assistant to the Undersecretary for Finance who coordinated the interagency group, summed up the experience, "We had 25 people from eight agencies reviewing comments and proposed drafts and it worked. It was amazing, it really worked."[84]

The system of rules went into effect in January 1988. Since then, the Bureau has remained active in issuing rule changes. Early in 1988, for example, it decided to do away with the "safekeeping exception" for financial institutions. Comments were received from the financial community, which did not like the change being proposed.   It was also reported that exceptions to recordkeeping rules that had previously been granted to a group of securities dealers were no longer needed for all but two of the firms, as the rest were complying with the rules.   No problems had resulted from the exceptions.[85]

It should be noted that the entrance of the Bureau into activities concerned with the Government Securities Act is a sharp departure from its previous responsibilities. In describing what would be involved in the Bureau's new regulatory obligations, Van Zeck, who headed up the Bureau's activities in this area, said quite honestly, "We haven't the faintest idea! Well, we have a faint idea and it's getting clearer every day." He added, "No one's ever done this before . . . no one's had the responsibility."[86]   In 1988, plans were being made to form a securities regulation staff in the Office of the Commissioner.[87]   If the past experience of the Bureau of the Public Debt in handling new chores is any gauge, it will do very well in entering this new era as a regulatory agency.

NOTES

1. Herbert Stein, <u>Presidential Economics</u> (New York: Simon & Schuster, 1984), p. 265.

2. Thomas J. Hailstones, <u>Viewpoints on Supply-Side Economics</u> (Richmond, Va.: Robert F. Dane, 1982), p. 168.

3. Hailstones, <u>Supply-Side Economics,</u> p. 188.

4. James D. Savage, <u>Balanced Budgets and American Politics</u> (Ithaca, N.Y.: Cornell University Press, 1988), p. 202.

5. Wallace G. Peterson, <u>Income, Employment and Economic Growth,</u> 6th ed. (New York: W.W. Norton, 1988), p. 614.

6. Peterson, <u>Income,</u> pp. 616-617.

7. Michael G. Rukstad, <u>Macroeconomic Decision Making in the World Economy</u> (Chicago: Dryden Press, 1986), p. 303.

8. Peterson, <u>Income,</u> p. 617.

9. Rukstad, <u>Macroeconomic Decision Making,</u> p. 105.

10. U.S. Department of the Treasury, Bureau of the Public Debt, "Debt Reaches 1,000,000,000," <u>PD News,</u> January 1982, p. 1.

11. Rukstad, <u>Macroeconomic Decision Making,</u> p. 266.

12. Rukstad, <u>Macroeconomic Decision Making,</u> p. 332.

13. Anthony S. Campagna, <u>U.S. National Economic Policy, 1917-1985</u> (New York: Praeger, 1987), p. 541. See also Campbell R. McConnell, op. cit., p. 330; and Wallace G. Peterson, op. cit., p. 615.

14. Hailstones, <u>Supply-Side Economics,</u> pp. 138, 297.

15. Savage, <u>Balanced Budgets,</u> p. 259.

16. Savage, <u>Balanced Budgets,</u> p. 198.

17. Rudolf G. Penner and Alan J. Abramson, <u>Broken Purse Strings</u> (Washington, D.C.: Urban Institute Press, 1988), p. 29.

18. U.S. Department of the Treasury, Bureau of the Public Debt, <u>Monthly Statement of the Public Debt of the United States,</u> September 30, 1988, p. 1.

19. U.S. Department of the Treasury, Bureau of the Public Debt, "Bureau Spotlight: Division of Investor Accounts," <u>PD News,</u> October 1982, p. 7.

20. U.S. Department of the Treasury, Bureau of the Public Debt, "Bureau Spotlight: The Office of Financing," <u>PD Newsletter,</u> July 1982, pp. 4-5.

21. Peter D. Strenlight (Senior Vice President, Federal Reserve Bank of New York), statement given to U.S. House Subcommittee on Domestic Monetary Policy, Federal Reserve <u>Bulletin</u>, April 1982, p. 223.

22. U.S. Department of the Treasury, Bureau of the Public Debt, <u>Information about Marketable Treasury Securities (Bills, Notes and Bonds) Sold at Original Issue,</u> Pamphlet, Revised July 1986.

23. Frank J. Fabozzi and T. Dessa Fabozzi, <u>Bond Markets, Analysis and Strategies</u> (Englewood Cliffs, N.J.: Prentice-Hall, 1989), pp. 93, 113.

24. U.S. Department of the Treasury, Bureau of the Public Debt, "Treasury Endorses Stripping," <u>PD News,</u> Spring 1985, p. 1.

25. Sandy Pfau, "To Strip or Not to Strip," <u>PD Newsletter,</u> February 1987, p. 3.

26. U.S. Department of the Treasury, Bureau of the Public Debt, <u>Monthly Statement of Public Debt,</u> September 30, 1988, p. 24.

27. Bob Reed, "$7,413,100,688 and Counting . . . ," <u>PD Newsletter,</u> April 1987, p. 6.

28. Federal Reserve System, <u>Bulletin,</u> June 1983.

29. U.S. Savings Bond Division, <u>The Savings Bond Question and Answer Book,</u> p. 1.

30. U.S. Department of the Treasury, Bureau of the Public Debt, "Savings Bond Update," <u>PD News,</u> August 1983, p. 2.

31. U.S. Department of the Treasury, Bureau of the Public Debt, "The Debt Goes Abroad," <u>PD News,</u> Spring 1985, p. 1.

32. U.S. Department of the Treasury, *Treasury Bulletin,* Winter Issue, March 1988, Table FD-5.

33. U.S. Department of the Treasury, Bureau of the Public Debt, *Bureau of Public Debt-Talking Points,* Report (Washington, D.C.:   BPD Files 120.9   IDF, June 10, 1982).

34. U.S. Department of the Treasury, Bureau of the Public Debt, "The Commissioner's Treasury Bill Committee," *PD News,* June 1982, p. 5.

35. U.S. Department of the Treasury, Bureau of the Public Debt, Commissioner of the Public Debt, *Monthly Status Report for July 1984* (Washington, D.C.:   BPD files).

36. U.S. Department of the Treasury, Bureau of the Public Debt, Commissioner of the Public Debt, *Monthly Status Report for August 1986* (Washington, D.C.:   BPD Files).

37. Commissioner, *Monthly Status Report,* July 1984.

38. U.S. Department of the Treasury, Bureau of the Public Debt, Commissioner of the Public Debt, *Monthly Status Report for February 1985* (Washington, D.C.:   BPD files).

39. Commissioner, *Monthly Status Report,* July 1984.

40. U.S. Department of the Treasury, Bureau of the Public Debt, *Establishment of New Bureau Office* (Washington, D.C.:   October 15, 1984), memorandum located in BPD files.

41. U.S. Department of the Treasury, Bureau of the Public Debt, *Project NEW: Requirements Analysis* (Washington, D.C.:   No date), p. ii, located in BPD files.

42. U.S. Department of the Treasury, Bureau of the Public Debt, Division of ADP Management, *Project NEW* (Washington, D.C.:   August 10, 1984), study located in BPD files.

43. John Englund, "New Computer Installed," *PD News,* October 1986, p. 8.

44. U.S. Department of the Treasury, Bureau of the Public Debt, "Book Entry Evolution," *PD News,* Spring 1984, p. 3.

45. Federal Reserve System, "Developments in Consumer Electronic Fund Transfers," _Bulletin_, June 1983, p. 395.

46. August Bequai, _The Cashless Society: EFTS at the Crossroads_ (New York: John Wiley & Sons, 1981), pp. 28-30.

47. U.S. Department of the Treasury, Bureau of the Public Debt, "TREASURY DIRECT," _PD News_, Special Edition, September 1986.

48. Bequai, _EFTS_, p. 15.

49. Federal Reserve System, "Developments in Consumer EFT," p. 396.

50. Federal Reserve System, "Developments in Consumer EFT," p. 395.

51. U.S. Department of the Treasury, Bureau of the Public Debt, "TREASURY DIRECT."

52. U.S. Department of the Treasury, Burea of the Public Debt, "What is This Thing," _PD News_, Fall 1984, p. 8.

53. U.S. Department of the Treasury, Bureau of the Public Debt, "TDAB Breaks New Ground in Automated Data Processing to Save Treasury Millions," _PD News_, July 1985, p. 3.

54. U.S. Dept. of Treasury, BPD, "What Is This Thing," p. 8.

55. U.S. Dept. of Treasury, BPD, "TDAB Breaks New Ground," p. 4.

56. U.S. Dept. of Treasury, BPD, "TDAB Breaks New Ground," pp. 3-4.

57. U.S. Dept. of Treasury, BPD, "TDAB Breaks New Ground," p. 4.

58. U.S. Dept. of Treasury, BPD, "TREASURY DIRECT."

59. U.S. Dept. of Treasury, BPD, "TREASURY DIRECT."

60. U.S. Dept. of Treasury, BPD, "TREASURY DIRECT."

61. Sandy Pfau, "Continuing the Partnership: Cleveland FRB Helps Develop PARS," _PD News_, March 1988, pp. 5-6.

62. U.S. Department of the Treasury, Bureau of the Public Debt, _Functional Chart,_ Savings Bond Operations Office, February 1981, pp. 1-9.

63. U.S. Department of the Treasury, Bureau of the Public Debt, "In Almost Heaven," _PD News,_ October 1982, p. 3.

64. U.S. Dept. of Treasury, BPD, "In Almost Heaven," p. 4.

65. U.S. Department of the Treasury, Bureau of the Public Debt, Savings Bond Operations Office, _Annual Report_ (Washington, D.C.: Fiscal Year 1983), p. 12.

66. U.S. Department of the Treasury, Bureau of the Public Debt, _Progress Report on Major Projects - first half of FY 1984_ (Washington, D.C.: April 28, 1984), memorandum from W.M. Gregg, Commissioner of the Public Debt, to Carole Jones Dineen, Fiscal Assistant Secretary. Located in BPD files.

67. U.S. Department of the Treasury, Bureau of the Public Debt, _Commissioner's Monthly Status Report For December 1987,_ BPD files, item 10.

68. U.S. Department of the Treasury, _Treasury News Press Release,_ December 16, 1987.

69. U.S. Department of the Treasury, Bureau of the Public Debt, _Commissioner's Monthly Status Report for September 1987,_ BPD Files, item 10.

70. Bureau of the Public Debt, _Monthly Status Report for September 1987,_ item 6.

71. U.S. Department of the Treasury, Bureau of the Public Debt, _Commissioner's Monthly Status Report for April 1988,_ BPD files, item 4.

72. U.S. Treasury, _Treasury News Press Release,_ September 22, 1987.

73. Bureau of the Public Debt, _Monthly Status Report for September 1987,_ item 5.

74. U.S. Department of the Treasury, Bureau of the Public Debt, _Commissioner's Monthly Status Report,_ January 1988, item 1.

75. U.S. Department of the Treasury, Bureau of the Public Debt, _Commissioner's Monthly Status Report for March 1988,_ BPD files, item 10.

76. Bureau of the Public Debt, <u>Monthly Status Report for April, 1988,</u> item 3.

77. Fabozzi and Fabozzi, <u>Bond Markets,</u> p. 3.

78. E. Gerald Corrigan,"Statement by the President, Federal Reserve Bank of New York, before the Subcommittee on Securities, U.S. Senate," Federal Reserve <u>Bulletin</u>, July 1985, pp. 520-21.

79. Corrigan, <u>Bulletin,</u> July 1985, p. 523.

80. Paul Volcker,"Statement by the Chairman of the Board of Governors of the Federal Reserve System, before the Subcommittee on Telecommunications, Consumer Protection and Finance, U.S. House of Representatives," Federal Reserve <u>Bulletin</u>, August 1985, p. 621.

81. Gail Schlifer, "Interview with Ellen Seidman," <u>PD News,</u> September 1987, p. 4.

82. U.S. Department of the Treasury, Bureau of the Public Debt, "Van Zeck Appointed Deputy Commissioner," <u>PD News,</u> June 1987, p. 4.

83. U.S. Department of the Treasury, Bureau of the Public Debt, "The Government Securities Act of 1986," <u>PD News,</u> Special Section, August 1987, GSA-2 to GSA-4.

84. Schlifer, "Ellen Seidman," pp. 4-5.

85. Bureau of the Public Debt, <u>Monthly Status Report for April 1988,</u> item 2.

86. U.S. Dept. of Treasury, BPD, "Van Zeck Appointed," p. 4.

87. U.S. Department of the Treasury, Bureau of the Public Debt, <u>Long-Range Plan</u>, (Washington, D.C.: 1988 edition), p. 4.

11

The Debt in Historical Perspective

Throughout its history the government of the United States has been in debt. During much of that time, the size of that debt has been of great concern to Americans. As such, fears of excessively large government debt were often expressed. Those fears, however, appear to have been unwarranted. The public debt has grown, but the government and the nation have survived. To cite one example, the current generation of Americans is supposed to be suffering from the burden of the debt from World War II. Instead, that debt seems almost trivial alongside the present debt of $2.9 trillion, and no one seems worried about the earlier debt. Instead, worry has shifted to the present debt and the burden it may be imposing on the present and future generations, if any.

In this chapter, the recent growth in the public debt will be put in perspective by comparing it to the debt growth of other periods. From the vantage point of that historical perspective, it will be seen that the debt explosion of the 1980s does not represent an extraordinary period of debt growth. It has been an explosion, but not a big bang, for there have been other periods when the growth of the public debt has been equally large.

A comparison of the debt growth of different time periods requires that some standard of measurement be devised. Unfortunately, there is not an acceptable standard to gauge the size of the debt,[1] so several will be employed. First, the debt will be examined in comparison with the size of the federal government. Second, the debt will be examined in terms of its relationship to GNP. Third, the actual growth rate of the debt in the 1980s will be contrasted to other periods, with special attention given to World War II. Fourth, the relationships between debt, deficits, and interest rates will be explored. Fifth, a hypothetical plan for paying off the debt will be provided, along with consideration of what repayment of the debt might mean to the economy.

DEBT AND GOVERNMENT SIZE

Americans have had mixed feelings about the size and scope of their national government. Few politicians have run successful campaigns on a platform of more government activity, as no one wishes the government to grow larger. But we all would like the government to do more for us--supply more money for roads, for better education, and for improved national defense. Despite our reservations, we have allowed the federal government to take on ever greater responsibilities.

As a result of this tendency, during the course of this century we have seen an increased expansion in the size and scope of activities of the federal government. Measuring this increased activity in a financial manner, we find that in 1900 the federal government's finances were less than 5 percent of the gross national product, while in 1988 that figure had risen to more than 20 percent.   The annual federal budget has gone, in absolute terms, from around $500 million in 1900 to approximately a trillion dollars in 1989. Even if these figures were adjusted for inflation, this represents an extremely large increase.   Total debt owed by the federal government rose slowly at first, but at an increasing rate over the last several decades, until it has reached a 2000-fold increase over its $1 billion level of 1900.

Not surprisingly, the public debt has grown in parallel with increases in the size of government. But that growth has not occurred at a steady rate. Before the Civil War, the debt remained small and constant, rising during wars and declining after them. The debt remained small because the government's scale of operations and its budget remained small. But there was a slight upward trend, for wartime expansions of the federal government budget were never reduced to prewar levels.   In the War of 1812 and the Mexican War, the lowest postwar budgets were about twice the amount of the budget immediately before the war.

After the Civil War, the pattern was altered slightly. When that war ended, the scale of government declined, as it had previously, but its proportion to its prewar size was greater. The lowest postwar budget (1877) was almost four times the prewar budget of 1860. Still, the debt was reduced, although it took some very high tariffs to do so. This pattern continued after the next major war, World War I. The federal government's budget fell, but at its postwar lowest (1927) it remained about four times its prewar level (1916). Debt reduction took place, again helped by high tariffs. Nevertheless, there was taking place a subtle process of incremental growth in federal government activities--a process of three steps forward and two steps back.

The point at which that growth accelerated is 1940, when the government began preparing for World War II. Large increases in the public debt had previously taken place when the country went to war. The expansion of government finance to pay for World War II was so extensive as to be one where a quantitative change became qualitative as well. On a per capita basis, the debt increased from $400 in 1941 to $1,907 in 1945.[2]

The post-World War II era marked another shift in the pattern of government size and debt repayment. As had happened after the Civil War and World War I, the size of the government budget declined, but it remained at about three and one-half times its prewar level. The change came in the attitude toward the debt. Immediate concerns over a debt reduction policy soon were abandoned, and the debt began its upward rise that has continued until today.

One way of looking at the growth of the debt is to compare it to the government's annual budget. This comparison is especially useful for demonstrating trends in debt buildups when the country goes to war. As noted above, during all our wars the government budget has risen, financed mainly through borrowing; as the war ended, the budget was reduced. As would be expected, the debt-to-budget ratio was low during the war and increased afterward. In fact, the actual figures are fairly consistent. In the last year of the Civil War, the debt was twice the budget, but with a return to peace it rose to seven times the budget; comparable figures for World War I are 1.5 and seven, and for World War II, three and nine. What this means is that while the size of the government budget kept spurting upward during and after wars, the debt apparently did little more than keep pace.

At the present time, the debt is 2.6 times the budget, which means that the government is in a condition comparable to where it was during one of its major wars. More will be said below on comparing the 1980s to a war. Now our attention will turn to a different way of gauging the debt.

DEBT AND GNP

Perhaps the best way of measuring the public debt is to compare it to total income in the economy, another definition of GNP. Economists favor this comparison because it gives an idea of how well the nation can handle the public debt.[3]   Just as an individual can support a greater amount of debt when he or she is making more money, so, too, the nation can take care of a larger debt when its total income is going up.   For example, if the public debt is a very small percentage of GNP, it would be possible, at least hypothetically, to pay off the debt with a onetime across-the-board income tax. The higher the debt, the less possible this becomes.

At the end of World War II, for example, the public debt was about 120 percent of GNP, meaning it was not possible to pay it off with a onetime tax.   Previous wars had not required such large expenditures: During the Civil War the debt-to-GNP ratio rose to 30 percent, the same figure that can be calculated for World War I. After each of these wars, the ratio fell.   The same result can be seen after World War II.   From 1945 to 1975, the economy grew much faster than the public debt, so the ratio fell to 26.8 percent; from 1975 to 1980, the percentage went up slightly (see Table 11.1). Since 1980, however, this percentage has risen significantly, putting it at levels not seen since the mid-1960s (see Table 11.2).

Table 11.1
Gross Federal Debt Held by the Public (percent of GNP, selected years)

1945	1950	1955	1960	1965	1970	1975	1980
108.4	82.6	59.5	47.6	39.6	29.4	26.8	27.8

Source: Robert Eisner, How Real Is the Federal Deficit (New York: Free Press, 1986), pp. 18-19.

Table 11.2
Gross Federal Debt Held by the Public (percent of GNP for the 1980s, 1980-88)

1982	1984	1986	1987	1988
29	35	41	43	43

Source: Economic Report of the President, 1989.

The increase in debt as a proportion of GNP can be accounted for by the budget deficits that have occurred in the 1980s. It has also been added to high interest rates during this time; when there are deficits and the interest rate on the debt is higher than the percentage increases in GNP, as has been the case during the 1980s, the debt-to-GNP ratio must go up.

This rise does not mean that the debt is getting too big. It should be recalled that the same ratio rose to 120 percent during World War II and was close to 40 percent during the Civil War and World War I. To make a comparison between the present and the past based on historical information, measures of the growth of the debt are needed. Several of these will be considered in the next section.

COMPARATIVE GROWTH RATES

A useful starting point in looking at the debt growth of the 1980s is to look at its growth in absolute amount and in terms of the percentage rate of its growth. This information is contained in Table 11.3. By adding up those figures and compounding the rates of increase, the total effect is that the debt increased by 2.6 times between 1981 and 1988, an absolute increase of $1.6 trillion and an average annual change of 15 percent. This would appear to be a very substantial growth rate.

Table 11.3
Growth in Government Debt (change from previous year)

Year	1982	1983	1984	1985	1986	1987	1988
Billions of $	144	235	195	251	303	224	252
Percent change	10	14	21	14	16	17	11

Source: Calculations based on data in Federal Reserve Bulletin, January 1989.

The annual change in the debt also gives a clearer picture of the real deficit of the government. A comparison of the figures in Table 11.3 with the figures in Table 10.1 will show that the annual increases in the debt have been larger than the federal government's reported deficit. The reason for this difference has to do with the way the federal government records its

budget. Presently the government employs what is called
a unified budget, which means that its reported budget
includes the transactions of its trust funds.[4] The most
important of these trust funds is that for Social
Security.   During the 1980s, the Social Security Trust
Fund has been showing a surplus because the social
security tax was raised in order to keep social security
solvent for at least the next 40 years.   Money held in
the Social Security Trust Fund is used to purchase
government securities.   The surplus funds borrowed in
this way from the Social Security Trust Fund, when
reported on a unified budget basis, reduce the actual
deficit being run by the other components of the budget.
The unified budget deficit gives an accounting of how
much money the federal government must borrow from the
public in financial markets, but the annual change in
the public debt tells how much the government has really
borrowed.[5]

Long ago, as noted in chapter 2, opponents of the
first Bank of the United States worried that Congress
was creating the means to lend to it.   Events proved
them wrong. It is doubtful that the advocates of Social
Security envisioned that they were creating a fund for
lending to the government, but it would appear that they
were more successful, at least for now.   It follows,
however, that historical comparisons of growth in the
debt are more relevant than annual budget deficits.

Table 11.4 compares the overall growth of the debt
for 1981-88 with several other periods of rapid debt
growth in U.S. history. As that table shows, the total

Table 11.4
Debt at End of Period vs. Debt at Start
(selected periods)

War of 1812	2.9
Mexican War	2.9
Civil War	42.4
World War I	8.6
Great Depression	2.7
World War II	6.3
Reagan Years	2.6

Source: Calculations based on data in U.S. Department
of Commerce, Historical Statistics of the
United States, Part 2 (Bureau of the Census,
1976), pp. 1117-18.

---

increase in debt of the last eight years has not been substantial in terms of a multiplicative increase. It is nowhere near the increases undertaken during major wars, and more in line with minor wars such as the Mexican War and the experience during the Great Depression.

Additional light can be shed on the magnitude of the current debt and its recent increase by giving a more detailed comparison with the previously, most recent debt buildup, World War II, as provided by Table 11.5. As noted earlier, the size of the debt compared to GNP was much higher at the end of World War II than it is currently. Moreover, the debt grew much faster at an average annual rate during the war than it has recently, and if the debt is adjusted for inflation, in this case by using the GNP deflator, the absolute growth of the debt during the war was about equal to that of the Reagan years, and the change took place during a shorter time period.

Table 11.5
Comparative Figures on the Public Debt

	World War II	Reagan Years
Average Annual Increase (%)	43	15
Debt/GNP, end of period (%)	120	43
Change in Debt (Billion 1982 $)	1,058	1,051

Source: Calculations based on data in U.S. Department of Commerce, Historical Statistics of the United States, Part 2 (Bureau of the Census, 1976), pp. 1117-18.

Under this comparison, the Reagan years do not seem to have been an especially burdensome period in terms of debt growth, although it should be noted that when the debt is adjusted for inflation, using the GNP deflator in 1982 dollars, it stood at $1.3 trillion at the end of World War II and $1.1 trillion in 1981--a decline in real terms. By 1988, however, the real debt had grown to $2.2 trillion. Not only has the recent debt growth been faster than the growth in GNP, it has also been faster than the inflation rate; both trends are departures from the experience of the previous 35 years.

If the growth of the public debt in the 1980s compares favorably with buildups during major wars, why should it be a concern? In all our major wars, the increase in public debt has been absorbed quite readily by the economy, while the debt itself has been managed and administered effectively by the government agencies responsible for those tasks. Why not just admit that the 1980s, too, have been a period of war--the drug war, the war on poverty, military maneuvers in Grenada and the Persian Gulf, Star Wars, the war to outspend the Soviet Union on defense, and the all-important war against high taxes? Then the rapid increase of the debt might at least seem justified. The economy seems capable of supporting this debt, and the Treasury and the Bureau of the Public Debt have done very well in managing and administering it.

A problem, however, is that previous wars saw the enemy surrender, and it is not so clear when truce will be called in many of the wars of the 1980s. The Gramm-Rudman-Hollings Act was intended to call such a truce, but it is still not clear that it will work. And what will the "peacetime" budget look like? Will it decline, so the debt-to-budget ratio will return to the range encountered after previous wars?

More important, as noted in chapter 1 and as has been argued throughout this book, large expansions of government borrowing during previous wars have not been costless. When taxes lagged behind government spending in major wars, the cost has been imposed on the public through either inflation or high interest rates, a topic to which we now turn.

INTEREST RATES AND THE DEBT

In the 1980s, many would argue that high interest rates and above-average inflation have been the price paid for government borrowing, at least until now. On the face of it, it does appear that interest rates have increased over the last three decades. Interest rates on short-term Treasury securities have ranged from 5 to 16 percent in the 1980s, with long-term rates in the 7.5 to 14 percent range; comparable figures for the 1970s are 3 to 12 percent short-term and 5.5 to 10 percent long-term; for the 1960s, 2.25 to 7.75 percent short-term and 3.75 to 7.75 percent long-term.

Looked at from a longer perspective, however, the evidence is not quite as clear. During previous debt expansions, interest rates have varied as follows: Revolutionary War, 4 to 6 percent; War of 1812, 5.4 to 7 percent; Civil War, 6 to 7 percent; World War I, 4 to 5 percent; Great Depression, 1 to 2 percent; and World War II, 1 to 2 percent. On this evidence it would appear that the more the government borrowed, the lower interest rate it paid.[6] Other factors are at work here.

In a very general way, the rate of interest depends on both the demand for and supply of loanable funds. The federal government is only one of many borrowers, and its impact on the interest rate will depend on how much is available to lend and how many others are trying to borrow. During the Great Depression, for example, there were few borrowers so the government deficits of that period had little impact on interest rates. When World War II began, as noted in chapter 7, interest rates were pegged at low rates because the Federal Reserve monetized the debt (i.e., made more loanable funds available). During the 1980s, as the economy has expanded it is possible that government borrowing has had an impact on interest rates, but that impact was offset by the increase in the supply of loanable funds that came from foreign countries.[7]

Interest rates are also influenced by inflation, as suppliers of loans add a premium to their interest rate charges to compensate them for expected future inflation. This factor, too, might explain why interest rates have been higher over the last 10 to 12 years than they had previously been. The low interest rates of the 1930s may have been due to its being a period of deflation. It is very difficult, as economist Paul Craig Roberts points out, to draw any firm conclusion about the size of the debt and deficit and the level of interest rates.[8]

To some extent, the high interest rates that were seen in the early and late 1980s have been a part of the Federal Reserve's efforts to fight inflation with a tight monetary policy. But the debt issues that have been made during this time have not helped. In the mid-1980s, interest rates were lower because the Federal Reserve eased its restraint on the money supply as the inflation rate came down. Lenders responded to lower inflation by reducing the inflation premium they were charging. These other factors may have been as important as the growth in the public debt in terms of determining interest rates.

Whatever caused the interest rates to rise, the fact remains that the higher the interest rates the government must pay, the higher everyone else in the economy must pay. This can lead to the "crowding out" of business investment,[9] higher home mortgage rates, and a rise in the exchange rate of the dollar with a corresponding decline of industries that must compete in foreign markets.[10] In terms of the debt itself, high interest rates also have an ominous implication. As economist Philip Cagan explains the problem, "Interest payments on the debt add to future deficits, requiring ever larger budgetary adjustments to control the deficits at some later date, while growing debt and deficits tend to raise the interest rate."[11] Higher

interest rates will lead to more debt and thus even
higher interest rates. This cycle will continue until
something is done about the deficits and the debt,
unless the Federal Reserve tries to reduce the debt
burden with inflation, a scenario that seems very
unlikely under present circumstances.
     This discussion of interest rates, along with
previous comparisons between the present debt with past
debt expansions, calls into question whether fears over
the size of the public debt are necessary. That such
fears exist is obvious. As Robert Heilbroner and Peter
Bernstein point out, in a 1988 survey of voters, 44
percent believed that deficit reduction was the most
important task facing the Bush administration that took
office in 1989. To put those fears into context, the
next section will present a deficit and debt reduction
plan to show how readily the economy can handle the debt
if its members want to.

A DEBT REDUCTION PLAN

     In order for the deficit and the debt to be
reduced, surpluses must occur in the federal
government's budget, either through reductions in
spending or increases in taxes; in the long run a
combination of both coupled with a growing economy will
do the job. So far budget reductions and tax increases
seem unlikely to happen. As noted in chapter 10, in
1985 Congress enacted the Gramm-Rudman-Hollings Act,
which required a balanced budget by 1991; as of this
writing, it is clear that the goals of the act will not
be met.[12]
     As the deadline for deficit reduction for the 1991
budget approached, however, realization dawned in
Washington that something would have to be done. A team
of negotiators representing the president and the
Congress began meeting in the Summer of 1990 to prepare
a deficit reduction plan. After wasting much time
debating the merits of a capital gains tax reduction, at
the last possible minute on September 30, just before
mandatory across budget reductions mandated by the
Gramm-Rudman-Hollings Act would have been made, the
negotiators did agree on a deficit reduction plan. That
plan was not accepted by Congress. After several weeks
of wrangling, Congress did pass a budget plan. Under
the plan, the budget deficit estimated for fiscal year
1990 would be reduced by $40 billion and a total of $500
billion in deficit reductions would be made over the
following five years. These reductions would be paid
for with a combination of tax increases, especially
excise taxes on gasoline and alcohol, and program cuts
in medicare and military spending.

The 1990 deficit reduction plan will not do much in terms of reducing the public debt. Projections show that the deficit for 1991 may total as much as $250 billion, even with the reduction, and it is not likely that it will diminish until much later during the five-year program. Even then the projected deficit for 1995 is still in the range of $150 billion. If the economy enters into a recession, as appears very likely at this time, or if the present war-like conditions in the middle-east turn for the worse, the deficit will be even larger over the next five years. The public debt can only continue to increase under these circumstances, probably doubling by the end of the century.

Additional tax increases seem out of the question. As described above, tax increases at the beginning of a recession can only serve to make things worse. Besides, President Bush wants to keep his promise to the American people to have no new taxes. The problem may rest with the American people, however. As David Stockman once put it, "The problem is that this democracy is somewhat ambivalent about what it wants. It wants low taxes and substantial public spending."[13] In his own assessment of the tax situation, President Bush has said that we have "more will than wallet."

But is this so? Or is it more likely that we have the wallet but not the will? To make an estimate of the nation's ability to eliminate the deficit and reduce the debt, a hypothetical experiment will be undertaken. To avoid any charge of political bias, this experimental plan will be patterned after the debt reduction plan proposed after the Civil War by Secretary of the Treasury Hugh McCulloch, as described in chapter 4. That plan relied on tariffs and excise taxes, not very large sources of tax revenue today. In keeping with current notions of broadening the tax base, however, the McCulloch plan will be extended across the board to all commodities.

In the 1980s, imports have grown from a $300 billion annual rate in 1980 to a $650 billion annual rate in 1989. Throughout the last four decades of the nineteenth century, tariffs averaged around 40 percent of dutiable items. Had similar tariff rates been enacted across the board in the 1980s, they would have added $120 to $260 billion to the government's revenue, enough to have balanced the budget. Could the economy have sustained such high tariff rates? The answer is probably yes, since the exchange rate of the dollar declined by nearly 40 percent from 1985 to 1989. The resultant price increases are similar to what a 40 percent tariff would have caused, and still imports continued to increase throughout the decade. The revenues from those higher prices could have gone directly to the Treasury in the form of tariff collections, instead of being borrowed from foreigners as has been the case.[14]

With tariffs taking care of the budget deficit, an excise tax could then be used to reduce the debt. During the 1980s personal consumption expenditures have risen from about $2 trillion a year in 1981 to nearly $3.5 trillion a year in 1989. Taking the current level of expenditures, a national sales tax on consumer goods of 4 percent, to pick a number as an example,[15] would raise $140 billion per year. Assuming that interest rates remain at their present level of 9 percent and no annual increases in GNP, $140 billion a year would pay off the public debt in 20 years. A reduction in interest rates and growth in GNP would make the payback period even shorter; if government spending increased in step with these tax increases, or if these tax increases greatly altered economic behavior, then the experiment would be less likely to succeed.

It should be recalled, however, that McCulloch's version of this policy did result in a 25-year string of federal government surpluses that cut the existing public debt in half. Taking a longer view, the only periods of consistent government surpluses have been during times when tariff rates were high, such as in the 1830s, 1850s, and the 1920s. Not that a policy of high tariffs is being advocated here; the above calculations represent little more than some jottings on a cocktail napkin to show how easily we can afford to pay off the debt, although larger policy experiments than this have resulted from less. It could be worse. The point of this little exercise is to show that we do have the wallet to reduce the deficit and pay off the debt.

But how much of the debt should be paid off? To answer this question, consider what the economy would be like without the public debt. First, the Federal Reserve currently holds about $230 billion of the debt; paying off the debt would require it to take in and retire an equal amount of dollars. It would then lose its ability to conduct open market operations as a tool for influencing the money supply. Some might applaud this result, recognizing as well that any efforts to establish "free banking" are very unlikely as long as the Federal Reserve must exist to help the Treasury manage and administer the public debt. Second, many banks, insurance companies, and pension funds purchase government securities as a secure investment. What type of securities will they use in place of those bonds? Third, at a more commonplace level, what will replace U.S. savings bonds as gifts? The point is that the public debt pervades the financial and social aspects of life in the United States in ways that are not always appreciated.

In fact, it may not be possible to pay off the

public debt, even if the will to do so existed.   As noted above, government trust funds hold their assets in the form of government securities.   In 1989 these trust funds held $660 billion in government securities. Starting in 1985, the trust funds began showing a surplus.   In the case of the Highway Trust Fund it could be that the government has decided to lend the money to itself rather than spend it.   With the Social Security Trust Fund the increase is due to increased Social Security tax rates for individual taxpayers.   Estimates now indicate that the Social Security Trust Fund will have a surplus of as much as $12 trillion by the year 2033,[16] but that those funds will be exhausted by 2046.[17]

This figure raises two troubling questions.   If the debt is not reduced, how will the money be raised to liquidate these funds when they are needed to pay retirement benefits to the baby boom generation?   Taxes on the rest of the population?   Borrowing from them?   It would appear that a frugal choice would be for the government to begin running a surplus from the rest of its budget to build up the funds necessary to accomplish this liquidity.   But if there is a series of budget surpluses, and they are used to pay off a portion of the public debt, what will the Social Security Trust Fund do with its $12 trillion surplus?   Will it be permitted to purchase corporate stocks and bonds?   Place deposits in banks?   Above it was noted that with the Social Security System, the government had created a means for it to borrow.   Now it would appear that it may have created the necessity to borrow as well.

As described in earlier chapters, surpluses in the federal government's budget can cause problems as vexing as deficits.   The troubles caused by the mounting surpluses of the 1830s and 1880s should remind us that paying back the debt can create as much of a burden on the economy as borrowing it.   So if anything is done about the present situation of high deficits and public debt, it will make the next 50 years of public debt management and administration as interesting and complicated as the previous two centuries.

NOTES

1. For a discussion of the problems of measuring the debt and the deficit, see Robert Eisner, How Real Is the Federal Deficit (New York: Free Press, 1986), pp. 1-47, and Robert Heilbroner and Peter Bernstein, The Debt and the Deficit (New York: W.W. Norton, 1989), pp. 29-45, 69-98.

2. The Committee on Public Debt Policy, Our National Debt (New York: Harcourt, Brace, 1949), p. 9.

3. See for example Heilbroner and Bernstein, Debt and Deficit, pp. 41-44.

4. There is also a problem in looking at the government's budget because it does not list capital items separately from current expenditures. See Heilbroner and Bernstein, Debt and Deficit, pp. 59-65, and Eisner, How Real Is Deficit, pp. 26-40.

5. The data in Tables 11.1 and 11.2 exclude public debt held by government trust funds and the Federal Reserve Banks. Inclusion of those holdings would increase the debt/GNP ratio to slightly over 50 percent.

6. The interest rates cited reflect the stated rates the securities paid at par. The actual yield on the securities would depend on whether the securities sold at par; it was not unusual before auction sales for securities to sell at prices significantly above or below par, as has been noted in earlier chapters.

7. See the discussion of this issue in Michael J. Boskin, Reagan and the Economy (San Francisco: ICS Press, 1987), pp. 185-189.

8. Paul Craig Roberts, "Why the Deficit Hysteria Is Unjustified," in Robert H. Fink and Jack C. High, eds., A Nation in Debt (Frederick, Md.:   University Publications of America, 1987), pp. 83-86. See also Heilbroner and Bernstein, Debt and Deficit, pp. 102-104.

9. For analysis that finds evidence to support the crowding-out effect, see Richard J. Cebula, The Deficit Problem in Perspective (Lexington, Mass.: Lexington Books, 1987), pp. 43-55. See also Eisner, How Real Is Deficit, p. 58, and Heilbroner and Bernstein, Debt and Deficit, pp. 104-111, for the opposite view.

10. Phillip Cagan, "Financing the Deficit, Interest Rates and Monetary Policy," in P. Cagan, ed., The Economy in Deficit, 1985 (Washington, D.C.:   American Enterprise Institute, 1985), p. 217.

11. Phillip Cagan, "Introduction," in Cagan, Economy in Deficit, p. 3.

12. Howard Gleckman, "The Bottom Line: Gramm-Rudman Isn't Working," Business Week, April 10, 1989, p. 36. See also Preston J. Miller, "Gramm-Rudman-Hollings Hold on Budget Policy: Losing Its Grip?" Federal Reserve Bank

of Minneapolis, <u>Quarterly Review,</u> Winter 1989, pp. 11-20.

13. Cited in Norman J. Ornstein, "The Politics of the Deficit," in Cagan, ed., <u>Economy in Deficit,</u> p. 311.

14. We are ignoring, of course, the problems that tariffs might have caused in terms of the retaliatory measures, if any, that might have been taken by our trading partners. Nor do we wish to raise the bogeyman of the country being in debt to foreigners. Taking the longer view, the foreign-held component of the public debt was 15 percent in 1789, 13 percent in 1866, and 12.8 percent in 1988.

15. This example is not too far fetched. The Japanese government recently imposed a 3 percent consumption tax on its citizens. The debt and deficit experience in Japan recently has been similar to that of the U.S., with Japan's deficits in the 1980s running at about 5 percent of GNP; as a result, the debt/GNP ratio has gone from about 35 percent to over 40 percent during the last decade.

16. Heilbroner and Bernstein, <u>Debt and Deficit,</u> p. 73.

17. Spencer Rich, "Social Security Funds 'Financially Sound,'" <u>The Washington Post,</u> April 25, 1989, p. A6.

Bibliography

Abbott, Charles C. The Federal Debt: Structure and
    Impact. New York: Twentieth Century Fund, 1953.
Anderson, Bette B. Internal memorandum. Washington,
    D.C.: BPD File D-120.9, December 20, 1980.
_____. Internal memorandum. Washington, D.C.: BPD
    File D-120.9, December 24, 1980.
Anderson, Gary M. "The U.S. Federal Deficit and
    National Debt: A Political and Economic History."
    In Buchanan, James M., Rowley, Charles K., and
    Tollinson, Robert D., eds., Deficits. New York:
    Basil Blackwell, 1987.
Anderson, William H. Financing Modern Government.
    Boston: Houghton Mifflin, 1973.
Author Unknown. "A Record Home for Millions." Business
    Automation, June 1963.
Baziluik, Linda. "Division of Securities Operations:
    Look Where We've Been." Public Debt Newsletter,
    1973-75.
Bequai, August. The Cashless Society: EFTS At the
    Crossroads. New York: Wiley, 1981.
Bolles, Albert S. The Financial History of the United
    States, From 1774 to 1784. New York: D. Appleton,
    1892.
Boskin, Michael J. Reagan and the Economy. San
    Francisco: ILS Press, 1987.
Buchanan, James M., and Flowers, Marilyn. The Public
    Finances. 6th ed. Homewood, Ill.: Richard D.
    Irwin, 1987.
Cagan, Phillip. "Financing the Deficit, Interest Rates
    and Monetary Policy." In Cagan, P., ed., The
    Economy in Deficit, 1985. Washington, D.C.:
    American Enterprise Institute, 1985.
Cambridge Planning and Analytics, Inc. DATADISK.
    Cambridge, Mass.: 1989.

Campagna, Anthony S.   U.S. National Economic Policy,
    1917-1985. New York: Praeger, 1987.
Cebula, Richard J. The Deficit Problem in Perspective.
    Lexington, Mass: Lexington Books, 1987.
Chandler, Lester V. The Economics of Money and Banking.
    4th ed. New York: Harper & Row, 1964.
Corrigan, E. Gerald.   "Statement by the President,
    Federal Reserve Bank of New York, before the
    Subcommittee on Securities, U.S. Senate." Federal
    Reserve Bulletin, July 1985.
Council of Economic Advisors.   "The Full Employment
    Surplus Concept." In Smith, Warren J., and Teigen,
    Ronald L., eds., Readings in Money, National Income
    and Stabilization Policy. Homewood, Ill.: Richard
    D. Irwin, 1970.
Crenson, Matthew A., and Rourke, Francis E. "By Way of
    Conclusion: American Bureaucracy since World War
    II." In Galombos, Louis, ed., The New American
    State. Baltimore: Johns Hopkins University Press,
    1987.
DeConde, Alexander.   A History of American Foreign
    Policy. New York: Scribner, 1963.
Dewey, Davis R. Financial History of the United States.
    New York: Longmans, Green, 1934.
Dorfman, Joseph.   The Economic Mind in American
    Civilization 1606-1865. New York: Viking, 1946.
Eisner, Robert. How Real Is the Federal Deficit. New
    York: Free Press, 1986.
Eisner, Robert, and Pieper, Paul J. "How to Make Sense
    of the Deficit." In Fink, Robert H., and High,
    Jack C., eds., A Nation in Debt. Frederick, Md.:
    University Publications of America, 1987.
Englund, John.   "New Computer Installed." PD News,
    October 1986.
Fabozzi, Frank J., and Fabozzi, T. Dessa.   Bond
    Markets, Analysis and Strategies.   Englewood
    Cliffs, N.J.: Prentice Hall Inc., 1989.
Federal Reserve System.   "Developments in Consumer
    Electronic Fund Transfers." Bulletin, June 1983.
Federal Reserve System. Bulletin, July 1985.
Federal Reserve System. Bulletin, August 1985.
Federal Reserve System. Bulletin, January 1986.
Federal Reserve System. Bulletin, January 1989.
Ferguson, James, E. The Power of the Purse. Chapel
    Hill, N.C.: University of North Carolina Press,
    1961.
Friedman, Milton, and Heller, Walter. Monetary vs
    Fiscal Policy. New York: W.W. Norton, 1969.
Friedman, Milton, and Schwartz, Anna. A Monetary
    History of the United States. Princeton, N.J.:
    Princeton University Press, 1963.

Gaines, Tilford C.   Techniques of Treasury Debt
    Management. New York: Free Press of Glencoe,
    1962.
Glass, Secretary Carter. Memorandum. Washington, D.C.:
    Bureau of the Public Debt, January 6, 1920.
Gleckman, Howard. "The Bottom Line: Gramm-Rudman Isn't
    Working." Business Week, April 10, 1989.
Gordon, Robert A. Economic Instability and Growth: The
    American Record. New York: Harper & Row, 1974.
Gurney, Gene, and Gurney, Clare. The United States
    Treasury: A Pictorial History. New York: Crown,
    1978.
Hacker, Louis.   "Secretary of the Treasury."   In
    Cochran, T. C., and Brewer, T. B., eds., Views of
    American Economic Growth: The Agricultural Era.
    New York: McGraw-Hill, 1966.
Hailstones, Thomas J.   Viewpoints on Supply-Side
    Economics. Richmond Va.: Robert F. Dane, 1982.
Hamby, Alonzo, ed.   The New Deal: Analysis and
    Interpretation. New York: Weybright and Talley,
    1969.
Hammond, Bray.   Banks and Politics in America.
    Princeton, N.J.: Princeton University Press, 1957.
Harris, Seymour E.   The National Debt and the New
    Economics. New York: McGraw-Hill, 1947.
Heckman, M. P. Memorandum. Bureau of the Public Debt
    Files, February 19, 1962.
Heilbroner, Robert, and Bernstein, Peter. The Debt and
    the Deficit. New York: W.W. Norton, 1989.
Hibbs, Douglas A., Jr. The American Political Economy.
    Cambridge, Mass.: Harvard University Press, 1987.
Hickman, Frederick W.   Memorandum to H.J. Hintgen.
    Washington, D.C.: Bureau of the Public Debt, File
    120.611, April 3, 1973.
Hintgen, H. J.   Circular letter. Washington, D.C.:
    Bureau of the Public Debt, File D-120.9, March 20,
    1972.
Hintgen, H. J.   Draft Memorandum. Washington, D.C.:
    Undated.
Hintgen, H. J.   Memorandum to all Employees.
    Washington, D.C.: June 16, 1967.
Hintgen, H. J.   Memorandum to D. M. Merritt.
    Washington, D.C.: Bureau of the Public Debt, File
    D-120.9, June 26, 1963.
Holsopple, Ellie. "Learning a New Alphabet with the
    OSAS Reorganization." PD News, January 1988.
Kilby, E. L. Memorandum. Washington, D.C.: March 19,
    1949.
Kilby, E. L.   Memorandum to William W. Parsons.
    Washington, D.C.: March 17, 1958, Copy in Bureau
    files.
Kilby, E. L. Report of Commissioner E. L. Kilby to the
    Secretary of the Treasury.   Washington, D.C.:

December 1, 1952.

Kirkland, Edward Chase. _Industry Comes of Age_. Chicago: Quadrangle Books, 1967.

Lee, Susan Previant, and Passell, Peter. _A New View of American History_. New York: W.W. Norton, 1979.

Leffingwell, R. C. Memorandum to Carter Glass. Washington, D.C.: Public Debt Files, Important Data File D-120.94, November 11, 1919, vol. 1.

Lekachman, Robert. _The Age of Keynes_. New York: Random House, 1966.

McConnell, Campbell R. _Economics_. New York: McGraw-Hill, 1987.

McGeoghegan, Michael. Letter. Public Debt Files, November 20, 1974.

Miller, Preston J. "Gramm-Rudman-Hollings' Hold on Budget Policy: Losing Its Grip?" Federal Reserve Bank of Minneapolis, _Quarterly Review_, Winter, 1989.

Mitchell, Wesley Clair. _A History of the Greenbacks_. Chicago: University of Chicago Press, 1903.

Morse, Jarvis M. _Paying for a World War_. Located in Bureau of the Public Debt files, Undated.

Murphy, Henry C. _National Debt in War and Transition_. New York: McGraw-Hill, 1950.

Musgrave, Richard A., and Musgrave, Peggy B. _Public Finance in Theory and Practice_. New York: McGraw-Hill, 1980.

Myers, Margaret G. _A Financial History of the United States_. New York: Columbia University Press, 1970.

Ott, David J., and Ott, Attiat F. "Fiscal Policy and the National Debt." In Smith, Warren J., and Teigen, Ronald L., eds., _Readings in Money, National Income and Stabilization Policy_. Homewood, Ill.: Richard D. Irwin, 1970.

Paine, Thomas S. _Common Sense and Other Political Writings_. Indianapolis, Ind.: Bobbs-Merrill, 1953.

Penner, Rudolph G., and Abramson, Alan J. _Broken Purse Strings_. Washington, D.C.: Urban Institute Press, 1988.

Peterson, Wallace G. _Income, Employment and Economic Growth_ 6th ed. New York: W.W. Norton, 1988.

Pfau, Sandy. "Continuing the Partnership: Cleveland FRB Helps Develop PARS." _PD News_, March 1988.

Pfau, Sandy. "To Strip or Not to Strip." _PD Newsletter_, February 1987.

Polk, James K. Handwritten copy of letter to Robert J. Walker, April 11, 1845, located in files at the Bureau of the Public Debt.

Poulson, Barry W. _Economic History of the United States_. New York: Macmillan, 1981.

Reed, Bob. "$7,413,100,688 and Counting . . ." _PD_

Newsletter, April 1987.

Remini, Robert. _Andrew Jackson and the Bank War_. New York: W.W. Norton, 1967.

Rich, Spenser. "Social Security Funds 'Financially Sound.'" _The Washington Post,_ April 25, 1989.

Roberts, Paul Craig. "Why the Deficit Hysteria is Unjustified." In Fink, R., and High, J., eds., _A Nation in Debt_. Frederick, Md: University Publications of America, 1987.

Roosevelt, Franklin D. _Third Plan on Government Reorganization_. Washington, D.C.: House Document No. 681, 76th Congress, April 2, 1940.

Rose, Mary K. Memorandum. Parkersburg W.Va.: February 21, 1975.

Rosencrans, W. S. Letter to the Secretary of the Treasury, dated October 15, 1888, copy in files of the Bureau of the Public Debt.

Rukstad, Michael G. _Macroeconomic Decision Making in the World Economy_. Chicago: Dryden Press, 1986.

Sanders, Donald H. _Computers in Society_. New York: McGraw-Hill, 1981.

Savage, James D. _Balanced Budgets and American Politics_. Ithaca, N.Y.: Cornell University Press, 1988.

Schlesinger, Arthur M., Jr. _The Age of Jackson_. Boston: Little, Brown, 1950.

Schlifer, Gail. "Interview with Ellen Seidman." _PD News,_ September 1987.

Snyder, John L. Letter from John L. Snyder, Secretary of the Treasury, to Senator John L. McClellan. Washington, D.C.: August 2, 1949.

Sorkin, Alan E. _Monetary and Fiscal Policy & Business Cycles in the Modern Era_. Lexington, Mass.: Lexington Books, 1988.

Stein, Herbert. _Presidential Economics_. New York: Simon & Schuster, 1984.

Strenlight, Peter D. "Statement given to U.S. House Subcommittee on Domestic Monetary Policy." Federal Reserve _Bulletin,_ April 1982.

Studenski, Paul, and Kroos, Herman E. _Financial History of the United States_. 2nd ed. New York: McGraw-Hill, 1963.

Swanson, David F. _The Origins of Hamilton's Fiscal Policies_. Gainesville, Fla.: University of Florida Monographs, Winter 1963.

Taus, Esther R. _Central Banking Functions of the United States Treasury, 1789-1941_. New York: Columbia University Press, 1943.

Taus, Esther R. _The Role of the U.S. Treasury in Stabilizing the Economy_. Washington, D.C.: University Press of America, 1981.

Taylor, George R. ed., _Hamilton and the National Debt_. Boston: D.C. Heath, 1950.

The Committee on Public Debt Policy. Our National Debt.
    New York: Harcourt, Brace, 1949.
Timberlake, Richard H., Jr.   The Origins of Central
    Banking in the United States. Cambridge, Mass.:
    Harvard University Press, 1976.
Tobin, James. "A Keynesian View of the Budget Deficit."
    In Fink, Robert H., and High, Jack C., eds., A
    Nation in Debt.   Frederick, Md.:   University
    Publications of America, 1987.
U.S. Congress. House. Reorganization Act of 1939, 76th
    Congress, 1939. H. Report. 120.
U.S. Congress. Senate. Reorganization Act of 1939,
    76th Congress, 1939. S. Report. 142.
U.S. Congress. Senate. Reorganization of the Federal
    Government, 82nd Congress, 1952. S. Doc. 91.
U.S. Congress. House. Report on the Condition of the
    Office of the Treasurer of the United States, 42nd
    Congress, May 2, 1872.
U.S.   Congress.   Senate.   Select   Committee   on
    Retrenchment of the Senate, 40th Congress, March 3,
    1869.
U.S. Department of Commerce, Bureau of the Census.
    Historical Statistics of the United States, Part 2,
    1976.
U.S. Department of the Treasury. Annual Report of the
    Secretary of the Treasury, 1815.
U.S. Department of the Treasury. Annual Report of the
    Secretary of the Treasury, 1835.
U.S. Department of the Treasury. Annual Report of the
    Secretary of the Treasury, 1837.
U.S. Department of the Treasury. Annual Report of the
    Secretary of the Treasury, 1847.
U.S. Department of the Treasury. Annual Report of the
    Secretary of the Treasury, 1863.
U.S. Department of the Treasury. Annual Report of the
    Secretary of the Treasury, 1864.
U.S. Department of the Treasury. Annual Report of the
    Secretary of the Treasury, 1865.
U.S. Department of the Treasury. Annual Report of the
    Secretary of the Treasury, 1866.
U.S. Department of the Treasury. Annual Report of the
    Secretary of the Treasury, 1870.
U.S. Department of the Treasury. Annual Report of the
    Secretary of the Treasury, 1875.
U.S. Department of the Treasury. Annual Report of the
    Secretary of the Treasury, 1876.
U.S. Department of the Treasury. Annual Report of the
    Secretary of the Treasury, 1878.
U.S. Department of the Treasury. Annual Report of the
    Secretary of the Treasury, 1894.
U.S. Department of the Treasury. Annual Report of the
    Secretary of the Treasury, 1895.
U.S. Department of the Treasury. Annual Report of the

Secretary of the Treasury, 1917.
U.S. Department of the Treasury. Annual Report of the
     Secretary of the Treasury, 1918.
U.S. Department of the Treasury. Annual Report of the
     Secretary of the Treasury, 1919.
U.S. Department of the Treasury. Annual Report of the
     Secretary of the Treasury, 1941.
U.S. Department of the Treasury. Annual Report of the
     Secretary of the Treasury, 1942.
U.S. Department of the Treasury. Annual Report of the
     Secretary of the Treasury, 1943.
U.S. Department of the Treasury. Annual Report of the
     Secretary of the Treasury, 1944.
U.S. Department of the Treasury. Annual Report of the
     Secretary of the Treasury, 1945.
U.S. Department of the Treasury. Annual Report of the
     Secretary of the Treasury, 1946.
U.S. Department of the Treasury. Annual Report of the
     Secretary of the Treasury, 1947.
U.S. Department of the Treasury. Annual Report of the
     Secretary of the Treasury, 1948.
U.S. Department of the Treasury. Annual Report of the
     Secretary of the Treasury, 1949.
U.S. Department of the Treasury. Annual Report of the
     Secretary of the Treasury, 1950.
U.S. Department of the Treasury. Annual Report of the
     Secretary of the Treasury, 1951.
U.S. Department of the Treasury. Annual Report of the
     Secretary of the Treasury, 1952.
U.S. Department of the Treasury. Annual Report of the
     Secretary of the Treasury, 1953.
U.S. Department of the Treasury. Annual Report of the
     Secretary of the Treasury, 1954.
U.S. Department of the Treasury. Annual Report of the
     Secretary of the Treasury, 1955.
U.S. Department of the Treasury. Annual Report of the
     Secretary of the Treasury, 1956.
U.S. Department of the Treasury. Annual Report of the
     Secretary of the Treasury, 1959.
U.S. Department of the Treasury. Annual Report of the
     Secretary of the Treasury, 1960.
U.S. Department of the Treasury. Annual Report of the
     Secretary of the Treasury, 1961.
U.S. Department of the Treasury. Annual Report of the
     Secretary of the Treasury, 1962.
U.S. Department of the Treasury. Annual Report of the
     Secretary of the Treasury, 1963.
U.S. Department of the Treasury. Annual Report of the
     Secretary of the Treasury, 1965.
U.S. Department of the Treasury. Annual Report of the
     Secretary of the Treasury, 1966.
U.S. Department of the Treasury. Annual Report of the
     Secretary of the Treasury, 1967.

U.S. Department of the Treasury. _Annual Report of the Secretary of the Treasury_, 1968.

U.S. Department of the Treasury. _Annual Report of the Secretary of the Treasury_, 1969.

U.S. Department of the Treasury. _Annual Report of the Secretary of the Treasury_, 1970.

U.S. Department of the Treasury. _Annual Report of the Secretary of the Treasury_, 1971.

U.S. Department of the Treasury. _Annual Report of the Secretary of the Treasury_, 1972.

U.S. Department of the Treasury. _Annual Report of the Secretary of the Treasury_, 1973.

U.S. Department of the Treasury. _Annual Report of the Secretary of the Treasury_, 1975.

U.S. Department of the Treasury. _Annual Report of the Secretary of the Treasury_, 1976.

U.S. Department of the Treasury. _Annual Report of the Secretary of the Treasury_, 1977.

U.S. Department of the Treasury. _Annual Report of the Secretary of the Treasury_, 1978.

U.S. Department of the Treasury. _Annual Report of the Secretary of the Treasury_, 1979.

U.S. Department of the Treasury. _Annual Report of the Secretary of the Treasury_, 1980.

U.S. Department of the Treasury. _File D100.4, Subject: Treasury Department_. Washington, D.C.: 1936.

U.S. Department of the Treasury. _A History of the United States Savings Bond Program_. Washington, D.C.: September 1984.

U.S. Department of the Treasury. _Progress in Management Improvement_. Washington, D.C.: FY 1968.

U.S. Department of the Treasury. _Public Debt Accounting_. Washington, D.C.: 1976.

U.S. Department of the Treasury. _Report of the Register of the Treasury_. Washington, D.C.: 1889.

U.S. Department of the Treasury. _Report of the Register of the Treasury_. Washington, D.C.: 1892.

U.S. Department of the Treasury. _Report to the Secretary from the Fiscal Assistant Secretary_. Washington, D.C.: December 1, 1952.

U.S. Department of the Treasury. _Treasury Bulletin_, February 1972.

U.S. Department of the Treasury. _Treasury Bulletin_, December 1980.

U.S. Department of the Treasury. _Treasury Bulletin_, Winter Issue, March 1988.

U.S. Department of the Treasury. _Treasury News Press Release_, September 22, 1987.

U.S. Department of the Treasury. _Treasury News Press Release_, December 16, 1987.

U.S. Department of the Treasury. "Wrestling with Leviathan--How Treasury Manages the Debt." _Treasury Papers_, October 1976.

U.S. Department of the Treasury, Bureau of the Public
    Debt. Administrative History of War Activities of
    the Chicago Office of the Bureau of the Public
    Debt. Chicago: circa July 1946.
U.S. Department of the Treasury, Bureau of the Public
Debt. "Book-Entry Evolution." PD News, Spring   1984.
U.S. Department of the Treasury, Bureau of the Public
    Debt.   Bureau of Public Debt-Talking Points.
    Washington, D.C.: BPD Files 120.9 IDF, June 10,
    1982.
U.S. Department of the Treasury, Bureau of the Public
    Debt.   "Bureau Spotlight: Division of Investor
    Accounts." PD News, October 1982.
U.S. Department of the Treasury, Bureau of the Public
    Debt.   "Bureau   Spotlight: The   Office   of
    Financing." PD Newsletter, July 1982.
U.S. Department of the Treasury, Bureau of the Public
    Debt.   Commissioner's Monthly Statement of the
    Public Debt of the United States. September 30,
    1988.
U.S. Department of the Treasury, Bureau of the Public
    Debt.   Commissioner's Monthly Status Report for
    July 1984. Washington, D.C.: BPD files.
U.S. Department of the Treasury, Bureau of the Public
    Debt.   Commissioner's Monthly Status Report for
    February 1985. Washington, D.C.: BPD files.
U.S. Department of the Treasury, Bureau of the Public
    Debt. Commissioner's Staff Papers for March 1985.
    Washington, D.C.: BPD files.
U.S. Department of the Treasury, Bureau of the Public
    Debt.   Commissioner's Monthly Status Report for
    August 1986. Washington, D.C.: BPD files.
U.S. Department of the Treasury, Bureau of the Public
    Debt.   Commissioner's Monthly Status Report for
    September 1987. Washington, D.C.: BPD files.
U.S. Department of the Treasury, Bureau of the Public
    Debt.   Commissioner's Monthly Status Report for
    December 1987. Washington, D.C.: BPD files.
U.S. Department of the Treasury, Bureau of the Public
    Debt.   Commissioner's Monthly Status Report for
    January 1988. Washington, D.C.: BPD files.
U.S. Department of the Treasury, Bureau of the Public
    Debt.   Commissioner's Monthly Status Report for
    March 1988. Washington, D.C.: BPD files.
U.S. Department of the Treasury, Bureau of the Public
    Debt.   Commissioner's Monthly Status Report for
    April 1988. Washington, D.C.: BPD files.
U.S. Department of the Treasury, Bureau of the Public
    Debt.   "The   Commissioner's   Treasury   Bill
    Committee." PD News, June 1982.
U.S. Department of the Treasury, Bureau of the Public
    Debt. Data File D-120, History of the Public Debt
    Organization. Washington, D.C.: 1952.

U.S. Department of the Treasury, Bureau of the Public
     Debt.   "The Debt Goes Abroad."   PD News, Spring
     1985.

U.S. Department of the Treasury, Bureau of the Public
     Debt.   "Debt Reaches 1,000,000,000." PD News,
     January 1982.

U.S. Department of the Treasury, Bureau of the Public
     Debt.   Description of Parkersburg Office
     Responsibilities and Functions. Washington, D.C.:
     October 18, 1974.

U.S. Department of the Treasury, Bureau of the Public
     Debt. Draft Memo P.D. 2694 (8.57). Washington,
     D.C.: April 1976.

U.S. Department of the Treasury, Bureau of the Public
     Debt. Draft Memo P.D. 2994 (88.57). Washington,
     D.C.: 1976.

U.S. Department of the Treasury, Bureau of the Public
     Debt.   Establishment of New Bureau Office.
     Washington, D.C.: October 15, 1984.

U.S. Department of the Treasury, Bureau of the Public
     Debt. Field Notes, No. 1, 1978.

U.S. Department of the Treasury, Bureau of the Public
     Debt. Field Notes, No. 2, 1978.

U.S. Department of the Treasury, Bureau of the Public
     Debt. Field Notes, No. 3, 1978.

U.S. Department of the Treasury, Bureau of the Public
     Debt. Functional Chart, Savings Bond Operations
     Office. Parkersburg, W.Va.: February 1981.

U.S. Department of the Treasury, Bureau of the Public
     Debt. "The Government Securities Act of 1986." PD
     News, Special Section, August 1987.

U.S. Department of the Treasury, Bureau of the Public
     Debt.   History of the U.S. Savings Bond Office.
     Parkersburg W.Va.:   circa 1975 (in Parkersburg
     office files).

U.S. Department of the Treasury, Bureau of the Public
     Debt. History of War Activities, Bureau of the
     Public Debt. Washington, D.C.: 1949.

U.S. Department of the Treasury, Bureau of the Public
     Debt. "In Almost Heaven." PD News, October 1982.

U.S. Department of the Treasury, Bureau of the Public
     Debt.   Information about Marketable Treasury
     Securities (Bills, Notes and Bonds) Sold at
     Original Issue. Revised July 1986.

U.S. Department of the Treasury, Bureau of the Public
     Debt. Internal Memorandum. Washington, D.C.:
     Undated.

U.S. Department of the Treasury, Bureau of the Public
     Debt. Internal Memorandum. Washington, D.C.:
     October 18, 1974.

U.S. Department of the Treasury, Bureau of the Public
     Debt. Long-Range Plan. Washington, D.C.: 1988
     edition.

U.S. Department of the Treasury, Bureau of the Public
     Debt. _Personnel Reports of Full-Time Employees_.
     Washington D.C.: BPD File D-200.5.
U.S. Department of the Treasury, Bureau of the Public
     Debt. _Progress Report on Major Projects - First
     Half of FY 1984_. Washington, D.C.: April 28,
     1984.
U.S. Department of the Treasury, Bureau of the Public
     Debt. _Project   NEW   Requirements   Analysis_.
     Washington, D.C.: Undated, located in BPD files.
U.S. Department of the Treasury, Bureau of the Public
     Debt. _Public Debt News_, First Quarter, 1972.
U.S. Department of the Treasury, Bureau of the Public
     Debt. _Public Debt News_, First Quarter, 1973.
U.S. Department of the Treasury, Bureau of the Public
     Debt. _Public Debt News_, Spring Issue, 1975.
U.S. Department of the Treasury, Bureau of the Public
     Debt. _Public Debt News_, June 1979.
U.S. Department of the Treasury, Bureau of the Public
     Debt. _Public Debt News_, October 1982.
U.S. Department of the Treasury, Bureau of the Public
     Debt. _Request for Purchase of Computer Equipment_.
     Parkersburg, Wa.Va.: September 1969.
U.S. Department of the Treasury, Bureau of the Public
     Debt. _Savings Bond Symposium_. Parkersburg, W.Va.:
     1955. (Bond manual in Parkersburg office files)
U.S. Department of the Treasury, Bureau of the Public
     Debt. "Savings Bond Update." _PD News_, August
     1983.
U.S. Department of the Treasury, Bureau of the Public
     Debt. _Schedule for Assisting Displaced Employees
     Find Jobs_. Chicago: November 11, 1974.
U.S. Department of the Treasury, Bureau of the Public
     Debt. _Summary of Decisions Made and Action Taken
     to Upgrade the EDP System in Parkersburg, West
     Virginia_. Parkersburg, W.Va.: September 28, 1962.
U.S. Department of the Treasury, Bureau of the Public
     Debt. _Summary of Its History and Principal
     Functions, etc._ Washington, D.C.: May 1954.
U.S. Department of the Treasury, Bureau of the Public
     Debt. "TDAB Breaks New Ground in Automated Data
     Processing to Save Treasury Millions." _PD News_,
     July 1985.
U.S. Department of the Treasury, Bureau of the Public
     Debt. "Treasury Endorses Stripping." _PD News_,
     Spring 1985.
U.S. Department of the Treasury, Bureau of the Public
     Debt. "TREASURY DIRECT." _PD News_, Special
     Edition, September 1986.
U.S. Department of the Treasury, Bureau of the Public
     Debt. Untitled and undated (circa 1976) report.
     Washington, D.C.: BPD files.
U.S. Department of the Treasury, Bureau of the Public

Debt. "Van Zeck Appointed Deputy Commissioner."
PD News, June 1987.

U.S. Department of the Treasury, Bureau of the Public
Debt. "What Is This Thing." PD News, Fall 1984.

U.S. Department of the Treasury, Bureau of the Public
Debt, Division of ADP Management. Project NEW.
Washington, D.C.: August 10, 1984.

U.S. Department of the Treasury, Bureau of the Public
Debt, Field Office. Newsletter, March 1, 1977.

U.S. Department of the Treasury, Bureau of the Public
Debt, Savings Bond Operations Office. Annual
Report. Washington D.C.: Fiscal Year 1983.

U.S. Government Printing Office. The Public Debt
Service. Washington, D.C.: April 1921.

U.S. Government Printing Office. "Regulations Governing
United States Savings Bonds, Series EE and HH."
Federal Register, December 26, 1979.

U.S. Government Printing Office. Statistical Abstract
of the United States. Washington, D.C.: 1985.

U.S. Savings Bond Division. The Savings Bond Question
and Answer Book.

U.S. Secretary of the Treasury. Commissioner of Public
Debt: Report to the Secretary of the Treasury,
December 20, 1940.

Volcker, Paul. "Statement by Chairman of the Board of
Governors of the Federal Reserve System, to
Subcommittee on Telecommunications, Consumer
Protection and Finance, U.S. House of Rep."
Federal Reserve Bulletin, August 1985.

Waage, Thomas O. "Service and Supervisory Functions of
the Federal Reserve System." In Prochnow, Herbert
V., ed., The Federal Reserve System. New York:
Harper & Row, 1960.

White, Leonard D. The Federalists. New York: Free
Press, 1965.

White, Leonard D. The Jeffersonians. New York: Free
Press, 1965.

White, Leonard D. The Republican Era. New York:
Macmillan, 1958.

Index

advance refunding, 134
Articles of
     Confederation, 15
Association of Primary
     Dealers in U.S.
     Government
     Securities, 188
automated clearing
     house, 191
automatic stabilizers,
     4, 110
automatic data
     processing, 159,
     166
average maturity length,
     154

Bank of England, 22
banking system, 8, 21,
     31, 32, 56. See
     also Federal
     Reserve System
Banking Act of 1935, 98
banknotes, 21, 34, 56,
     61, 74-75, 77;
     expansion, 22;
     issue of, 31
Bernstein, Peter, 216
Biddle, Nicholas, 36,
     39, 40-41
Bland-Allison Act, 63
Bonds, U.S. See
     government
     securities; savings
     bonds

bonds: yield on, 97
Boutwell, George, 62
branch drafts, 36
Broughton, William S.,
     81, 83
Buchanan, James, 5
Budget and Accounting
     Act of 1921, 83
Budget, U.S. Government,
     4, 131-2, 148-52;
     surplus in, 12, 75,
     97, 101, 114-5,
     132-3. See also
     deficit
Bureau of the Public
     Debt: formed, 87;
     World War II and
     101-105; Division
     of Savings Bonds,
     101-2, 193-5;
     number of
     employees, 116,
     122, 138, 157; use
     of computers, 122-
     4, 139-40, 162,
     185-93; Management
     Analysis Office,
     142; West Virginia
     Office, 123, 139,
     160
Bureau of Engraving and
     Printing, 65, 163
Bureau of the Budget, 83
Bush, George, 217

Cagan, Philip, 215
Carlisle, John, 64
Carter, Jimmy, 151-52,
      165, 173, 176
Central Bank, 31
Chase, Salmon P., 52-56,
      62
Cheves, Langdon, 36
Civil Service Act of
      1883, 67
Clay, Henry, 38
Cleveland, Grover, 64
Clymer, George, 13
Cobb, Howell, 46
COBOL, 162
Coinage Act of 1792, 21
Commissioner of the
      Internal Revenue,
      55
Commissioner of the
      Public Debt, 81,
      189. See also
      Broughton, William
      S.; Gregg, Richard;
      Gregg, William;
      Hintgen, H. J.;
      Kilby, E. L.
competitive bids, 153,
      181
Congressional Budget and
      Impoundment Control
      Act, 149; Budget
      Committee, 149;
      Congressional
      Budget Office, 150,
      179
Congress, U.S., 17, 23,
      25, 36, 40, 44;
      distributes
      surplus, 41; Civil
      War finances, 52,
      54, 55; reduces
      taxes, 62, 176;
      deficit reduction
      plan, 216
Constitutional
      Convention, 15, 19
Continental dollars, 13
Continental Congress,
      12-13, 15;
      financial
      committee, 11; lack
      of taxing power, 12

Cooke, Jay, 55
Corrigan, Gerald, 197
Cortelyou, George, 75
Council of Economic
      Advisors, 131, 133,
      175
Crawford, William, 35-36
credit: tightening of,
      46, 63, 177
crowding out, 7, 215
Cuba, 74
Cubes, 183
Current Tax Payment Act
      of 1943, 92
Customs Service, 67

debt administration, 6,
      8 , 81, 101, 136,
      153, 156; defined,
      7
debt management, 20, 58,
      74, 110-12, 119,
      133-5, 152;
      defined, 7; and
      banks, 74; during
      World War I, 77-9;
      during World War
      II, 92-100; during
      the 1980s, 185
debt ownership, 96, 120,
      135, 155
debt reduction plan:
      hypothetical, 216
deficit, budget, 9, 24,
      36, 43, 47; during
      Civil War, 53;
      during World War I,
      80; during Great
      Depression, 85;
      during World War
      II, 91-3; Keynesian
      view of, 110-11,
      129-31, 148; during
      Viet Nam War, 133;
      during 1980s, 177-
      9; reduction plan,
      214-6
demand: total, 110
Deposit Act of 1936, 42
Division of Securities
      Operations, 183
Division of Currency,
      57, 65

Divisions of Loans and
    Currency, 66, 77,
    81, 102-3, 159
Doctrine of Implied
    Power, 23
Drysdale Government
    Securities, Inc.,
    197
Duer, William, 19

economic conditions and
    budget deficit, 4
Economy Recovery Tax Act
    of 1981, 176
Eisenhower, Dwight, 111,
    118, 131
electronic data
    processing, 123,
    139
electronic fund
    transfer, 189-90
Employee Incentives
    Awards Program, 141
Employment Act of 1946,
    109
E.M.S. Government
    Securities, Inc.,
    197-98
equal employment
    opportunity, 162
exchange rate: of
    dollar, 215
E-Z Clear, 194

Fairchild, Charles, 63
Federalist
    Administration, 11,
    15, 21, 24, 25, 29,
    37
Fessenden, William P.,
    56
Federal Reserve System,
    5, 112-3, 148, 151,
    176, 187, 189;
    formation of, 76;
    fiscal agent for
    treasury, 76, 135-
    6, 141-2, 153, 163-
    4, 181-3;
    operations during
    World War II, 98-
    99; 1951 accord
    with treasury, 117.

See also monetary
    policy; money
    supply; open market
    operations
Federal Woman's Program
    Coordinator, 162
Fillmore, Millard, 46
First Bank of the United
    States, 22-23, 31,
    34; acting like a
    central bank, 31;
    as fiscal agent for
    the government, 31;
    charter debate, 23;
    failed recharter,
    32
Fiscal Bank of the
    United States, 43
fiscal policy, 4, 52,
    60, 150-1;
    Keynesian view of,
    110, 130; during
    Kennedy
    administration,
    130; supply-side,
    173. See also
    budget, deficit;
    U.S. government
Fiscal Service of the
    Treasury, 87, 115
Fiscal Assistant
    Secretary, 102
Folger, Charles J., 63
Ford, Gerald, 150-51
Fordney-McCumber Tariff,
    82
foreign debt, 20, 32,
    61, 155, 186
foreign exchange, 32
foreign investors, 184
Franklin, Benjamin, 12
Friedman, Milton, 100
functional finance, 9,
    110, 129
Funding Act of April 12,
    1866, 61
Funding Act of 1790, 18

Gallatin, Albert, 25,
    30-32, 38, 53;
    opinion on
    management of
    public debt, 30;

plan of debt
    reduction, 30
Gilder, George, 175
Glass, Carter, 81
gold, 61
government securities,
    2, 6, 7; interest
    rates of, 7;
    marketable, 7;
    negotiable, 7;
    nonmarketable, 7
Government Securities
    Act, 196-9
    government trust
    funds,   142
Gramm-Rudman-Hollings
    Act, 179, 214, 216
Great Depression, 9, 84
greenbacks, 54, 56, 59,
    61, 63, 65;
    declared
    unconstitutional,
    62
Gregg, Richard, 194
Gregg, William, 194
Guthrie, James, 46

Hamilton, Alexander, 12,
    19, 24, 25; named
    treasury secretary,
    16; Revolutionary
    War debt
    assumption, 17-18;
    views on national
    bank, 22
handicapped persons, 104
Hard Money, 53
Harding, Warren G., 82
Harris, Seymour, 100,
    110
Harrison, Willian Henry,
    43, 64
Heilbroner, Robert, 216
Heller, Walter, 130,
    132, 175
Hepburn v. Griswold, 62
highway trust fund, 219
Hintgen, H. J., 140,
    159, 162
Homestead Act, 60
Hoover, Herbert, 85,
    115, 151; Hoover
    Commission, 115

House of
    Representatives, 16
Humphrey, George, 119

imports, 217
Incentive Awards
    Program, 165
income: transfer of, 96
Independent Treasury,
    43, 45-46, 52-53,
    61, 74, 119, 121;
    Independent
    Treasury Act of
    1840, 43; Second
    Independent
    Treasury Bill, 43
Industrial Revolution,
    60
inflation, 5, 12, 59,
    93, 111, 119, 133,
    148; during Civil
    War, 54; during
    World War I, 80;
    during World War
    II, 100-101; during
    1970s, 150-1;
    during 1980s, 173,
    176-7
interest rates, 6, 134,
    177, 179-80, 182-
    84, 186; and
    economic
    conditions, 7; and
    the debt, 214; and
    the Revolutionary
    War, 214;
    influenced by
    inflation, 214;
    interest rate risk,
    97; stabilization,
    96
investment, 6

Jackson, Andrew, 37-38,
    40, 43; veto of
    Second Bank of the
    United States, 40;
    pays public debt,
    41
Jacksonians, 29
Jefferson, Thomas, 18,
    23, 25, 30-32, 37;
    opinion of balanced

budget, 29; trade
    embargo, 31
Jeffersonians, 29, 31–
    32, 37, 52; debt
    management program,
    37
Johnson, Lyndon, 130,
    132–33
Jones, William, 35–36
Julliard v. Greenman, 62

Kemp, Jack, 178
Kennedy, John F., 130–
    132
Keynes, John Maynard,
    85, 109–10, 174
Keynesians, 111, 130,
    147–50, 173, 178–79
Kilby, E. L., 114, 116,
    122–24
Knickerbocker Trust
    Company, 75

Laffer, Arthur, 174–75;
Laffer Curve, 174, 178
Lee, Susan, 85
legal tender, 5;
    interest-free
    notes, 53; Legal
    Tender Act, 54
Liberty Loans Act of
    1917, 81; First,
    78; Second, 79
Lincoln, Abraham, 52
loans: from France, 13;
    from the
    Netherlands, 13
Loan-Office
    Commissioners, 13
Louisiana Purchase, 30

Madison, James, 17–18,
    22, 32, 34
magnetic tape, 164
magnetic ink character
    recognition, 194
marketable treasury
    issue, 153, 157–58
Marshall, John, 36, 40
McAdoo, William Gibbs,
    78
McCulloch, Hugh, 57, 59–
    62, 217–18

McCullough v. Maryland,
    36
McKinley Tariff of 1890,
    64
Mellon, Andrew, 82–83
Meritorious Service
    Award, 161
Merrill Lynch & Co.,
    Inc., 182
microfilm recording,
    115, 124, 139
Minter, Tom, 183
Mitchell, Wesley, 54
monetary policy, 112,
    176–77; of Federal
    Reserve, 215
money markets, 40
money supply, 2, 5, 33,
    42–3, 46, 63, 74;
    increase during
    Revolutionary War,
    12–3; increase
    during World War
    II, 93–94, 100–101.
    See also Federal
    Reserve System,
    greenbacks,
    inflation, monetary
    policy
Morgan, J.P., 64
Morgenthau, Henry, 86–
    87, 93, 98
Morris, Robert, 14, 16,
    22
Murphy, Henry C., 101

National Association of
    Securities Dealers,
    198
national banks, 56, 63,
    74; National Bank
    Act, 56
National City Bank, 64
national road, 36
New Deal, 86
Ninomiya, Calvin, 197
Nixon, Richard, 148–50

offering cycle, 182
Office of Automated
    Information
    Systems, 187
Office of Economic

Opportunity, 132
Office of Financing,
    180-82
Office of Price
    Administration, 100
Office of the
    Commissioner, 199
Office of the
    Comptroller of the
    Currency, 56, 74
Office of the Registrar,
    35, 57-58, 66, 68,
    77, 81, 102, 124
Office of Tax Policy,
    158
OPEC, 147, 150
Open Market Operations,
    46, 63-64, 98-99,
    117, 133, 135, 157
optical character
    recognition, 194

Paine, Thomas, 12
Panama Canal, 74
paper dollars: increase
    is similar to tax,
    12
Parker v. Davis, 62
Passell, Peter, 85
Patton, Eugene, 75
Payroll Deduction
    Savings Plan:
    initiated, 95
pensions: to
    Revolutionary War
    veterans, 36
pet banks, 41
Philippines, 74
political patronage, 67
Polk, James K., 43, 45
Progressives, 73
Project NEW, 187
public credit:
    confidence in, 18
public debt, 1, 2, 132,
    151, 173, 176, 188;
    monetizing of, 5,
    98; burden of, 5-6;
    as percent of GNP.
    2, 210; growth in,
    92, 173, 188 210;
    total of U.S.: as
    of 1790, 20;   as of

1801, 24; as of
1811, 30; as of
1815, 33; as of
1828, 37; paid off
in 1835, 41; as of
1849, 46; as of
1860, 51; as of
1865, 59; as of
1899, 65; as of
1919, 80; as of
1940, 86; as of
1946, 109; as of
1960, 130; as of
1980, 152; growth
in during 1980s,
211-214; as of
1990, 1. See also
debt
administration;
debt management;
debt ownership
Public Debt Accounting
    and Reporting
    System, 192
Public Debt Electronic
    Committee, 123
Public Debt Service, 83,
    87; Division of
    Savings Bonds, 87
public finance, 3, 8
public land: sales of,
    38
Pure Food and Drug Act,
    74

Reagan, Ronald, 29, 82;
    economic policies
    of, 173-177
Recessions, 4, 36, 42,
    47, 64, 82, 86,
    111; in 1973, 150;
    in 1980, 152; in
    1981, 177
Reed, Robert, 183
Refunding Act of 1870,
    62-63
Remini, Robert, 40
Republicans, 52, 60, 73,
    82, 111, 178
Resumption Act of 1875,
    62
Revenue Act of 1964, 132
Revolutionary War, 1

Roberts, Paul Craig, 215
Roosevelt, Theodore, 73
Roosevelt, Franklin D.,
    85-87
Rush, Richard, 37, 38

Salomon Brothers, 182
Samuelson, Paul, 110
Savage, James D., 29
savings bonds, 95, 105,
    134-37, 141, 154,
    159, 165, 180, 184;
    first offered, 87;
    program moved to
    Chicago, 103;
    Savings Bond
    Operations Office,
    161, 164, 193;
    Series E punchcard
    introduced, 123,
    139; Tax Savings
    Bonds, 94
Schwartz, Anna, 100
Second Bank of the
    United States, 34-
    36, 38-41;
    chartered, 35;
    constitutionality
    of, 36; Jackson's
    veto of
    rechartering, 40
Securities and Exchange
    Act of 1933, 198
Securities and Exchange
    Commission, 196-99
Selective Service, 92
Shaw, Leslie M., 75-76
Sherman Act, 74
sinking fund policy, 20
Smith, Adam, 22
Smoot-Hawley Tariff of
    1930, 85
Snyder, John, 112, 117-
    18
Social Security Trust
    Fund, 219
Social Security
    Administration, 189
specie, 39; resumption
    of payment, 34, 42,
    46, 53; suspension
    of payment, 62-63
specie circular, 42

speculators in U.S.
    securities, 17-19
spending: defense, 109;
    government, 109
Sproul, Alan, 113
state banknotes, 39, 45
state debts: assumption,
    18
state-chartered banks,
    23, 33
Stockman, David, 178,
    217
Strips, 183
Superintendent of
    Finance, 14
supply-side economics,
    174, 177
Supreme Court, 62
surplus: distribution to
    states, 41
    government, 36, 41,
    218; Treasury, 38

Taney, Roger, 41
Tariff of Abominations,
    37
tariffs, 4, 30, 46, 52,
    64, 78; as revenue
    policy, 15, 33, 60,
    62, 78; compared to
    budget surpluses,
    60
Taus, Esther, 35, 42, 75
taxes, 3, 5, 33, 52, 78;
    inflation as, 5,
    80, 100; power to
    tax given to
    congress, 16;
    constitutionality
    of income tax, 64;
    trickle down tax
    policy, 82; during
    World War II, 92;
    reduced in 1948,
    111; reduced in
    1963, 130-3;
    reduced in 1982,
    174-5. See also
    fiscal policy,
    tariffs
Tax Commissioner, 55
Taylor, Zachary, 46
thrift stamps, 79

Timberlake, Richard, H.,
    36, 76
Tobin, James, 148, 178
treasury auctions, 153,
    180-81, 187, 196;
    automated, 191-92
treasury bills:
    authorized, 84
Treasury Department, 7,
    24, 31, 46, 60, 78,
    112, 129, 135, 153;
    formation of, 16;
    operations during
    Civil War, 57-8;
    early expansion of,
    65-7; central
    banking function
    of, 75-6;
    reorganizations of,
    81, 83, 87;
    operations during
    World War II, 95-
    98; relations with
    Federal Reserve,
    97, 116-8, 141;
    advance refunding
    plan, 134. See
    also Bureau of the
    Public Debt; debt
    management; fiscal
    policy; treasury
    auctions; treasury
    secretary
Treasury Direct, 184,
    187-93
Treasury-Federal Reserve
    Task Force, 163,
    183
treasury notes, 33-34
Treasury Secretary: See
    Boutwell, George;
    Carlisle, John;
    Clymer, George;
    Chase, Salmon P.;
    Cobb, Howell;
    Cortelyou, George;
    Crawford, William;
    Fairchild, Charles;
    Folger, Charles J.;
    Gallatin, Albert;
    Glass, Carter;
    Guthrie, James;
    Hamilton,

Alexander;
    Humphrey, George;
    McAdoo, William
    Gibbs; Mellon,
    Andrew; Morgenthau,
    Henry; Rush,
    Richard; Shaw,
    Leslie M.; Snyder,
    John; Taney, Roger;
    Vinson, Fred;
    Walker, Robert J.;
    Wolcott, Oliver;
    Woodbury, Levi
treasury securities,
    190; book-entry
    form, 141, 157,
    163, 165, 183-8,
    190-2, 197;
    automated book-
    entry, 190. See
    also debt
    management;
    government
    securities; savings
    bonds; treasury
    auctions
Trent Affair, 53
trickle-down tax
    policies, 82,
Truman, Harry S., 111-
    12, 117

Underwood Tariff of
    1913, 78
unemployment rate, 92,
    147-8, 150, 173,
    177
United States
    Constitution, 1,
    12, 16, 19, 23;
    Sixteenth
    Amendment, 78
United States
    Government, 3, 22,
    52, 175, 207;
    borrowing, 5;
    budgeting
    procedure, 24;
    finances as
    percentage of GNP,
    208; growth in,
    208; impact on
    interest rate, 214

Univac 1110 Computer
    System, 162

Van Buren, Martin, 43,
veterans bonus, 85
Victory Fund Committee,
    101
Victory Loan, 81
Vinson, Fred, 111
Volcker, Paul, 197

wage and price controls,
    149
wages: real wages during
    Civil War, 54
Walker, Robert J., 44-
    46, 55
War Finance Division,
    101
War Loan Organization,
    79
War Savings
    Certificates, 79
War Savings Staff, 101

War Savings Stamps, 79
wars, financing of:
    Revolutionary War,
    11-14; War of
    1812, 33; Mexican
    War, 44-5; Civil
    War, 52-6, 58-9;
    Spanish-American
    War, 64; World War
    I, 77-80; World War
    II, 92-9; Korean
    War, 117; Viet Nam
    War, 133, 135
Washington, George, 16,
    22
Whig Party, 43, 46
Windom, William, 67
wire transfer, 135, 163,
    189
Wolcott, Oliver, 24, 25
Woodbury, Levi, 41-43

Zeck, Van, 191, 198-99

ABOUT THE AUTHORS

DONALD R. STABILE is professor of economics and director of the Center for Economic Education at St. Mary's College of Maryland. He is the author of <u>Prophets of Order: The Rise of the New Class and Socialism in America</u>. Dr. Stabile holds a B.S. from the University of Florida and an M.A. and Ph.D. from the University of Massachusetts at Amherst.

JEFFREY A. CANTOR is associate professor of business administration at Lehman College of the City University of New York. He has written over 40 articles in areas related to public and historical research and research methodology, in addition to a history of the U.S. Department of the Treasury's Bureau of the Public Debt. Dr. Cantor holds a B.S. and M.A. from New York University and a Ph.D. from Florida State University.